Dedication

You are what you read.

Dedicated to the many authors whose books have contributed to the making of me — and therefore this book. Among them:

> Margaret Atwood
>
> Jacques Barzun
>
> Peter Berger
>
> Benjamin Bloom
>
> Marion Zimmer Bradley
>
> C.J. Cherryh
>
> Grey Owl
>
> Gluckel of Hameln
>
> Gilbert Highet
>
> Walt Kelly
>
> Lao Tzu
>
> Ursula LeGuin
>
> Dorothy Sayers
>
> Michael Polanyi
>
> David Riesman
>
> Edward Sapir
>
> Sei Shonagon
>
> Virginia Woolf

May you, its readers, be nourished by this book.

# Contents

## A Great Balancing Act: Equitable Education for Girls and Boys

Introduction: Becoming Mindful . . . . . . . i

Chapter One: The "Curriculum" of the Real World . . . . . . . 1

Chapter Two: Undercurrents of Gender: The Hidden Curriculum and the Null Curriculum . . . . . 13

Chapter Three: Ways of Knowing: Girls and Boys Coming into Their Own . . . . . 39

Chapter Four: The Formal Curriculum: Becoming Inclusive . . . . . 47

Chapter Five: History . . . . . 55

Chapter Six: Science . . . . . 75

Chapter Seven: English Literature and Language . . . . . 83

Chapter Eight: Mathematics . . . . . 99

Chapter Nine: Arts . . . . . 113

Chapter Ten: Computers . . . . . 121

Chapter Eleven: The Informal Curriculum: Athletics . . . . . 125

Chapter Twelve: The Informal Curriculum: Leadership . . . . . 131

Chapter Thirteen: Parents and the Home Curriculum . . . . . 137

Bibliography . . . . . 145

## BECOMING MINDFUL

■ ■ ■ ■

> *…I ask myself and you, which of our visions will claim us*
> *which will we claim*
> *how will we go on living*
> *how will we touch, what will we know*
> *what will we say to each other.*
>
> —*Adrienne Rich, 1976*

*Introduction*

"Who am I?" and "What can I become?" are questions of great urgency for children and adolescents. Their own lives and the society of the future will be affected by their answers. The ideas they absorb from those around them about being male or female will be of decisive importance in the answers they are able to construct.

During their most impressionable years, young people are shaped by their parents and by the schools where they spend many thousands of hours. Their vision of themselves, other people, their world, and their options in dealing with others and the world, is influenced by the pointers they get about gender, by the expectations they pick up concerning how to be a woman or a man in this society.

We make a difference whether we want to or not. We influence the young by the kinds of people we are, the ideas and values we hold, the language we use; by the actions we take and avoid taking; by what we require, encourage, discourage, and forbid them to do; by what we keep silent about, are unmindful of, or ignore.

The recent flood of new information on structuring experience along gender lines, and on the female component of human experience, has profound implications for the education of boys as well as girls, in and out of school. It has already affected what is taught and how it is taught in the formal academic disciplines. It has suggested new ways of looking at messages sent by the informal curriculum of athletics and extracurricular activities, and the hidden curriculum of a school's overall climate, outside as well as inside the classroom.

The degree to which there is biological programming for the observable intellectual, personality, and behavioral differences between females and males is still an open question. But the evidence is overwhelming that these differences can either be promoted or de-emphasized. There is no doubt that in our society gender differences are mostly promoted. Girls and boys receive different messages from parents, peers, schools, teachers, and media — messages that the adults who transmit them may not even be aware they are sending.

Expectations created by the different messages about gender-appropriate attitudes and behavior can, and often do, limit aspirations, stunt the development of abilities, limit choices, interfere with learning, and systematically disadvantage a group.

Gender stereotyping limits boys as well as girls. Significant changes have taken place in the demands on men and women in the workplace and family in the last generation or two. Gender-stereotyped responses to those changes are to the disadvantage of both women and men. Moreover, they interfere with learning. According to the evidence, new information that does not fit in with the receiver's preconceived stereotypic ideas tends to be forgotten or distorted, making for gaps and errors in knowledge.

Changes have also occurred in the basic assumptions in several fields of learning. In science, for instance, there is greater emphasis on interconnections, global thinking, and the development of intuition. In literature, there is less rigid adherence to textual analysis at the expense of examining how works of art are rooted in the cultures that produced them. These and other changes, while slow to get into textbooks, are affecting teaching down to younger students' level; some of the changes are more in tune with the generally preferred thinking and learning styles of girls than of boys. There are features of our educational arrangements that, perhaps increasingly, place boys at a disadvantage. Too often, however, girls are more handicapped.

Recognizing the educational implications of gender differences means having to decide what actions, if any, to take that will lead to increased ability by individuals, whether girls or boys, to fulfill their potential without being limited by their own, and others', stereotyped expectations.

*I*n current scholarship on women and gender, there are three basic mind-sets, which it is useful to recognize and take into account as background to decision-making. The first concentrates on girls, and sees the benefits of the "differentness" assigned to them. It focuses on their strengths, the worth of their contributions to society, and of those special capacities, insights, intellectual and personality traits, approaches and styles historically allotted to them and not to males. People with this mind-set focus on the celebration of the feminine as valuable, and on gaining recognition that female-associated characteristics and competencies are equal in value and importance to male-associated ones. (An example might be the argument for including women in the highest-level peace-negotiations because of their special expertise in nurturing, caring, and conciliating).

The second basic mind-set also concentrates on girls, but sees the "differentness" assigned to them by their socialization as a disadvantage, because of social devaluation of the "feminine" relative to the "masculine." It focuses on helping females individually and as a group to overcome handicaps placed on them by societal sexism. The intention is to bring girls "up to par" with boys in socially valued competencies, and thereby to gain equality in adulthood between women and men. (An example might be assertiveness training for girls).

The third mind-set recognizes that gender-stereotypic socialization has created deficiencies not only in girls, but also in boys. In the past, in a society that valued male-associated characteristics more than female-associated ones, lack of the latter was not as serious for males as lack of the former was for females. However, social and intellectual changes that are resulting in greater need for female-associated intellectual and personality traits make their rejection by males increasingly problematic.

**Because it values diversity and emphasizes choice, this third mind-set is the most complex of the three. People with this mind-set emphasize:**

- enabling both boys and girls to add attitudes and behaviors previously considered the domain of the opposite sex to their own repertoire of competencies
- helping both girls and boys to recognize the appropriate contexts within which their varied competencies are most effective
- working towards more equitable relationships between males and females
- encouraging the viewing of differentness in positive ways

These three mind-sets are not mutually exclusive. All may be drawn on and selectively used, depending on context. Some will be more relevant than others as a guide to action in a particular set of circumstances.

However, the first mind-set is indispensable. Unless there is individual and societal recognition of the value of females and female-identified intellectual and personality traits, girls and women will never be "up to par" with boys and men. However distinguished their performance, they would still be devalued by some because of their inescapable femaleness. And males would remain reluctant to add anything female-identified to their own repertoire of competencies, and fear and deny characteristics within themselves that are perceived as "feminine," to their own loss.

Schools, teachers, and parents who are trying to decide on what action to take in their own particular circumstances need to be alert to each of the three mind-sets, and use them as guides to action when and as each is relevant. They need also to recognize that there is, on every available measure, considerable overlap between males and females: some girls are more competitive than many boys, some boys are more nurturing than many girls. In striving to become aware of educationally relevant gender differences, educators and parents must not lose sight of all that is gender shared. We must keep in mind that differences are statistical and have very limited predictive validity about any one individual student. Therefore, to the extent that we differentiate between individuals on the basis of group characteristics, we are doing a disservice to the individual.

We must accept that identical treatment of boys and girls is not always desirable or equitable. They have been socialized into systematic differences in learning and communications styles, in their ways of relating to other people, in their assumptions and expectations. Not recognizing the differences when they are salient means failing to ensure that boys and girls can both build on their strengths, remedy their weaknesses, and become more flexible in their repertoire. Educators and parents must become knowledgeable about: statistically widespread and reliably documented (rather than popularly assumed) differences between boys and girls; when differences are educationally relevant, and in what ways; and what options there are for remedying any negative impact of the differences.

To accomplish this, a searching look through the lens of gender at all aspects of young people's education — in and out of school — is indicated. Decisions may then be made about what might be desirable changes, keeping in mind that not making a decision is a decision in itself.

**In schools, an inclusive review would turn the searchlight on the following:**

- the **formal curriculum** of subject-matter disciplines, the ways they are taught and tested, and the classroom dynamics as they are learned or not learned
- the **informal curriculum** of athletics, leadership, and extracurricular activities
- the **hidden curriculum** of the school's climate, things not deliberately taught or instituted, but which are the cumulative result of many unconscious or unexamined behaviors that add up to a palpable style or atmosphere
- the **null curriculum** — that which is missing from all other curricula, not as a result of conscious decision to exclude it, but merely because it has never occurred to anyone to consider whether or not it should be there

In homes, parents' searching look at gender would need to review the home curriculum, including what is being deliberately and overtly taught, what the hidden curriculum is that may have unintended results, and what the null curriculum, those things never even considered because never thought of, might be.

Both educators and families need to consider, as they review how they themselves influence and are influenced by, gender-related ideas and behavior, the gender "curriculum" of the real world, and the preferred ways of knowing of girls and boys.

*T*eachers from preschool to high school, as well as parents, need information about what difference gender makes to the students they teach, how they teach, and what they teach. They need it because they deal with the young during the time that self-images and world-views, both vitally affected by notions about gender, are being formed. They also need practical, what-to-do-Monday-morning suggestions about what they can do to enhance learning, self-actualization, and life-experience chances for both girls and boys, and to minimize the chance of one or the other gender being educationally disadvantaged. Such information is not readily available; this book is intended to fill the gap.

While focusing on gender, this book also deals with diversity, of which gender is an element. Women as a group have shared much with other groups historically subordinate due to race, ethnicity, and other factors. They have faced barriers on the path to various socially valued goals, and the continuation of such barriers due to often unconsidered messages of exclusion. In those cases where differences other than those of gender (such as race and ethnicity) have been reliably documented and have educational implications, they have been included in the information provided.

This book is for everyone connected with schools: teachers, librarians, curriculum coordinators and planners, directors of studies, subject-area specialists, division and department chairs, heads, principals and superintendents, trustees and school boards. It is also for parents, whose direct and indirect influence is enormous, and whose collaboration with schools and the adults in them is so vital for the best education of the young.

The book presents recent research-based information about educationally relevant gender-related differences between girls and boys. It identifies many of the messages sent by parents, teachers, schools, peers, and media to young people about how they should think, feel, and behave as males and females, and explains the various ways in which what is taught and how it is taught may have a different impact on boys and girls. It may be useful in everyday interactions and in attempts to understand and influence attitudes and behavior. It can help with curriculum revision, formulating policy and practice, and long-range planning.

*T*his book also offers practical, versatile, adaptable, family and classroom-tested, and subject-relevant suggestions on how to avoid trammeling either girls or boys, how to overcome negative aspects of gender-stereotyping, and how to maximize learning potential for both boys and girls. It suggests ways to consider whether gender-stereotypic thinking and behavior might inadvertently be promoted, or one gender or the other disadvantaged, in such areas of life in and out of school as: styles of communication; allocation of time and space; ways of relating, teaching, counseling, and coaching; approaches to discipline and social life; and courses offered, subject matter covered, issues discussed, texts and testing methods used. It also offers possible strategies for change and specifics on how change might be put into effect.

Re-visioning the various curricula in school and home with gender in view can be done in small increments, step by step. But it cannot be done quickly. The process has to be deliberate, multifaceted, consistent, and cumulative.

Those who have set their feet on the path of this enterprise have tended to take three to five years to arrive at the point at which they began to feel reasonably satisfied with what they have accomplished. In starting out, experience suggests it is helpful to avoid biting off more than one can chew. Do what is easy and interesting first to assure success in early efforts. Remember that doing something, however small, is still better than doing nothing. Set goals that are both short-term (a month to several months) and long-range (about two to four years). Be flexible; if something is not working, try another approach or address a different area. Support, and be supported by, others engaged in the same or a similar enterprise. Articulate your own resistance; left vague, it can result in malaise and spun wheels. Brought to light, it can be addressed. Don't be turned away from the whole enterprise by one or two readings, authors, speakers, consultants, or other sources that make this work sound too complicated, extreme, uncomfortable, irrelevant, or weird. Share failures as well as successes with colleagues, family, or friends — feeling isolated when making any change can be terribly discouraging.

## HOW TO USE THIS BOOK

*T*he following recommendations are intended to guide readers to sections of ***The Great Balancing Act*** that will be of particular interest to them:

**All readers, including parents:**

**CHAPTER ONE:** *The "Curriculum" of the Real World*
**CHAPTER THREE:** *Ways of Knowing: Girls and Boys Coming into Their Own*

In **CHAPTER TWO:** *Undercurrents of Gender* the sections on:
> ➤ Crosscurrents in Communication
> ➤ Testing the Waters

**CHAPTER TWELVE:** *The Informal Curriculum*: Leadership

**Teachers of all grade levels and subject-area specialists:**

You can find sections about the disciplines and subject matter of interest to you via headings or subheadings. The order in which the disciplines are presented is deliberate, and is intended to model an attempt to defuse a binary division into the female-stereotypic humanities on the one hand and the male-stereotypic math/science axis on the other.

The following sections, relevant to all disciplines and subject matter, present pedagogical information:

> ➤ for suggestions that "promote in-depth understanding . . . " look under the **What Schools and Teachers Can Do** heading in the **SCIENCE** and **MATHEMATICS** chapters
> ➤ for suggestions on running discussion groups, look in "build on known connections between discussion and deepening understanding . . . " under the **What Schools and Teachers Can Do** heading in the **MATHEMATICS** chapter
> ➤ for suggestions on promoting gender equitable class contributions, look in "to improve students' ability to communicate . . . " under **What Schools and Teachers Can Do** in the **ENGLISH** chapter.

**Librarians:**

The **Resources** sections in each chapter are likely to be of interest.

**Trustees, board members, administrators, and coaches:**

Find relevant sections by looking through the headings and subheadings.

The help of all those who have contributed to the making of this book with good ideas and moral support is gratefully acknowledged; and like bread cast upon the waters, it is offered up to fellow educators and fellow parents in the hope that those who consume it will be nourished by it.

—*Anne Chapman*

## CHAPTER ONE

## THE "CURRICULUM" OF THE REAL WORLD

*You will come to a place where the streets are not marked.*
*Some windows are lighted. But mostly they're darked.*
*A place you could sprain both your elbow and chin!*
*Do you dare to stay out? Do you dare to go in?*
*How much can you lose? How much can you win?*
*Step with care and great tact*
*and remember that Life's*
*a Great Balancing Act.*

> —*Dr. Seuss, 1990*

The real world of work and family has changed radically in only the last generation or two. Demands on men and women in these two significant spheres of life have changed as well — and traditional, gender-stereotypical responses to the new demands can be damaging for both women and men. This in itself is a good reason for examining the gender messages we, as adults in schools and families, may be sending (or not sending) to children and adolescents. The "curriculum" of the real world is one that they will all have to follow. Being alert to its gender-relevant features will help us to consider how best to prepare young people for its challenges, many of which are out of sync with traditional assumptions.

According to the traditional concepts developed among, but influential beyond, the white middle classes, girls are both assumed and supposed to be cooperative, nurturing, passive, and dependent supporters; boys, competitive, active, and independent leaders. Girls are conceptualized as shyer, more intuitive, emotional, artistic, and verbal than boys, who are seen more as aggressive, analytically intellectual, mechanically inclined, and good at math. Girls are supposedly heading for the humanities, boys for the sciences; girls are thought of as focused on marriage, children, and personal relationships, boys on a career and the freedom to be their own man.

These stereotyped ideals are still promoted. Running counter to them is still penalized. Parents, teachers, and others who influence the young need to weigh the costs of continuing to do so in the changed world that has already arrived.

### A GIRL GRADUATING FROM HIGH SCHOOL IN THE NEXT FEW YEARS WILL FACE:

- ➤ the absolute certainty of encountering situations in which being aggressive and competitive are to her advantage
- ➤ the virtual certainty of working for pay outside the home for decades of her adult life **(1)**
- ➤ the virtual certainty that she will be called upon, in the course of her working life, to exercise skills and attitudes that have been traditionally considered "masculine" **(2)**
- ➤ the virtual certainty of living alone for substantial periods of her life **(3)**
- ➤ the strong probability of divorce **(4)**
- ➤ the virtual certainty that, if she is divorced and has children, she will be the custodial single parent with major financial responsibility for herself and her children **(5)**
- ➤ the strong probability of conflict between career and family obligations **(6)**
- ➤ the strong possibility of working in lower-paid occupations and being paid less than a comparably qualified man **(7)**
- ➤ the strong possibility of being sexually harassed on the job **(8)**
- ➤ the increasing possibility of earning more money than her husband **(12)**

**A BOY GRADUATING FROM HIGH SCHOOL IN THE NEXT FEW YEARS WILL FACE:**

- the absolute certainty of encountering situations in which being aggressive and competitive are damaging to him
- the virtual certainty of being married to a woman who works for pay outside the home during most of their married life **(1)**
- the virtual certainty of being called upon, in the course of his working life, to exercise skills and attitudes traditionally considered "feminine" **(9)**
- the strong probability of divorce **(3)**
- the strong probability of conflict between career and family obligations **(10)**
- the strong probability, if divorced with children, of remarrying and having to contribute to the emotional, as well as the financial, well-being of two sets of offspring; and the small, but increasing, probability that he will be the sole custodial single parent **(11)**
- the increasing probability of having a wife who earns more than he does **(12)**
- the small but not insignificant possibility of being sexually harassed on the job **(8)**

## BY THE NUMBERS: WHAT GIRLS AND BOYS FACE IN THE REAL WORLD

1 • Eighty-one percent of all 25- to 64-year-old women with four years or more of college were in the labor force in 1991; some not working at that point would have done so earlier, or would do so later (Statistical Abstracts 1994, 397).
 • The labor force participation of women is approaching that of men: in 1992, of women aged 20-64 with no child under 18, 85 percent worked outside the home; of men with the same characteristics, 89 percent; 95 percent of all married fathers, and 73 percent of all married mothers worked (Hayghe 94, 25).
 • The average woman worker could expect to spend twenty-nine years of her life in the labor force, compared to thirty-nine years for the average man (U.S. Department of Labor 1988, 1).
 • The traditional family of a husband who is the sole breadwinner, a full-time homemaker wife, and children, now makes up only 10 percent of U.S. families (Aburdene and Naisbitt 1992, 217).
 • In only 21 percent of U.S. families in 1990 was there a husband working full time year round, with a wife who was a full-time housewife — down from 70 percent in 1940 (Lugaila 1992, 53; Kalish 1992, 2).
 • Sixty-eight percent of wives with children under 18 were in the labor force in 1993, compared to 18 percent in 1950 (Statistical Abstract 1994, 402; U.S. Department of Labor 1980, 27).
 • In 28 percent of married-couple families with children, both spouses worked year-round full time (Lugaila 1992, 53).
 • Women workers' contribution to household income is substantial: dual-worker families' median income was $47,000, husband-only earners' $30,000, and female-headed households' $17,000 in 1990 (Kalish 1992, 2).
 • Married women working full time contributed a median of 41 percent of the family's income in 1993 (Lewin 1995).

2 • Mathematics, traditionally a "masculine" subject that women were not supposed to be good at, is increasingly a necessity for an ever-wider variety of jobs, and especially for the better-paid jobs. (For more on women and mathematics, see the **MATHEMATICS** chapter of this book.)
 • To achieve leadership positions, women have to be able to compete; to give orders to people even if their subordinates are older, more experienced, and male; to express anger, say no,

to fail and not give up, to fight for what they believe in (see chapter on **LEADERSHIP**). Of course, many women do all this and more just fine; but, unlike men, they are not specifically socialized to do so. Indeed, some are negatively socialized for it. They are brought up to feel guilty for behaving in such ways: nice girls don't . . .

➤ **3** • A quarter of American households were people living alone in 1992, two-thirds of them women. In 1940, only 8 percent of households was a single-person one (U.S. census Bureau, cited in *Education Week*, 1993, 3; Haub 1992, 7).

• Among those over 65, 42 percent of the women and 16 percent of the men lived alone in 1990 (Women's Action Coalition 1993, 44).

• The percentage who never marry has doubled to 10 percent since 1950 (Aburdene and Naisbitt 1992, 220).

➤ **4** • Half of all marriages contracted since 1970 could end in divorce (U.S. Census Bureau estimate). There was one divorce for every two marriages during the 1980s; and according to the Census Bureau, if the rate were to decrease in the later 1990s it would only do so marginally (Lugaila 1992, 8; Norton and Miller 1992, 9).

➤ **5** • About half of divorced women with children were awarded child support in 1990 (For college-educated, the figure was 71 percent in 1983, the latest break-out available). Of these, a quarter received no payment, and only half received full payment (Lugaila 1992, 41).

• The average child support payment among all those who did receive payment was $2,995, with white women on the average receiving 38 percent higher payments than average, and college educated women about 67 percent higher than the average (Education Week 1991, citing Census Bureau).

• One in eight families in 1991 was headed by a single parent, who was five times more likely to be a woman, and three times more likely to be African American (Kalish 1992, 2-3).

• The percentage of children living with only one parent more than doubled from 1960 to 1990, among whites 7 percent to 19 percent, among African Americans 22 percent to 55 percent (Lugaila 1992, 37).

➤ **6** • Forty percent of mothers adjusted their work schedules to meet child-care needs, even when fathers were the primary care-givers while mothers worked (1993 report by the Population Reference Bureau cited in Cohen 1993).

• The "mommy track," offered in the last decade by organizations, is "ostensibly intended to make it easier for married women with children to continue managerial and professional jobs, [offering] flexible working hours and generous maternity leave to women but not men in dual-career marriages to ameliorate that pressures of family and work. But women are penalized for taking advantage of these policies, because once they do, their commitment to achieving top-level positions is called into question" (Lorber 1994, 234).

• Fewer than 2 percent of private-sector companies and 9 percent of government agencies offer employer-sponsored day care for children of those who work there (Women's Action Coalition 1993, 42).

• However, the number of "large U.S. employers that provide some kind of day-care assistance" grew from eleven in 1972 to nearly 4,000 in 1992 (Brown ed. 1993, 19).

• Nine out of ten women will be caregivers for either children or parents or both (Women's Action Coalition 1993, 42).

➤ **7** • Within the college-educated population, both men and women continue to be influenced in their choice of field of study, which has decisive influence on their future career, by gender stereotypes (engineering and computer science for boys, education and health services for girls).

• In the top six intended areas of college study among 1985 high school graduates only two (business and commerce, and social sciences) were chosen by similar proportions of boys and girls. The same levels of imbalance were shown in 1994 (Admissions Testing Program 1985, 9; The College Board 1994, vi).

• Most jobs still tend to be gender-segregated. In 1990, women were over 80 percent of secretaries, waitresses, health aides, those waiting on tables, and sewing machine operators; under 20 percent of physicians, police officers, engineers, and construction trade workers (Ries and Stone 1992, 340).

• Women also work in fewer occupations than men; they are heavily concentrated in thirty of the 400 to 500 main job categories in the U.S. (Unger and Saundra 1993, 166).

• Boys' gender-stereotypical choices lead to high-paid occupations, girls' to low-paid occupations; women's lifetime earnings are higher if they work in a predominantly male occupation.

• Within what is apparently the same occupation, gender-stereotyped expectations continue to influence specialization. For instance, women may now be doctors as well as nurses; but more women are pediatricians, and more men neurosurgeons; men who go into nursing "tend to specialize in the more lucrative areas and become administrators" (Lorber 1994, 198; Unger and Saundra 1993, 168).

• In the early 1990s, in corporations where women were 37 percent of all employees, women were 17 percent of those in all levels of management, and 7 percent of those ranked assistant vice-president or higher. Similar proportions existed in public-sector jobs (Lorber 1994, 227-228).

• Only thirteen of the Fortune 500 companies had a woman as one of their five highest-paid executives, and women held fewer than 1 percent of the firms' top 2,500 jobs (*Wall Street Journal* 1994, 1).

• Women were 3 percent of all managers at the 1,000 largest U.S. companies; and among 986 chief executives in those companies, there were two women (Schmittroth 1991, 27).

• Among all full-time wage and salary workers, women's earnings were 71 percent of men's; and among women in high-income occupations, the gap was bigger. In 1955, women's earnings were 64 percent of men's (U.S. Department of Labor 1993, 6,1; U.S. Department of Labor figures reported in Lewis 1991, 12; U.S. Department of Labor 1980, 52).

• In 1989, men were still four times more likely to be earning $48,000 or more a year than women (Ryscavage 1994, 6). Among teachers, taking every possible variable into account (such as teaching load, experience, years of education etc.) for equivalent work with equivalent expertise there was still a wage-gap to the disadvantage of women (*Education Week*, 1989, 12).

• While the number of woman-owned businesses more than tripled in the decade of 1977 to 1987, so at the latter date women owned 30 percent of all businesses, their firms accounted for under 15 percent of all receipts generated by American companies; and over a third had total receipts of under $5,000 (Ries and Stone 1992, 347-8).

➤ **8** • Offensive remarks were experienced by 35 percent, and inappropriate touching by 26 percent of the workers in the sexual harassment survey of 8,500 workers conducted by the U.S. Merit Board, a federal agency, in 1987 (Aburdene and Naisbitt 1992, 86).

• Half the American Management association's over 500 members had to deal with sexual harassment in the last five years (Aburdene and Naisbitt 1992, 86).

- Almost 90 percent of the Fortune 500 companies surveyed by the National Council for Research on Women had received sexual harassment complaints; over a third had been sued; nearly a quarter had been repeatedly sued. Based on the research, it is estimated that about half of all women will experience sexual harassment at some point during their academic or working life (Women's Action Coalition 1993, 53).
- Men filed 6 percent of sexual harassment complaints between 1981 and 1989 (Quoted in Wolf 1991, 300, n.43). Figures on men's actual experience of harassment in the workplace do not seem to be available; but although most harassment is of women, there is plenty of anecdotal evidence for harassment of men (some, but not all, of it homophobic).

➤ 9 • Recommended and valued leadership style has been changing in the last generation or so towards female-stereotypical attitudes and behaviors such as supporting, encouraging, soliciting input from all, facilitating, empathizing, being responsive. The traditional hierarchical pyramid structure, derived from the military and sports ("the business metaphors of the industrial age") still seen as indispensable by the authors of *Megatrends* in 1982, by 1992 was seen by the same authors as being replaced by "networks, lattices and webs"; and the "masculine way" of management changing in the direction of "creating a nourishing environment for personal growth" becoming a manager's top responsibility (Aburdene and Naisbitt 1992, 88-97; confirmed by numerous other sources). Of course, many men do all this and more just fine; but, unlike women, they are not socialized to do so.

➤ 10 • Fathers participate in childcare more, and consider it more important. In 1991, one-fifth of preschool children were cared for by fathers while their mothers worked outside the home, up from one in seven during 1965-1988. The increase was attributed, in part, to greater acceptance by society of men undertaking childcare (Cohen 1993). The trend is expected to continue (Information Please Almanac 1995, 436).
- Between 1965 and 1986, men's share in childcare rose by 50 percent, though still low compared to women's (United Nations 1991, 102).
- In ranking career, husband-companion, and father as the role they felt would give them the greatest satisfaction, twice as many male college students in 1990 than in 1980 gave fatherhood as their top choice (Willinger 1993, 122).
- Husbands do more housework: 20 percent of husbands in dual-earner couples were found to be fully involved in sharing traditionally female-identified household chores in a national sample in 1994 (Starrels 1994, 473). The number of hours spent by men doing household chores and preparing meals doubled from 1965 to 1986 (United Nations 1991, 102).
- In dual-earner families, men in 1993 spent about seven hours a week in cooking, washing, cleaning; four hours running errands and paying bills; and seven more hours in household and automobile maintenance — a total of eighteen hours a week. Their working wives spent thirty four hours a week on activities in the same categories (Presser 1993, 5).
- In a small (160 couples) recent study of spouses both of whom worked full time all year, and who believed in gender equality, the husbands were found to do eight hours of housework per week to the wives' twelve (Cited in Lorber 1994, 189).
- Men increasingly are willing to balance job commitment with family commitment: Nearly half the men in one 1989 survey said they would put off career advancement in return for more family time.
- The ratio of men to women who took family leave went from 1 to 400 to 1 to 50 at AT&T in the decade from 1980 to 1990. Nearly two thirds of the men at DuPont favored leave from men to care for sick children in 1991, up from 40 percent in 1986; and those favoring leave to care for newborns doubled, to one third.

- In Sweden, only 2 percent of new fathers availed themselves of parental leave when the law giving this option was passed in 1975. The figure in the early 1990s was 27 percent (All four sets of data quoted in Aburdene and Naisbitt 1992, 224-225).

➤ 11
- Remarriage is common: Almost half of all marriages in 1992 were second, third, or higher order marriages (Information Please Almanac 1995, 430).
- Stepchildren are significant in numbers, and will be more so: 7.3 million children lived in step-families in 1990; one third of married couples will have a stepchild or an adopted child by 2010 (Aburdene and Naisbitt 1992, 219).
- More children live with their fathers only: Among all races, the percentage of children living with their fathers only tripled between 1970 and 1990, though at the latter date it was still only 3 percent (Census figures cited in Ries and Stone 1992, 256).

➤ 12
- Among dual-earner couples, the wife's income not infrequently is larger than the husband's. In 1993, women earned more than men in 23 percent of the married-couple families where both spouses worked, up from about 15 percent a decade ago (Lewin 1995).

*I*n the changed world that has already arrived, our young man will also be about twice as likely as the young woman to die of heart disease, a condition closely linked to the competitive, so-called Type-A personality. Risk-taking, acting out aggressiveness, and high stress will lead to his being about three times more likely to die in an accident, of alcohol or drug dependency, or by suicide; about seven times more likely to be arrested for drunk driving or for a violent crime; and nine times more likely to be a murderer. It is perhaps not surprising that his life expectancy is seven years shorter than hers (Laudan 1994, 27, 99, 150, 173; Sadker and Sadker 1994, 221; Statistical Abstracts 1994, 853).

The lives of both will have been colored by stereotypes. Between them, they will have to come to terms with the dysfunctional aspects of those stereotypes in the lives they lead as adults.

### TRADITIONAL STEREOTYPES CONTINUE TO BE INFLUENTIAL

That such stereotypes are still alive and well, in spite of some measurable changes in people's attitudes about the roles and rights of women and men, has been documented by a number of studies in the late 1980s and early 1990s (Deaux and Kite 1993, 127; Unger and Crawford 1992, 138).

Among much other evidence, it is notable that in 1989, 32 percent of male and 20 percent of female first-year college students agreed with the statement that married women's activities are best confined to home and family; and in a very large national sample, 33 percent of the men and 39 percent of the women agreed that it is much better for all involved if a man achieves outside the home, and a woman takes care of home and family. However, in 1977 the latter figures were 69 percent agreement for men and 64 percent for women; and in the same period of time, agreement that it's more important for a wife to help her husband's career than her own declined by half among both women and men (Schmittroth 1991, 17, 20).

Also in 1989, a study of expectations of graduating seniors at the University of California at Berkeley showed that the overwhelming majority of both women and men hoped to marry, have children, and pursue a career. Nine tenths of the women planned on graduate degrees and half anticipated earning at least as much as their husbands, expecting to interrupt their careers between six months and twelve years to raise children. In real world terms, they were "talking career but thinking job"; whereas the men were "talking family but thinking career," being willing to "help" in the home but believing that housework and childcare were the wife's responsibility (Machung 1989 cited in Martin 1995, 169).

In a 1990 poll of Fortune 1000 chief executive officers, nearly 80 percent of the 241 respondents said there are "identifiable barriers that keep women from reaching the top" in the workplace. And 81 percent of those acknowledging the existence of barriers identified them as stereotypes and preconceptions (Fierman 1992, 503; originally in *Fortune*, July 30, 1990).

Much of the stereotyping and the preconceptions that need to be overcome arise from:

> ➤ the "clone syndrome," which leads all people (both women and men) to be uncomfortable with those who are "different," and to want to associate with those as similar to themselves as possible
> ➤ lack of experience on the part of many men of working with women in any but subordinate positions
> ➤ lack of experience on the part of many women with working as an equal member, or leader, of a high-status male work-group
> ➤ perceptions of "differentness" as inferiority by those often who unwittingly assume themselves to be the norm
> ➤ frequent viewing by men of women's communication, leadership, and interpersonal styles as inferior, unsuccessful, or erroneous versions of men's styles rather than as different, equally valid, or more valid, styles

*E*ducation can help young people to prepare to meet and overcome the attitudes that reinforce stereotypes and preconceptions, and can provide experiences that counter them. Context-appropriate suggestions for doing so are incorporated in the "What Can Be Done" sections in various parts of this book.

But the issue is not as simple as replacing the expectation that "women's place is in the home" with the expectation that "women's place is in the workplace," or even that it is in both. It is just as undesirable to make women feel that they should be in the labor force when they have the option and the desire to devote themselves full-time to their family as it is undesirable to make mothers feel they should not work outside the home.

Nor is it enough to help girls acquire attitudes and competencies stereotypically considered "masculine." Given the realities, boys also need help. Boys need to recognize the value and importance of attitudes and competencies stereotypically considered "feminine" not just in the family context but for success in the workplace as well; and, perhaps more importantly, they need also to stop being afraid of having or acquiring attitudes and competencies considered "feminine" themselves.

The first is almost a prerequisite for the second. As long as women and whatever is "feminine" are devalued, men will have good reason to avoid becoming in any way their like; and this is to men's as well as women's disadvantage.

The most realistic, as well as the most equitable, educational option is to counteract attitudes and behavior that devalue and disadvantage girls, women, and whatever is female-identified and to help both girls and boys interact as equals, and relate to each other in non-stereotypical ways as valued collaborators, worthy opponents, and interesting individuals. This can be done by promoting their growth into women and men who are capable of functioning competently in both the home and the workplace, and in varying combinations of the two. Boys and girls must be given the ability to function in nontraditional ways, and be supported in the choices they make, whether traditional or not. To bring this about, it is vital that, as educators, we avoid closing the door to some options for either boys or girls by what we *don't* do. We must also avoid squeezing the young into one particular option by what we *do* do.

It is also important for us to alert young people to the costs associated with each of the choices before them; none come without costs as well as rewards. The girl who blithely assumes that she will be a superwoman who can be it all, do it all, and have it all, who intends to have a distinguished professional career in a prestigious field, while being the kind of mother her own grandmother and Dr. Spock would be proud of, while helping her husband in his career, being active in volunteer work, undertaking an ambitious program of personal growth, and working on cellulite-free thighs, needs to have adults around her who can get her to consider how this is to be accomplished, and at what cost. Increasingly, boys need the same guidance as they yearn to take more equal roles in family life, take on their full share of parenting, and support their wives in their professional careers while making resounding successes of their own.

Young people need help in recognizing, and resisting, the ways media promote stereotypes, and in perceiving the self-interest that prompts media to favor those images of gendered human behavior that are profitable to advertisers. The difficulty of those trying to help the young to handle the new challenges they will be facing is compounded by the mass media, which swamp with gender-stereotypical messages both young people and all those who deal with and have expectations of them. Children get a double dose of the gender-stereotyping messages from the media. Some they absorb in their own watching. Others influence the adults with whom children interact — adults who gain much of the information they have about children from the media.

Media messages have real effects. Numerous studies have documented that television viewing has an impact on children's social learning, attitude formation, and behavior (Katz and Ksansnak 1994, 281; Strate 1994, 92; Mortimer 1994; Barry 1993). More specifically, there is evidence that those who watch TV a lot have more stereotyped views of sex roles, and describe themselves and their aspirations in more stereotypical ways, than those who watch less, from three-year-olds on up (Unger and Crawford 1992, 117; Greenfield 1984, 33). Adults also are affected. For instance, women's interest in political participation and public achievement declined after they viewed media images of women in traditional roles (Unger and Saundra 1993, 163). This is part of the reality that has to be recognized and taken into account in educational decision-making.

Television is probably the most significant of the mass media. In 1994, children aged 2-11 watched television twenty-three hours and forty-one minutes per week, and teens watched twenty-three hours and thirteen minutes per week (Nielsen ratings cited in Lazarus and Lipper 1994, before page 1); and 60 percent of nine-year-olds as well as 47 percent of seventeen-year-olds watched over three hours a day (NAEP Trend Assessment reported in *Education Week* , 1994, 4).

What those of any age watching TV see is highly stereotyped gender role presentations. This is marked in programming of every kind, but is most blatant in advertising where both men and women are presented in traditional, limited, and often demeaning ways. Studies over a seventeen-year period have found little change in the traditional representations of gender roles in prime time, any more than they did in advertising — although very recently some non-stereotyped or gender-neutral ads have begun to put in an appearance (Lazier and Kendrick 1993; McClelland 1993).

Based on a study of over 1,000 television programs in 1992, network TV dramas focus on male characters in a ratio of 2:1, the same as in 1954. "Villains" are disproportionately male, young, lower class, and Latino/Hispanic or "foreign." Marriage hurts men and helps women in prime time; in children's programming it hurts both. On television, women age faster than men, and as they age, are more likely to be portrayed as evil and unsuccessful; for every "bad" old male, there are eight "bad" old females (Gerbner 1993).

Another study showed that women are five times more likely to be blondes, four time more likely to be provocatively dressed, and are significantly younger than men (who are four times more likely to be gray-haired). Women are twice as likely than men to be shown as married ( Davis D., 1990).

Male news anchors (64 percent) overshadow female ones; men are interviewed far more often than women both as the source of news (82 percent), and as authorities about news (80 percent). Men sell investments, women soap, and figure heavily as sex objects. In TV dramas, there has, however, been some movement away from the still predominant stereotype of women as domestic, emotional, indecisive, and dependent on men (Gerbner 1993; McClelland 1993).

The media replicate and reinforce traditional versions of masculinity. Men appear more often in action and drama programming, and less often in shows that feature emotions or interpersonal relations. Men drive, drink, and smoke more, use firearms, are athletic, make business calls, and do the problem-solving and planning for themselves and others. Beer ads portray masculinity as depending on acceptance of challenge, danger, and risk — and men in groups as licensed to act irresponsibly.

In 1989, a series of commercials for a first-aid product showed one ad with a father holding a little girl who had a scraped knee and telling her "Daddy will kiss it and make it all better" and the next a boy with the same injury being told by his mother "Hush . . . big boys don't cry" (Hall and Crum 1994; Fejes 1992; Strate 1992; Cushner, McClelland and Safford 1992).

Preschoolers — at the most impressionable age for developing gender-role concepts — watch on the average twenty-five to thirty hours of TV a week. They are catered to by specifically targeted "boys' programs" and "girls' programs," which focus on only a few, and those among the most damaging, of the most rigid gender stereotypes. On boys' shows, heroes win by violent and aggressive actions (one pair of researchers characterized boys' shows as "let's reach out and crush someone"). On girls' shows, heroes defend themselves with "rainbows, magic, and kindness." The lesson boys learn from TV is that aggression and violence are successful conflict-resolution techniques; girls, that they are personally powerless, and have to rely on others' chivalry to escape from conflict and danger (Hesse and Cross 1990, cited in Horgan 1995, 29).

Concerned parents, child-care providers, and those involved in early childhood education need to consider the implications of prolonged TV exposure on the young, and construct action plans based on their assessment.

*A*dults, by their own behavior towards the young, can encourage the development of gender-stereotyped attitudes and behaviors — or counteract it. Whether to encourage or to counteract is a judgment that has to be made by individuals. It is, however, best made consciously, deliberately, and taking into account potential advantages and disadvantages.

Children begin to develop gender-stereotyped concepts at two to four years of age. At this age, toddlers of both sexes are usually already convinced that "girls would clean the house when they were grown up, and boys would be the boss and would mow the lawn" (Archer and Lloyd 1985, 267).

Parents have been shown to treat sons and daughters differently from infanthood. Their behavior add up to encouragement of gender-stereotyped behavior and attitudes in their children. As the children get older, parents tend more deliberately to reinforce their children's differentiation along gender lines.

Girls are typically treated as more physically fragile; are looked and talked to more; and mothers give girls more verbal feedback and instruction when the baby tries to communicate. Adults who are not parents tend to respond to baby boys with physical activity, to girls with comforting and soothing.

As toddlers, girls are encouraged by parents to ask for help, to help others, and to stick close to their parents, who are also readier to respond to girls with help and to accompany them. Parents tend to discourage girls from manipulating objects, running, jumping, climbing; and supervise them more closely than boys.

Parents are less directive with sons than with daughters, give them more independence and freedom to explore the physical environment. Boys have increasing contact earlier with people who are not family, especially peers, who are more influential for boys than girls. Sons are both praised more and given more negative feedback and physical punishment. More attention is paid to boys' negative, and especially aggressive, behavior; the same behavior in girls tends to be ignored.

(Note: The information above is based on both large and small-scale studies, almost exclusively of the white middle classes. They are consistent with each other, and all but a few are from the 1980s and 1990s. Sources are Reid and Paludi 1993, 194-195; Unger and Crawford 1992, 235-236; Fagot and Hagan 1991, 618, 624, 627; Thorne 1989, 146; Feiring and Lewis 1988, 107; 1970s studies cited in Salamon and Robinson eds. 1987; Archer and Lloyd 1985, 220; Power 1985, 1522; Huston and Carpenter 1985, 144; Sprafkin 1983, 170; Johnson and Roopnarine 1983, 194 ).

The same "aggressive" behavior is perceived differently depending upon whom it is directed towards; it appears to be acceptable in boys when directed towards same-sex peers. For example, a snowball fight between two boys was interpreted in an experimental setting as less aggressive than the same behavior between two girls, or a girl and a boy (Unger and Crawford 1992, 235-236).

The consequences of aggression also appear to be differentially emphasized by parents. There is some small-scale but consistent research evidence that those children whose mothers at eighteen to twenty-four months drew their attention clearly, recurrently, and insistently to the distress of others, and discussed feelings with them, were subsequently more concerned about and altruistic towards others; and that mothers consistently talked more about feelings to their eighteen-month old daughters than to same-age sons (Dunn 1987, 36).

The impact of such adult behavior is suggested by the fact that, by age ten, boys have been reported to expect less disapproval from their parents for aggression than do girls of the same age; and adolescent boys to be more likely than girls to believe that aggression increases self-esteem and that victims do not suffer (Late 1980s studies cited in Unger and Crawford 1992, 250).

Males at all ages tend to be more committed to gender stereotypes than are females; and more pressure is put on them by adults and peers to conform to the stereotyped masculine role from preschool through adolescence and beyond (Katz and Ksansnak 1994; Fagot and Hagan 1991; Galambos, Almeida and Petersen 1990). In adulthood, it is parents with children at home who are most prone to gender-stereotyped beliefs and behavior; and the best predictor of gender-role flexibility for a child, and of his or her tolerance of gender-flexible attitudes in others, is the flexibility to be found in their social environment: their parents, other adults, and peers (Katz and Ksansnak 1994; Katz and Walsh 1991, 339). For boys especially, the example and behavior toward them of males in their environment is decisive.

Parents provide sex-stereotyped toys and reinforce their use, fathers being especially emphatic about ensuring sons' play with typical male toys. At ten months, girls and boys are about equally likely to play with blocks, but both parents have been found to be more likely to attend to the block play of sons than daughters. At eighteen months, studies show parents' gender stereotypical toy choices still did not consistently coincide with the toys the infants chose themselves when given a range of toys in a laboratory setting. By ages three and four, though, children chose gender-appropriate toys. They also used gender-role oriented thinking to justify other children's likes and dislikes about toys; though in justifying their own choices, they used more reasoning about what the toy would do. In situations of free choice, it appears that young children may prefer toys not associated with either sex (Unger and Crawford 1992, 238-239, 243; Goldstein 1992, 69; Robinson and Salamon 1987, 126; Archer and Lloyd 1985, 260).

The types of toys given to boys encourage high levels of physical activity, and play outside, away from home. Girls' toys, in contrast, are more domestically oriented and more likely to involve verbal interaction (Quoted in Vaughter, Sadh and Vozzola 1994, 87; Unger and Crawford 1992, 239).

Among toddlers, the preference of boys for "boys' toys" increases with age. Own-gender toy choice is generally less marked among girls at all ages. At about three and a half, both sexes are more likely to play with cross-gender toys in mixed-gender groups (Lloyd 1987, 154). The gradually developed heavy preference for gender-typed, and very different, toys and for the play-styles these toys encourage, contribute to the increasing gender-segregation of playgroups — which in turn further differentiates interaction and communication styles of girls and boys.

The heavy media promotion of toys has put additional pressure on gender-role stereotyping, making it difficult even for those parents who wish to resist. An example is the difference between "Adorable Transformables," toys recommended for girls four and over that include such items as a necklace with a toy dog on it that turns into a lipstick, and "Transformers," futuristic, militarily oriented toys very popular with boys five and over that transform from a metal robot warrior to a plane, tank or the like, and are associated with very violent TV cartoon shows (Miedzian 1991, 268-269; Carlsson-Paige and Levin 1990, 93).

Boys' "war-play" has in the three to five age group become of considerable concern to many parents, who however often reported that they "felt somewhat out of control in terms of regulating their sons' war toys."

This is not surprising, given the extremely heavy promotion of such toys on TV and elsewhere, and their explicit connection with masculinity (one is even called "He-man"). Ninety percent of video game players are estimated to be male, and most of the games deal with violence (sixty-six out of a hundred sampled recently "revolved around outright destruction") (Miedzian 1991, 269, 274). While there is a correlation between preference for toy weapons and aggressive behavior, it is not clear whether this is a cause-effect relationship (Goldstein 1992, 70).

Parents and other adults in children's lives can offer them other ways of "being a man" than engaging in machine-supported violence, and "being a woman" than consuming beauty-enhancing products (Helpful sources: Hunter College Women's Studies Collective 1995; Miedzian 1991; Carlsson-Paige and Levin 1990; Gerzon 1982, Chapter 15).

A number of research studies suggest that, just as parents, other adults, peers, and media contribute to, so can they also counteract and modify gender-typed behavior developed by children. Effective methods include giving children non-stereotypical toys and stories at home; modeling for them nontraditional behavior, and showing positive consequences that result; making sure that girls spend time in low-structure and boys in high-structure activities and situations (see **LEADERSHIP** section); counter-stereotypical television programming, stories, and films; teacher reinforcement; and curriculum change. The studies suggest that specific, focused intervention efforts work better between ages four and ten than in later childhood; and that boys' behavior is harder to change and responds better to male intervention (Katz and Walsh 1991, 338-339). It is also clear that the most effective intervention efforts are multi-faceted, consistent, and prolonged.

Gender-role expectations by parents, and the differential behavior that results, seem to be affected by race, ethnicity, and class. However, there are few studies that explore differences from the picture presented above, which is based almost exclusively on studies of white middle class families. Some studies of African American children suggest less stringent stereotyping of girls' behavior in general and in working class families in particular; and that girls with more nontraditional gender-role training were higher in achievement. Anecdotal evidence suggests that Asian-American and Hispanic-American parents expect even more gender stereotypical development from their daughters than do whites (Reid and Paludi 1993, 195).

Gender stereotyping affects not only attitudes and behavior, but learning ability and performance. A number of studies have shown that gender stereotypes limit the kinds of activities that children can engage in competently (Bradbard et al. 1986). There is more forgetting of information not congruent with gender-stereotypes — and the more so the more committed learners are to gender-stereotyped attitudes (Bigler and Liben 1990, 1441). There is more forgetting, and less accurate memory, for information culturally judged "masculine," or that is male-associated, by girls and vice versa (Liben and Signorella 1993; Loftus et al. 1987, 79-81). Boys perform better on tasks and games defined or labeled as being "masculine," and girls on those labeled "feminine," even when the game or task was neutral or the same (Mark 1983, 4; Skolnick 1982, 31) .Performance on history tests through high school follows gender-stereotypical lines, with boys performing better on test items to do with war, and girls on those about humanitarian concerns (Kneedler 1988). Children learn more about new objects labeled as being for their own gender than those labeled for the other (Martin and Little 1990). Both boys and girls tend to ignore people whose behavior does not match their gender-stereotyped ideas (Schan and Tittle 1985, 85), and hence do not attend to information or learning opportunities provided by such people.

■ ■ ■ ■

## CHAPTER TWO

## UNDERCURRENTS OF GENDER: THE HIDDEN CURRICULUM AND THE NULL CURRICULUM

*By broadening his conception of the forces that make up and control his life,
the average person can never again be completely caught in the grip
of patterned behavior of which he has no awareness.*

*—Edward T. Hall, 1959*

The hidden curriculum is that which we teach without meaning to do so. The null curriculum is that which we leave untaught without having given it a thought.

Just as we are not usually mindful of the air we breathe, we are also not usually aware of the nature of the environment in which we operate. We all have absorbed ideas about what is "gender-appropriate" from our upbringing and the culture around us. These ideas seep into our thinking and affect our attitudes and behavior though we may not realize it. As a result, assumptions about gender that we may not even be aware of influence the ways we organize the school as an institution, the style and atmosphere of the school, and the relationships of adults and students in the school community. The same goes for the family — and our arrangements embody and radiate the hidden and null curriculum.

Gender-oriented messages are potentially carried by all aspects of school and family life: from lunch table conversation to room decoration; from scheduling of space and time to ways of testing, and reactions to success and failure; from admission interview to college recommendation. It takes mindful attention to recognize when such messages are being sent, and what their implications are. Decisions can then be made about whether to ignore, add to, reduce, change, or eliminate them. In the absence of awareness, decisions, and deliberate action, the effects of such messages, not always either trivial or benign, will continue unchanged.

Messages are also sent about importance and unimportance by those attitudes, experiences, competencies, and topics that are ignored and omitted from the life of the school and the family.

The following suggestions are intended to help schools and families who are interested in how assumptions about gender may be influencing the climate for the young in their midst — and in the impact that gender aspects of the climate may be having on various individuals and groups within their community.

### ADMINISTRATION: CHARTING A COURSE THROUGH ALL WEATHER

The new scholarship on women and gender has had a significant impact on ways of thinking in a wide variety of contexts. Acquaintance with it can help to shed light on the (often unintended) gender-related messages that may be built into schools' policies and practices. The following are areas in which alertness to the potential relevance of gender may be helpful.

**Communication:** Helping both adult and student members of the school community to understand differences in male and female communication styles reduces the potential for miscommunication that can have a negative impact on relationships among adults, as well as those between adults and students, in the school community. (For gender-related communication styles and the problems they may cause, see the section, **CROSSCURRENTS IN COMMUNICATION**, page 16). A school might also consider from a hidden/null curriculum point of view such things as:

> ➤ messages communicated by methods of testing, such as grading on a curve (suggesting that competition is for ranking rather than achievement); all tests timed (suggesting that it's

more important to finish fast than to demonstrate understanding); high proportion of multiple choice tests (suggesting that memory for isolated facts rather than comprehension of relationships is valued)

- ➤ talking about "the track team" when referring to the boys' team, but to "the girls' track team" (suggesting that one is the norm, the other the exception)
- ➤ the implications about ways of thought, unarticulated assumptions, and the weight of history behind such things as describing one course as "black women's literature," and not describing another as "white men's literature"
- ➤ teaching of debating but not of attentive listening
- ➤ putting more emphasis on teaching about motherhood than fatherhood, or teaching about neither
- ➤ apologizing for some kinds of language when used in the presence of a girl or woman, but not of a boy or man

**Professional Development:** To keep abreast of new developments both in their own discipline and in pedagogy, faculty need opportunities for exposure to, time for absorption of, and support in integrating the new information and ideas on the topic of women and gender. Faculty teaching the same subject and grade level need time to discuss ways to use the new information on pedagogy and subject matter in their own teaching. Those supervising teachers need to become knowledgeable about the research on boys' and girls' styles of learning and communication, so they can both help and hold accountable those they supervise for using techniques known to be both effective and equitable.

A school might consider hidden/null curriculum aspects of the balance between subject matter and pedagogy in professional development, and opportunities provided and encouragement given to pursue them. The administration might consider maintaining a record by gender of participation in sabbatical, summer study, and faculty development programs, and in faculty travel to workshops and conferences. Consciousness of the need for childcare if some are to be able to participate, and provision made for it, are relevant here.

**Faculty Working with Parents:** While all faculty greatly appreciate knowing that the administration backs them up in their interactions with parents, it is important to avoid fighting their battles for them. This is especially true of female faculty, who are more likely both to prefer avoiding confrontations, and to be shielded from them even when that may not be their wish — or if it is, may not be in their best interest as developing professionals. How these issues are handled is part of the hidden curriculum.

Encouraging faculty to alert an administrator to situations in which they think they may either have overreacted, been too belligerent, or not been firm enough, gives the opportunity both to work with the faculty member to help them do better next time, and to work out a strategy that settles the problem without escalation.

**Scheduling:** A school's schedule may unintentionally promote gender stereotyping by putting what are expected to be male- or female-preferred elective courses into the same time slot (For example, AP physics and AP French, or technical drawing and dance).

**Advising:** Academic advisors, teachers, and guidance counselors, while no longer automatically steering girls and boys towards traditionally "female" and "male" courses and career paths, may more readily allow girls than boys to drop courses they don't like, or find difficult. They may be unaware of just how much consistent, repeated, and long-range effort it takes to counteract students' existing gender-stereotyped thinking. They may also need support in helping parents to understand and come to terms with their children's possible choices of nontraditional courses and colleges (girls wanting to major in physics at Cal Tech, boys in theater arts at Sarah Lawrence).

**Extracurricular Offerings:** These opportunities may be slanted more towards boys' interests than girls' (or vice versa), or there may be an absence, or dearth, of extracurricular offerings of comparable interest to both girls and boys.

**Awards:** School prizes and recognition may be more abundant in areas of boys' than of girls' accomplishments and interests, or vice versa. The school may offer rewards for competitiveness and winning, but not for maintaining morale, caretaking, nurturing, or improvement. Awards may have descriptions/parameters that unintentionally make it more difficult for girls than for boys to win them, or vice versa.

**Student Service Programs:** Student service programs may no longer be stereotyped (girls cleaning classrooms, boys raking leaves), but in cases where jobs are left to student choice, there may be not much encouragement for them to at least consider alternatives when they consistently make gender-stereotyped choices.

**Publications:** Language used in school communications and publications such as view books, the newspaper, the yearbook, the literary magazine, and so on may still use "man" and "he," on the assumption that these terms are generic, yet actually be sending a message of exclusion (See the material on "quirks of gendered language" in the section on **ENGLISH,** page 83).

**Publicity:** Publicity may be more vigorous for those events or achievements that are identified more closely with boys than those identified with girls (for example, football games or science fairs vs. dance recitals or art exhibitions).

**Dress:** Appearance-related concerns of girls (diet, dress) may be given too little attention in some cases, too much attention in others; and dress-codes favor, or be perceived to favor, one gender or the other.

**Parents:** Parent relations may be overly driven by stereotyped assumptions. The mothers' organization may always be asked to hold bake-sales, the fathers' to help with athletic events. Parent conferences may make it hard for fathers or employed mothers to attend, and communications with parents may neglect the noncustodial parent among the divorced. The null curriculum may include not sharing with parents what the school is doing in terms of pedagogy and curriculum that is gender-relevant, and not holding workshops, meetings, and lectures to inform parents about gender-relevant information that would help them help their children to achievement and fulfillment of potential.(Some suggestions for doing so are included in **What Schools and Teachers Can Do** sections).

**Numbers:** Keep in mind that the relative proportion of women and men in certain positions in the school send messages with gender implications, such as the numbers of trustees; teachers and administrators at various grade, seniority levels, and different subject areas; coaches; committee members and chairs of committees; commencement and assembly speakers; and nominees for and holders of awards.

**Salary and Perquisites:** Many schools have inherited systematic gender differences in salary, in nonsalary benefits, and in the provision of housing. To equalize the situation in this area is not easy, and may take some time. It should be noted that differences may be perceived as existing, when in fact they do not, or when their existence is accounted for by what may be equitable reasons. It is usually advantageous for a school to be as open as possible about differences in this area, and what is being done about them.

**Support for Change and Self-Examination:** A look at curriculum and school climate with gender in view opens doors to a view of other issues of interest and importance to schools. Among them are: learning and teaching styles; faculty professional development; interdisciplinary learning and course construction; interest in a more global and/or more inclusive curriculum; critical thinking and cognitive development; cooperative learning and peer teaching; media literacy; anti-violence education and conflict-resolution; mediation and peer counseling skills; dealing with harassment preventively; and preparation for the self-study and review associated with re-accreditation.

## CROSSCURRENTS IN COMMUNICATION

Gender differences in speech are far from absolute, though males and females are socialized towards different communication patterns that are congruent with gender stereotypes. Each pattern or style has both advantages and disadvantages; the male style, however, is more highly valued and culturally preferred.

Both genders can, and do, use both styles, but are predominantly associated with one or the other. Moreover, the circumstances in which either uses the other's style are mirror-images: the male style goes with confidence and competing for status; the female, with uncertainty and the search for harmony, regardless of the speaker's actual gender. Confident girls normally using the "male" style may adopt aspects of the "female" style in a class where they feel intimidated or incompetent; boys may use features of the "female" style in circumstances of emotional vulnerability.

Male speech patterns, especially in all-male groups, have been found remarkably constant at various ages and across subcultures including urban middle class and blue-collar as well as rural whites, and urban blacks. These patterns have three main characteristics: arguing, verbal posturing, and monologues.

Arguing, which variously features countering in kind to others' ribbing and needling; contradicting and deriding others' statements; personal put-downs and name-calling; shouting, insults, and threats, is a common feature of speech in all-male groups, and can go to great lengths over quite trivial issues. Such exchanges are not viewed as a sign of hostility or real conflict, but are accepted as normal and enjoyed among friends. "Signifying," or "dozens," a ritual exchange of insults common among African Americans, functions to create group solidarity; male bonding in all-male groups results from conversation conceptualized as a contest. Throwing down a challenge with a needling remark is interpreted as inclusive, friendly, an invitation to join the group in the fun of mock contest by showing you can take it and give as good as you got.

With verbal posturing, males typically make strongly assertive statements, indulge in competitive overstatement, boasting, and "devil's advocate" arguments, without personal stakes or involvement. They cultivate an impersonal, abstract style with little self-disclosure, while seeking to control the topic, frequently interrupting, and ignoring the comments of previous speakers.

The monologue is a way of asserting dominance by keeping center stage in the face of passive non-support (audience silence) or active challenge (attempted interruptions, hostile comments, and put-downs). Males more than females find it difficult to listen to others.

Females more often than males reinforce other speakers with minimal, uninterrupting comments ("Mmmm," "Right") and with nonverbal cues of attention (nodding, leaning towards speaker); and when interrupting, tend to do so to ask for clarification and elaboration, thereby sustaining the speaker rather than trying to take the floor.

Efforts are made to include others by use of inclusive pronouns and phrases; by explicit acknowledgment of, and responses to, other's statements, and invitations to others to speak; and by comments intended to keep conversational exchanges going, and all voices fully heard. Conflict and competition are expressed indirectly.

Females are more likely than males to use false starts, a questioning intonation when making statements, tentative delivery, hesitant pacing, an excessive number of qualifiers and tag questions ("....isn't it?" "....don't you?"), and a more personal style with considerable self-disclosure.

Minority students' class participation is affected by cultural factors. For Asian-American and Hispanic students, and especially women, there are cultural prescriptions against speaking up, and positive reinforcement for being quiet and obedient. African-American females are less likely than white to be dominated by males in verbal exchange situations; and one study noted that African-American students in general are more comfortable speaking out in class rather than raising their hand and waiting to be called on. Being ignored, or reprimanded for talking "out of turn" may extinguish their class participation.

(Sources for the paragraphs above are: Thorne 1993, passim.: Kramarae and Treichler 1990, 56; Tannen 1990, passim; Graddol and Swann 1989, Chapter 4; Lyman 1987, 155; Hall and Sandler1984, 5; Treichler and Kramarae 1983, 119-120; Maltz and Borker 1982, 204-213; Ong 1981 passim.; Eakins and Eakins 1978, Chapters 2 and 3; Jenkins n.d.).

Gender-related differences in communication styles have educational implications. Girls, and those boys who use the predominantly female-associated style, are at a disadvantage in the classroom. There is evidence that teachers of both sexes value more highly student comments and answers delivered in the assertive "male" style, even when the content is the same. Hesitant speakers carry less credibility; and are interrupted far more often, by teachers as well as peers. They are unable to finish what they had to say, and once interrupted tend to stay out of the discussion altogether thereafter. The resulting lack of participation reinforces passivity, reduces understanding (because of the failure to try out and clarify ideas), and may be directly penalized by teachers in grading as well. It also deprives the rest of the group of their potential contributions.

There are also disadvantages for students using the predominantly male-associated style. They would benefit from learning not to blurt out the first answer that comes into their head in the rush to beat others out; to sustain a speaker in order to gain all that he or she has to contribute; to listen thoughtfully, and to care not only about getting their own ideas heard and accepted, but also about understanding others' ideas, responding to them, and integrating them into their own thinking.

African-American boys' confrontational communication style may be interpreted as inappropriate challenge to authority (especially by white male teachers) and penalized. Their "turn-taking" style may also become an issue in that, instead of considering a "turn" to be someone's until they have finished, they are more likely to think of a "turn" as the making of one point. They may interrupt, before speakers with other styles have finished, annoyed because the previous speaker is "hogging the floor"; whereas the latter are likely to be annoyed since they feel "their turn" is being taken away from them (Kochman 1981, Chapters 2 and 3). Being alert to potential problems of this kind, and discussing the differences in style with students if it occurs, can help to improve communication.

Boys' more aggressive style leads to their tending to dominate class discussions, in terms both of frequency and time. Research in the 1980s showed that regardless of whether the class is English or mathematics, boys in fourth, sixth, and eighth grades are about eight times more likely than girls to call out answers; and teachers are more likely to let boys than girls "get away with" not raising their hands.

Differences in communication styles can lead to miscommunication problems between boys and girls, and women and men as well.

In cross-gender conversations, males and females may be at cross-purposes because the former typically perceive questions as requests for information or attempts at interruption; the latter, as conversational maintenance. Males shift topics quickly, which can leave females feeling frustrated and left behind; females develop and elaborate topics, shifting gradually, which can result in leaving males bored and tuned out.

Females tend to misinterpret as hostility males' attempts to signal friendliness and an invitation to join the group and become "one of the boys" by the kind of needling, challenging, or insults that they'd use with their male peers. (Some of this kind of "teasing" is hostile; the female perception may be, but is not necessarily, inaccurate.)

The female response to what is perceived as personal antagonism is likely to be visible hurt, annoyance, anxiety, or withdrawal. To males, this can seem a discomfiting, and even baffling, rejection of their friendly gesture. Males also tend to interpret females' refusal to respond with counter-challenge and thereby join the game of competing for status (due to unwillingness to compete, lack of interest in status, or simply incomprehension as to what the situation is about) as an indication of the females' position at the lowest end of the status scale and of their acceptance of such a position. When repeated, such experiences reinforce assumptions of general female inferiority, as does the labeling of boys at the bottom of the male hierarchy as "girls."

Crossed wires in communication can lead to increased difficulties on both sides in working together comfortably and equitably in groups, whether those groups are students in the classroom or adults in a faculty or business meeting (Sandler and Hoffman 1992; Tannen 1990; Sadker and Sadker 1987; Krupnick 1985; Hall 1982).

The problem is not differences in gender, nor even the cultural traditions surrounding gender; it is the fact that different styles of relating to others need to be reconciled, and even more so the fact that usually neither the boys and girls nor the adults around them who are supposed to interact, recognize that there is a need for recognition of differences, and for negotiating any changes needed to make the interaction reasonably comfortable for both.

There are gender differences in nonverbal communication by, and toward, females and males also.

In speaking, not only what is said but how it is said sends messages. A deep, well-projected, slowly cadenced voice is perceived by listeners as more confident and dominant than a high-pitched, thin, and rapid one, which is "heard" as less competent, submissive, and subordinate. The deep voice is the voice of power and authority. Whether an individual's voice is high or low is, in part at least, physiological, and connected with size of larynx and with hormone levels, which differ by sex and give mature men on the average the deepest voices. However, the ranges of women and men overlap considerably, and each individual can pitch his or her voice over a considerable range. The social expectation is that women have high voices, mature men low. In general, women tend to speak at the high end of their register, men at the low end of theirs. This is clearly to women's disadvantage, and girls can be alerted to this situation, and learn to use their lower register.

Eye contact is an important element of communication. Both a steady stare (often perceived and sometimes intended as a challenge) and complete absence of eye contact (often interpreted and sometimes intended as "you're too insignificant for me to see you") are perceived as signals of dominance. Both are behaviors more often engaged in by men, and among men, by those of higher status or greater power. Women (and men in subordinate positions) typically avert their eyes from another's stare, a signal interpreted as not taking up the challenge. This is certainly the safer route. For a woman, or a lower-status man, to stare back at a dominant male may, in some circumstances, actually put them in danger. However, averting the gaze is admission and confirmation of subordinate status.

Females, and males in subordinate positions, look (usually intermittently) at those they listen to more than at those they speak to. As listeners, they are watching the higher-status speaker for cues, and are also signaling dutiful attentiveness. This behavior is expected (usually unconsciously) by the higher-status speaker, as in a teacher saying to a student "Look at me when I am speaking to you!"

In a number of studies, the more a person looked at another while listening to them, the less powerful they were rated by others, both male and female. Women who were in the position of "experts," were of high status, or had a high level of control orientation, were found to look significantly less at those they were listening to than did those who did not have these characteristics. Looking at another while speaking to them, on the other hand, is characteristic of those with high status. The more looking while speaking and the less looking while listening, the higher the status and dominance; and the greater the interpersonal power such an individual is considered to have by others.

Women in secure, well-defined power positions show their power nonverbally as directly as do men. However, in mixed-gender situations when power situations are ill-defined, undefined, or unstable, men's visual behavior typically conveys dominance, and women's does not. Alertness to one's own behavior can avoid giving the impression of powerlessness or low status by looking habits.

There is a cultural component to the "language of the eyes." Researchers have noted that among African Americans, listeners avoid looking at the speaker, especially if the speaker is perceived as dominant. Puerto Ricans, Mexican Americans, Japanese, and Native Americans among others also have the pattern of looking down to show respect. There are gender as well as cultural differences in this area also; looking at the speaker while listening occurred most frequently among white females, and least frequently among African American males. All this has obvious implications for teachers who might measure attentiveness or respect by the extent that students make eye contact.

Another nonverbal message of power, importance, and status concerns the space claimed and controlled. There are differences in male and female body language that both signal and perpetuate their stereotypical roles. A number of studies have shown that expansive body postures are connected with dominance, and that those postures characteristic for men and boys take up more space than those considered correct for, and characteristically adopted by, women and girls; although socially weak males' postures resemble those of females.

From early childhood, boys range over a wider territory than do girls. They typically control more space: as much as ten times more on playgrounds. They also invade girls' space, and disrupt girls' games more often than happens the other way round. Girls play closer to, and are more watched over by, adults. Other people will stand and sit closer to females than to males — although the degree of socially approved closeness varies culturally. Walking towards another from opposite directions, it is the lower-status person who detours and gets out of the way; in cross-gender situations, females typically do so. Lack of control over territory goes with low status; and subordinates yield space to dominants, who are freer to move into another's territory. Moving in on someone communicates a challenge to their power or status; giving way both signals and reinforces subordination.

Since African-American culture sanctions closer personal distance as appropriate than does white culture, white teachers (especially men) may perceive the approach of an African-American boy closer than their own cultural comfort-distance as a challenge to their authority. African-American girls may interpret the greater distance to them maintained by whites as lack of caring, disdain, or dislike. (There is anecdotal evidence that such misunderstandings have in fact happened in schools.)

Space allocation in home and school in terms of the size of "own" room(s), offices/studies, lockers, toy chests, playing fields; who intrudes into whose space; and the amount of personal and possessions space habitually given to various people are part of the hidden curriculum, conveying messages about status and importance. Never talking about and paying no attention to the implications of differences in verbal and nonverbal communications is part of the null curriculum.

(The section above draws on information in Ellyson, Dovidio and Brown 1992; Smith-Lovin and Robinson 1992; Ridgeway and Diekema 1992; Graddol and Swann 1989, Chapter 2; Thorne 1989, 146; Hecht, Andersen and Ribeau 1989; Bull 1983, 75; Ellison, Dovidio and Fehr 1981, 64-75; Eakins and Eakins 1978, Chapter 6; Henley 1977, 37-38; 153-166).

## TESTING THE WATERS FOR GENDER UNDERTOW IN SCHOOL AND FAMILY

Gender-influenced assumptions, expectations, and actions permeate the atmosphere of every school and family. However, the traces of gender in what goes on rarely surface, although they become clear enough when looked for. What happens about conflict is one undercurrent of life that is gender marked — although, as always, the differences between girls and boys are far from absolute.

Among boys, conflict is more likely to be overt, and more easily tips over into action. The "presenting symptoms" tend to be noisy and clear: persistent verbal baiting, yelling, scuffling, hitting, breakage, fist fights. The causes are usually not hard to identify. Because the situation seems so obvious, it is rare for adults to try to identify any less obvious underlying causes; and when they do try, getting at them is difficult.

Boys consider it uncool, and indeed unmanly, to admit to being bullied; to being concerned over school performance, or relations with siblings; to feeling grief at the loss of a relationship; to feeling that they are betraying their own culture by fitting in so well with the school's, or being anxious at not fitting in; to being worried over bodily changes in adolescence. Such more covert problems may well be at the root of what, overtly, is "acting out," or a short fuse. Assuming, say, that a problem is settled by separating combatants and making them take turns may not get at the root of the matter. It's a judgment call in specific situations: sometimes the obvious is just that. But it's worth considering at least whether to take it further.

Seeking the opportunity for a quiet talk a while after a conflict has been settled allows a low-key approach that might lead to a boy's sharing of something he feels he should be able to handle himself, but that he could use, and perhaps really needs, help with.

Among boys, the presence of peers is likely to intensify rather than defuse conflicts, since ignoring or refusing a challenge, attempts at conciliation, compromise, backing down, or backing away are all typically perceived as weak, unmanly, contemptible. Boys from minority groups may feel particular pressure from peers, not only to engage with peer conflict, but also to resist Anglo-American middle class school values — which is likely to embroil them in conflict with school authorities.

It is worth working with boys to:

> ➤ discuss whether it really is considered "unmanly" by others to resolve rather than escalate conflict, and to seek alternative options before resorting to violence; if so, by whom, why, and with what degree of validity
> ➤ explore the part played by what they think their same-sex peers expect of them in their behaviors; and ways to check out, and evaluate, others' expectations rather than acting on unexamined assumptions
> ➤ teach conflict resolution and mediation techniques that give them alternatives and the confidence to choose them when circumstances warrant, such as how to deal with anger, and with peer pressure toward not backing down; how to listen carefully and understand another's opinions and feelings (you may ask boys in conflict to paraphrase the other's statement before talking themselves); to clarify jointly with an opponent what exactly the dispute or disagreement is about; and to come up with, examine, and negotiate options; to seek common ground; to explain that spectators who do not speak out against wrong action on the part of others are aiding and abetting the wrongdoer because silence will be taken for approval; to explore the pros, cons, and limits of not "ratting on" others; and to accept compromise as a good solution, because both parties get part of what they wanted, rather than a bad solution, because neither party got all they wanted.

Conflict among girls tends to be less overt, less obvious, and its existence may even be denied. Girls tend to have more of an investment in relationships than do boys, and to be more attuned to the dynamics of relationships, taking note of subtle changes in tone or body-language, and drawing inferences about the attitudes of others to each other, and to them.

With typically lower self-confidence and greater intimacy and therefore more emotional investment in same-sex friendships than boys (AAUW 1992, 11-12; Brown 1991, 67), girls are quick to perceive, or suspect, a slight. Concerned about a breach in the social fabric were they to confront the other person to check it out, they may nurse a grudge, or simmer with hurt, without admitting it — sometimes even to themselves. Adults can help them work out ways to test their assumptions about others' feelings towards them; and to become less dependent on others' approval.

On the plus side, girls' networks of friends or dorm-mates have a stake in the restoration of social harmony, and therefore will support compromises, win-win solutions, and emotional healing after the settlement of a conflict.

Moderating disputes may be difficult because the issues may be amorphous with a tendency to get mired in circumlocutory talk, and the stakes in denial of conflict are high.

Cutting through to what the core issue tends to be by asking students, "What do you feel?" "What would make you feel better?" and "What action would you like [the other person or persons] to take?" helps girls to get a handle on their emotions, become more direct, and both clarify what they want from other people, and become better able to express it. Teaching them conflict resolution techniques that depend on clear articulation of the terms of the dispute, or peer counseling that formally introduces a third party who needs clear and specific information about the conflict, can also help.

Girls may need help articulating feelings of anger and hostility; reassurance that there are safe ways of expressing such feelings; and understanding that they can experience, and admit to, the feelings without necessarily taking any action based on them.

Sometimes girls need to be pulled up short if they use what amounts to emotional blackmail: manipulation of others through tears, tantrums, hysterical outbursts, and other indirect attempts to get their way.

In cross-gender conflict, gender differences in conflict management may worsen problems and make for unsatisfactory settlements. For instance, in situations that involve breaking a promise, a study of adults found that men tended to start conflict with a question, women with an accusation; and for men, conflicts that began with an accusation by the offended party had more of a tendency to escalate, and were less likely to have a satisfactory outcome. Men were more likely to make excuses, women to apologize; and for women, it was apologies by the offender rather than excuses that resulted in satisfactory resolutions. Indeed, excuses by an offender decreased the chances that women would be satisfied with the conflict's resolution.

It appears that, for men, it is the initial reaction by the person who is offended that governs the outcome of the conflict; for women, it is the offender's subsequent behavior that does so (Miller 1991).

In mixed groups, women typically build on positive social behavior by giving positive messages themselves, maintaining and amplifying good feelings within the group. Men, on the other hand, respond to positive messages with task-oriented behavior, halting the development of empathy and emotional ties among group members. They also are far more likely than women to react with hostility and negative behavior to an initial disagreement or unfriendly act, especially if the initial behavior came from another man. Women are more likely to react to initial negativity by not reacting to it at all, especially if the initiator was another woman. In other words, men typically tend to escalate conflict, women to avoid it (Wood and Rhodes 1992, 101-102).

### Actions that may be considered

Alerting students to the gender differences in styles of interaction may help them to become more thoughtful about their own, and more understanding of others', behavior, and thereby reduce interpersonal tensions.

Girls are likely to give each other a great deal of emotional support, and feel a responsibility for each others' emotional well-being. This tendency needs watching. Caretakers may be depleting themselves to the point of interfering with their own work and even their health in attempts to help their friend or a classmate; the limits of their responsibility must be drawn for them clearly, and made to stick.

Be alert to, and consider avoiding, the common method of consoling a girl, which feeds into a stereotype. Avoid telling her: "There, there, it's all right, you've done your best," with its hidden, unintended messages of "You have license to fail, success is not important, only that you try," and "you have done your best, and still failed — therefore, you must lack the ability to succeed."

Some boys find it easier to discuss emotional problems with a woman; but it is very important for them to also have mature male father figures whom they feel they can talk with freely. Just reassuring them that it is all right to have the feelings, and to act as sounding board and sympathetic listener is often all that is needed.

Be alert to, and consider resisting, the style of consolation that reinforces the already powerful message of appropriate masculinity as repression of anxiety and vulnerability ("Don't worry," "You'll get over it," "You're tough, you can take it"). Consider instead validating the feelings as appropriate in the circumstances, and as being shared by others — especially other males ("Several of my advisees have had a similar experience; some found they became less miserable when they were able to talk about it." or "I've felt hurt like this myself when the coach grounded me").

Watch for the hidden message in excessive praise. Students may take it to mean that they have low ability. (A lot of praise implies that performance far exceeded expectation. If expectation was low, is that because ability is judged to be limited?) Differential praise for equivalent performance is especially to be avoided. Moreover, for praise to do the most good, it needs to be accompanied by detailed explanation of exactly what it was about the performance that was judged praiseworthy.

Bonding among boys tends to turn around common activities, often doing or watching sports together. Coming close to boys may be difficult for adults who do not share their interest in athletics. Teachers and parents may consider the possible benefits of creating a wider spectrum of activities through which boys can learn to relate.

Among girls, bonding tends to depend more on talk and the discussion of feelings than on activities in common. Girls generally have a very lively sense of how any group they are a part of functions as a community, such as their class, sibling group, or even the school. They may be quick to alert adults to low morale. Misinterpreting such alerting as "snitching" or seeking to curry favor with adults, and meeting it with disapproval, sends the message that emotional caretaking is not only not valued but is wrong.

Girls' emotional bonding is usually strongest with a small circle of friends. They are somewhat clique-prone, and adults might consider creating opportunities for girls to experience bonding with larger groups, such as clubs, teams, or girl scout troops.

Cross-gender friendship bonds are important in helping children develop competencies and attitudes that will stand them in good stead as adults. Cross-sex interaction is important. The exclusiveness of play with same-sex peers that increases through grade school is known to be associated with:

- ➤ devaluation of the other sex
- ➤ an avoidance of traits and activities associated with the other sex
- ➤ reinforcement of only a few favored (and stereotyped) ways of thought and behavior at the expense of other possibilities

Within single-sex groups, tactics used to achieve dominant status are congruent with the preferred play style, and become increasingly different. The differences have long-range implications for adult leadership and communication.

Dominant girls gain leadership in all-girl groups by verbal persuasion, and exercise influence by requests. Boys interacting with same-sex peers increasingly tend to shoulder others out of the way and make demands. The styles girls and boys have developed in single-sex groups during grade-school years that work within their own groups are increasingly ineffective, and counterproductive or alienating, with members of the other gender. The effects linger thereafter; and color the problems and misunderstandings experienced by adults in dealing with members of the opposite sex (Unger and Crawford 1992, 248-249). The influence of same-sex peers also keeps reinforcing commitment to gender-stereotyped thinking and behavior, especially for boys — and the rigidity of this commitment interferes with learning (see **THE "CURRICULUM" OF THE REAL WORLD**, page 11).

Adults can help boys and girls relate to each other in relaxed and friendly ways. Cross-gender friendship bonds can be nurtured most in a climate in which young people:

- learn to relate to those not of their own gender in a wide variety of ways—as colleagues, collaborators, competitors, leaders and followers, providers and requesters of help
- take part in activities, in groups that include varied ages as well as both genders
- interact in mixed-gender groups that are not heavily skewed towards one or the other gender
- take part in gender-neutral activities when in mixed groups
- participate as a mixed-gender group in some significant activity that encourages or demands cooperation (Outward Bound and orienteering activities, creation of a group art project or radio show, running an experiment or neighborhood work project) especially if the activity is one that lasts for some time and requires the group to meet and work together repeatedly
- have some principle of grouping other than gender explicitly invoked in the group's formation (counting off, interest in studying robins on the one hand and cardinals on the other, those eating a hot or a cold lunch)
- have situations created for them by adults in which they are free to interact without being stigmatized by other children for having chosen to do so themselves (for example, adults forming mixed-gender playgroups for younger children or naming those who will collaborate in a research report or the running of an experiment)
- are helped to differentiate between: liking as a friend, and romantic interest; a study-date and a "date" date; being a couple (as in "going with") and hanging out with (as in "buddies"); the salience of sexuality in different contexts, i.e. flirting at a dance as opposed to flirting in the laboratory
- are taught not to put others down for cross-gender interactions
- are consistently, explicitly, and continually reinforced for mixed-gender interaction (by comments such as "Langston and Amy are setting an example in how well they collaborate")
- see adults modeling, and hear adults address in discussions, positive nonsexual cross-gender relationships
- have adults actively intervene, when the dynamics of stereotype and power negatively affect relationships within the gender-mixed group

By adolescence, opposite-sex peers are a strong influence on how rigid or flexible in being bound by gender stereotyping both boys and girls are. There is some evidence that the greatest change in flexibility may occur in early adolescence. Having friends of the opposite sex who are tolerant about nontraditional gender roles and behaviors for themselves and others seems to be associated with greater open-mindedness about what is gender-appropriate in both boys and girls (Katz and Ksansnak 1994).

Adult behavior and ways of approaching the young are also influenced by gender, not infrequently in ways we are not alert to.

Men may want to consider that what they say about girls and women, how they react to the ways their students and children talk about them, and how they themselves behave towards females, sends powerful messages to young people about how an adult male should think, feel, and act towards the opposite sex. Because they are perceived as authorities, men have a particularly important role in setting the thermostat in terms of how chilly the climate will be for non-gender-stereotyped behavior.

Male students need to hear from their male teachers, dorm parents, and fathers that gender stereotyping is not just a "women's issue" but a human challenge deserving serious attention. Students will believe that faculty really think this to the extent that they see their male teachers supporting female colleagues and encouraging female students to excel (Jordan 1992, 144-145).

**Men might want to alert themselves to the following dimensions of gender influence:**

➤ the need for balance in emphasizing positive aspects of the masculine intellectual and personal styles and approaches, without neglecting to point out less positive aspects of masculinity and its expressions when talking with either boys or girls

➤ being conscious of themselves as overall role models for boys

➤ monitoring themselves for the ability to listen to another's problems without feeling that the onus is on them to solve the problem. Encouraging people with problems to talk, listening, asking how a situation is making them feel, what they would like the outcome to be, what ways they can think of that might lead to the desired outcome, and what the pros and cons of various solutions are is usually preferable to the best advice about what to do

➤ helping young people to opportunities that allow non-gender-stereotyped behavior and giving support to such behavior when it occurs

➤ in schools, and especially if young, avoiding the temptation to establish authority by "out-machoing" the male students who are most likely to challenge them; and not joining the boys in the jockeying for status that is common in male groups

**Women may want to consider:**

➤ being alert to the fact that what they say about boys and men, how they react to the ways their students and children talk about them, and how they themselves behave towards males, sends powerful messages to young people about how an adult female should think, feel, and act towards the opposite sex

➤ being alert to the fact that a deep voice and slow speech is a marker of authority in this culture, and that both can be cultivated (see **CROSSCURRENTS IN COMMUNICATION**, page 16)

➤ being conscious of themselves as role models for girls, illustrating one of the various options open to females with their own lives. Girls and boys would both benefit from hearing firsthand the pluses as well as the minuses of the option chosen, whether a combination of career and family, part-time work, choosing to stay single, be a full-time homemaker, or some other option.

➤ being alert to the need for balance in emphasizing the positive aspects of feminine intellectual and personal styles and approaches, without neglecting to point out less positive aspects of femininity and its expressions when talking with either girls or boys

➤ acquiescing to boys' tendency to consider a higher level of baiting, rivalry, badmouthing each other, and shouting as normal, acceptable, and even pleasurable than they themselves might be comfortable with (see **CROSSCURRENTS IN COMMUNICATION**, page 16), and to the fact that it may take awhile to develop a sense of when to step in, and when to radiate benign neglect

**All faculty and parents are likely to benefit from:**

➤ becoming familiar with differences in male and female styles of communication, and with common kinds of miscommunication (see **CROSSCURRENTS IN COMMUNICATION**, page 16).

➤ being willing and able to use both task-oriented and directive, and morale-oriented and supportive leadership styles, and being alert to the kinds of situations when one or the other or a combination of them is most appropriate (see **LEADERSHIP,** page 131).

➤ avoiding overreaction to challenge by the young for fear of not being perceived as "tough enough"

- ➤ becoming both knowledgeable and comfortable with discussing issues of sexuality and reproduction, love and romance, sexism and feminism, traditional and nontraditional lifestyles, dieting and health concerns
- ➤ handling both same-sex and opposite-sex students' (and other young people such as baby-sitters') possible crushes on them sensitively, and recognizing that what is coming across as deliberately seductive behavior from a girl (or a boy) may be an unself-confident child trying to make herself (or himself) liked — or may in fact be deliberately seductive behavior, even if the adult is married and no longer young. In either case, talking the situation over in confidence with another adult (in schools, the student's advisor, and/or the school counselor, the dean of students, or the dormitory head) is advisable.
- ➤ being circumspect in the use of physical contact with children or young people not one's own: a pat on the shoulder, a touch of the arm, let alone even the most innocent of hugs may mean something different to a student from what was intended. This does not mean faculty should never touch students; but it does mean that using judgment is indicated
- ➤ in schools, recognizing the possible dangers of over-involvement emotionally with a student, even in a nonsexual way
- ➤ being alert to one's students' and children's fear of the possibility of their own homosexuality, and to their homophobic reactions to others; making it clear to them that sexual preferences are separate from gender roles (boys may mistakenly be concerned, for instance, that playing with dolls, a liking for poetry, or enrollment in dance class shows that they are homosexual, or even that such behavior will turn them into homosexuals); becoming informed about current sociological, historical, biological and religious stands on the topic; and doing some reading by, as well as about, gay men and lesbian women so that they are able to discuss the issues with their students and children with a degree of comfort and competence
- ➤ exercising restraint in self-revelation, especially in schools. Learning about situations encountered by adults, and how adults think, feel, and react to them, can be an important part of students' education. However, not all students can handle sharing adult problems and adult reactions; doing so can be very upsetting to them. It can also be detrimental to the adult if their confidences are passed on to others, possibly becoming distorted in the process. As a rule of thumb, (certainly far from infallible): don't share what you would not be comfortable seeing in print in the school newspaper.

## DISCIPLINE: WEATHERING TURBULENCE

*T*he ways that discipline is handled in school and at home may be influenced by gender-associated expectations, and may have unintended effects.

For a start, an examination of the basic assumptions behind the approaches to discipline for the young may be useful. Teachers and parents might take a look at where their own ideas and policies stand as regards a balance between the "ethic of justice," which stresses rights, rules and laws, abstract right and wrong, regardless of the details of the situation, and tends to be associated with males, and the "ethic of care," which looks at the context of the action being evaluated, and how all involved will be affected, and tends to be associated with females. It's also useful to take a look at when they tend to use which mode. (For the ethic of justice and of care, see Gilligan 1982).

In schools, consider whether the community might not benefit from the introduction (if not already present) of peer mediation, not as a substitute for, but as an adjunct to, the discipline system. (For peer mediation in grades 6-12, see Cohen 1995, and/or contact School Mediation Associates, 134 Standish Road, Watertown, MA 02172; (617) 876-6074.)

Here are some gender-related discipline issues that the school, and parents, may want to take a look at and decide whether to take action about (see also the section **HARASSMENT**, page 27).

**Boys may:**

- have their pranks and minor transgressions winked at, because "boys will be boys," which can create a mistaken impression of immunity
- be more strictly held to the rules, out of concern for the assumed likelihood that, if boys are not stopped early, they will "go too far"
- be punished more severely than girls for the same offense.
- be penalized by society's narrower definition of appropriate clothing for males than females that may, unintentionally, result in school situations in a more restrictive dress code for boys; greater likelihood of boys being disciplined for breaking rules about clothing, since their dress codes can be simpler than girls', and transgressions more obvious; less likelihood of being allowed to wear clothing traditional in their culture (dashiki, sarong, burnoose)

**Girls may:**

- be held to stricter standards of tidiness, neatness, and decorum than boys, without any intention of creating a double standard
- "get away with" more because their transgressions may be less obvious and high-profile than boys'
- have their cold-shouldering and freezing out of peers ignored, whereas boys' more active taunting and verbal hassling of peers is penalized
- not be "called on" their use of tears or tantrums as a way to avoid responsibility, or as attempts to control others
- be less likely than boys to be scolded for pushing or shoving aside another child, since their actions are less likely to be interpreted as "aggression"

**Women and men who deal with young people may:**

- interpret disciplinary standards differently
- be consistently more lenient with girls (or boys)
- be reluctant to discipline girls ("They cry") or boys ("They get defiant and in your face")
- assess transgressions differently by gender (for instance, consider physical fighting between equals more serious for girls than boys, but bullying those younger or weaker more serious for boys than girls)
- tolerate more noise and boisterousness from one gender than the other
- assign different punishments to boys and girls (work-crew or grounding for boys, detention or curfew for girls)
- have different standards for what constitutes appropriately severe punishment for girls and boys

**Men may be more likely to:**

- perceive boys' transgressions as personal challenges to their authority
- show anger in disciplinary situations even when they feel disappointed, upset, anxious, or sad

- be harsher with young people they think are defying them
- be more willing to give girls a break

**Women may be more likely to:**

- be unwilling to confront boys in disciplinary situations when their authority might be challenged
- overreact in disciplinary situations in order to avoid appearing "soft"
- be anxious about the possibility of themselves becoming "too emotional" in a disciplinary situation
- find it difficult to show anger even when the situation warrants it

In dealing with boys' alcohol-related discipline, it may be helpful to recognize the very strong cultural linkage, promoted by the mass media and in other ways, between manliness and drinking. Drinking and getting drunk is often perceived by boys as an entree into manhood, a kind of initiation rite that needs repetition to be really valid, and to maintain both the drinker's own conviction that he is really a man, and his masculine image before his buddies (Postman et al. 1987).

Research shows that adult women tend to drink wine, to drink slowly, on special occasions, with family, and to celebrate special events. Anecdotal information from schools suggests however that girls' pattern of alcohol use is changing, and moving closer to boys'. In some ways, alcohol is a greater problem for girls because their generally lighter weight produces higher effects with less alcohol, and because of the sexual problems that drinking situations are likely to embroil them in.

Men and boys tend to drink with same-sex friends, acquaintances, or even strangers. They drink beer fast, irrespective of occasion, and drink for the effect of drinking — to get high or drunk. This activity is something that has become, since the 1840s, part of the concept of masculinity; and tends to be accepted by the culture in general as predictably "manly" behavior (Landrine, Bardwell and Dean 1988). Being willing to risk getting caught adds to the perception that the drinker is "being a man."

It is hardly surprising that adolescent boys, who need to prove themselves men, encounter a significant number of disciplinary problems that center around drinking.

**Schools and parents may consider adding to their drug and alcohol education:**

- a discussion of the male role and male gender stereotyping
- the power of stereotypes supported by mass media
- the question of whether what is perceived as peers' expectation actually exists
- dealing with peer pressure and expectations about "appropriately" masculine behavior that is actually inappropriate or damaging when it does exist
- alternative ways of "proving" masculinity

Finally, in schools the question of representation may be considered, in the person of the dean of students and her or his assistants, and the gender makeup of students and adults on the discipline committee.

### INTO THE STORM: HARASSMENT, SEXUAL AND OTHERWISE

Sexual harassment exists in schools from the elementary grades on up — and most of it is students doing it to each other. Although often dismissed as a joke, just teasing, or a minor irritant, it is no laughing matter. Harassers may be doing something illegal as well as mean; those harassed may have not only their dignity and feelings hurt, but their learning ability sapped. Harassment and other bullying behaviors have a very chilling effect on school climate.

While more of the harassed are girls, and more of the harassers are boys, the differences are smaller than stereotypes would lead one to believe. A large-scale national study of eighth to eleventh graders, conducted in 1993, found that nearly one in three girls, and nearly one in five boys, said that they were "often" sexually harassed, when the definition of such harassment was "unwanted and unwelcome sexual behavior that interferes with your life."

Moreover, two thirds of the boys and just over half the girls said that they have themselves harassed someone else at school.

The behaviors reported were not trivial. Two thirds of the girls and 40 percent of the boys had been grabbed, touched, or pinched in a sexual way; about a third of each had clothing pulled off or down. There were some gender differences, in that boys more often than girls experienced being called homosexual, the form of harassment they found most upsetting. Boys more frequently reported being shown, given, or left sexual pictures or messages, and being spied on while dressing. (The researchers asked about fourteen specific behaviors, half of them physical.)

Students reported that 80 percent of the unwelcome behaviors were student-to-student. Adult-to-student harassment was less widespread. However, a quarter of the girls reported harassment by a teacher or other school employee, African-American girls more frequently than whites or Hispanics (Sidel 1994, 33; Lawton 1993, 5).

The scope of the problem is confirmed by other evidence. Surveys at the college level consistently found 20-30 percent of all female students experiencing some form of sexual harassment, more severe in the case of African American and Hispanic women than whites, and by far most of it harassment by peers.

The evidence also confirms that sexual harassment is not only a "women's problem." Men, too, are subject to it, though at lower rates; and harassment occurs within as well as between genders. Harassing behavior, especially among males, is often related to trying to gain status with male peers by demonstrating domination over a female or a weaker male. Virtually all experts agree that most cases of peer harassment occur when boys or men are in groups, showing off to each other.

Among medical students at one institution three quarters of the women and a fifth of the men reported harassment. In a poll of high school juniors and seniors, a third of the girls and nearly a fifth of the boys said they knew classmates who had been sexually harassed. Data from one independent school show 32 percent of female faculty witnessing or experiencing some kind of harassment or overt gender bias of the harassment type; in a student survey from another, half the girls and a third of the boys said they had observed sexual harassment at their school.

(Sources for the section above are: Ginorio 1995, 11; Mee 1995, 5; Sidel, 1994,35,71; NAIS-CWIS 1993; Hughes and Sandler 1986,1; Dalton 1986, 52)

*D*ifferences of perception may facilitate, or contribute to, sexual harassment. Among adults, there is wide agreement on condemnation of sexual harassment. A two-year government study of nearly 20,000 federal employees found that, in the abstract, over 95 percent of the respondents were opposed to sexual harassment, and a quarter of both male and female respondents agreed that something could be sexual harassment even if the person doing it did not mean to be offensive. More concretely, a *TIME* magazine poll showed just over half the respondents agreeing that a man found to have engaged in sexual harassment of a woman should be fired from his job.(U.S.Merit Systems 1981, 61-67; Gibbs 1991, 63).

There is, however, considerable disagreement on just what constitutes sexual harassment. Men, more than women, tend to regard only the most blatant behavior as sexual harassment. They are more than twice as likely as women to feel that often the victim was, at least partially, responsible ("Wearing shorts like those, she's asking for it."), and that the whole issue is exaggerated (U.S.Merit Systems 1981, 61-67).

Several studies show that men are likely to misinterpret women's friendly behavior as sexual interest. Male observers of everyday interactions between men and women are more likely to view the women's behavior as sexy, flirtatious, and seductive, whereas women view the same behavior as merely friendly. The misperception may lead the man to react with sexual speech or action he thinks he has at least a minimal green light for, which in fact is unwelcome to the woman and is interpreted by her as harassing behavior (Project 1988, 3).

Similarly, one of the characteristics of male speech is that men use needling, ragging, provoking, putting the other person challengingly on the spot, and even put-downs as ways to indicate potential acceptance; the expectation is that the other person will prove himself or herself a good guy and worthy of inclusion in the group by replying in kind. Such exchanges are not intended, nor perceived, as unpleasant, and are generally enjoyed by both parties. Directed towards women, such verbal behavior may, but does not necessarily, carry more derogatory, demeaning, and hostile overtones. In either case, it is likely to be interpreted as a personal attack, and responded to with hurt, withdrawal, or anger, which is likely to escalate the ragging and the perception of women as weak and unable to "take it."

When asked to rate the seriousness of a list of behaviors ranging from winking to off-color and demeaning jokes, propositioning, breast-touching, groping, all the way to rape, on a scale of one to whatever number best represented the seriousness of rape compared to the wink, men's ratings ranged very widely. To them, these behaviors were not related at all, and the distance between them in seriousness was enormous. Women's ratings were along a relatively much narrower band, suggesting that to them all these sexualized behaviors were connected on a fairly short continuum, all of serious weight. To men, a number of these were not only pleasurable, but their expectation was that women too would find them so ("I wish someone would proposition me."). Indeed, a large-scale mid-1980s study found two thirds of the men saying that they would be flattered if asked to have sex by a woman coworker, whereas two thirds of the women said they would be insulted by a sexual invitation from a male colleague (Lorber 1995, 249).

The difference in perception applies not to gender alone. Racial or ethnic slurs defended with the classic "Hey, can't you take a joke?"; Jewish-American princess stories told in a gauche attempt to amuse seem like fun to the ones making the jokes or innuendoes. "Just kidding. . . " The targets, rightly or wrongly, are likely to perceive hostility, feel demeaned or even threatened, and experience discomfort, anxiety, pain or rage (Rowe 1985).

Activities such as fourth-grade boys teasing a peer by calling him "woman," or embarrassing girls to the point of tears by "rating" her physical attributes (AAUW 1992, 73-4), high school boys telling the joke: "What's long and skinny and goes from bedroom to kitchen? A woman's leash" (Sadker and Sadker 1994, 274), are often dismissed as just high spirits, not intended to hurt ("Boys will be boys. . ."). But whatever the intent, the hurt *was* inflicted.

Gender differences in perception extend to more serious sexual scenarios, including the issue of when does seduction turn into "scoring" and rape. A survey of almost 1,000 students at a Massachusetts college concerning date rape found that one in fourteen of the men had committed or attempted rape, and half of these said that they had some sense of pride at the time of the incident. While women who had been rape victims said that in 81 percent of the rapes the men used threats or mild force, while the women told him to stop, argued, and pleaded with him, only 58 percent of the men said the women asked them to stop, and only 35 percent that they had used threats. Whereas two thirds of the women said they physically resisted and struggled, according to the men, only 10 percent of women did so (Project 1990).

That attitudes towards sexuality and violence can be significantly changed by intervention programs is suggested by a large-scale 1988 study of sixth-to ninth-grade students. Before the two-year program began, 65 percent of the boys and 57 percent of the girls among the 1,700 students involved said it was acceptable for a man to force a woman to have sex with him if they had been dating for six months. A smaller percentage said that forced sex was permissible if the man had spent a lot of money — defined as $10-$20 — on her; and half the students said that a woman who walks alone at night in seductive clothes is inviting rape. After the awareness program, fewer than 25 percent of the students still thought that forced sex was acceptable under any circumstances (Project 1988, 9).

## ➤ What Schools and Teachers Can Do

Schools and teachers should educate themselves about sexual harassment, which is defined as sexually charged conduct that has the effect of "substantially interfering with an individual's work performance or creating an intimidating, hostile, or offensive working environment." (EEOC's 1980 legal guideline, cited in University of Michigan 1983, 2). It is more about power than about sex. It encompasses a wide range of behaviors of varying severity, that may all be called "sexual harassment" because of the negative effects on the one towards whom such behavior is directed — from overdone needling and off-color joking to invasive actions using physical force. Sexual harassment may — even when intended as good-natured, friendly camaraderie rather than hostility or deliberate intention to hurt — result in annoyance, distaste, or worse. It differs from flirtation, which feels good whereas harassment feels bad. It differs from nonhostile teasing, which unlike harassment does not result in its target feeling angry, helpless, humiliated, guilty, or scared. It may be rooted in attitudes towards women that sees them as a class, not as individuals, and as inferior and therefore "fair game." It may be an expression of hostility, anger, resentment towards women, or towards anyone perceived as weaker. It may be a way of gaining status with male peers, to be "one of the boys;" an attempt to prove one's masculinity, to bond with male peers by joining them in putting down women, or demonstrating solidarity as a male group. It resembles bullying. Both intimidate by using dominance, abuse power over another, take pleasure in someone else's discomfort/pain, and violate another's rights. But bullying lacks the extra dimension of singling out individuals because of their sex or alleged sexual orientation.

Sexual harassment will not go away if ignored, or just because the one harassed protests. It is made worse in the short run when complaints are met by the harasser with incomprehension, denial, derision, hostility, from "What's the matter, can't you take a joke?" to "How like a woman, making a fuss over nothing," or "Castrating bitch!" It is also made worse in the long run when bystanders, or others who hear about it, consider it a laughing matter, or allow it to pass without comment. They give harassment legitimacy and encourage the harasser with their behavior. This applies both to student peers and to adults.

Sexual harassment is everyone's problem. Harassers may not even realize their target does not enjoy their attentions, or may feel that their target is a legitimate victim, and that what they are doing is allowed or even approved. They will not find out that others find their behavior offensive, aggravating, hurtful, wrong, unless they are told so — not only by the one they are harassing, but also by bystanders, peers, (other) adults, and the school.

Sexual harassment is hard to address, because it is often amorphous and ambiguous. It may come down to one person's word against the other, and is difficult to "prove" in individual instances. It raises issues of freedom of speech. It may be counter-stereotypical, as in female students' blatant sexual advances making male faculty's jobs difficult. In male-to-female cases, it plays into the stereotype of the weak female unable to "take it," and is, to some extent, culturally sanctioned.

**To develop guidelines and/or policies to deal with sexual (and other) harassment, consider the following:**

- before instituting any guideline or policy, seek legal counsel
- treat student-to-student cases as discipline issues under the heading of harassment — which would also include boys or girls bullying or hazing younger students of either sex, harrying another student for their alleged sexual orientation, and badgering others on racial, ethnic, religious or other similar grounds

- use informal procedures first
- consider keeping (private) notes of conversations with complainants and alleged offenders, and anonymous notes of complaints and their resolutions as part of school records
- operate on the basis that the priorities are to first of all, do no damage; get the offense to stop; and to escalate slowly
- go the maximum distance in seeing if two people have misunderstood each other
- ask the complainant what she or he would like to have happen as a result of the complaint
- try to establish clearly, and check with both individually, what happened and what the people involved thought and felt. (Both may agree as to what happened; their interpretation of what it meant, and the way they feel about it, may be very different.)
- protect the privacy of both the offended and the alleged offender; but at some point it might be appropriate to ask whether they would like to have someone with them (friend, advisor, parent, colleague) while they talk about what happened
- make available psychological support for the complainant if it is indicated by the severity of the upset; and for the alleged offender, who may be innocent and traumatized by the accusation and its impact
- hold major punishments (suspension, dismissal) in abeyance, for serious, violent, or egregious cases or recidivists. Complainants are likely to be reluctant to come forward if they feel their complaint will result in immediate expulsion or dismissal for a schoolmate or colleague
- have a formal, legally checked, complaint procedure that is made public, for cases that are serious or repeat offenses

Consider taking ongoing and generic as well as ad hoc individual actions that address the issue of sexual (and other) harassment in school. Don't assume that because specific cases of harassment have not been reported, such behavior does not go on.

**The following suggestions target increasingly specific approaches:**

- do consciousness raising as an ongoing measure, in the absence of individual complaints
- stress values such as respect for others, tolerance, and the right of freedom from intimidation
- make issues of harassment a low key part of orientation for new students and faculty
- integrate sexual harassment and bullying issues with faculty and/or student workshops/ training in an ongoing, non-crisis way (case studies and question-answer formats have been found to work well with both adolescents and adults)
- integrate sexual harassment issues in subject-matter teaching already in the curriculum (teachers have done so as part of tenth grade study of *Tess of the D'Urbervilles* and *I Know Why the Caged Bird Sings*)
- address the issue of homophobia in the context of harassment, as well as other contexts (e.g. when teaching *The Color Purple* in English, or, in biology, introducing reliable research on the topic) since being called homosexual is very common and is among the forms of harassment found most upsetting by students, especially boys
- dissociate non-gender-stereotyped behavior from homosexuality (boys often fear that stereo-typical female behavior, from showing emotions to belonging to the drama club, means that they are, or will be perceived as, homosexual; girls, that showing strong interest in athletics or competitiveness will have that effect)
- get information on the issue, as on other issues, out into the community as part of keeping everyone informed about contemporary problems that affect us all

- in cases of hearsay, ambiguous, or less serious instances, try the generic approach, which preserves maximum confidentiality and avoids confrontation while making the point as well as reinforcing the school's stand against harassment. This might be issuing a blanket reminder for the group of which the alleged offender is a member and that can plausibly be treated as a group for this purpose (upperclass students, the senior class, the faculty, administrators) about what constitutes harassment in your institution, and why there is a policy against it, perhaps taking the opportunity to (re)distribute copies of the policy, hold a workshop or have the reminder come in the context of an invited speaker or a follow-up on something in the news that is relevant.

- working with individual cases, suggest a personal statement to the offender by the one harassed (this preserves maximum confidentiality and avoids compromising the alleged harasser in cases where this makes sense). Such a statement could be an oral, polite but firm, request for the harassment to stop: "I want you to stop telling me jokes like this. It makes me uncomfortable, and I don't want to hear them." Alternatively it could be writing a three-part letter to the offender, which includes specific description of behavior found offensive; a description of feelings; and a description of what offender is asked to do.

(The suggestions above draw on information from the following: Pitsch 1995; Lawton 1993; About Women 1993, 1992, 1991; Project 1990, 1988; Rowe 1985)

*B*e alert to court cases and official findings that could be relevant for the school as an institution or in working with students/faculty towards an understanding of the issues.

For example, students who have been sexually harassed by a teacher are entitled to seek monetary damages from the school (Ruling by the Supreme Court: *Franklin v. Gwinnett County School District* 1992; cited in About Women 1992, 5). Students who were sexually harassed by their peers may also recover monetary damages from schools (Ruling by a U.S. District judge: *Doe v. Petaluma* 1993, cited in Pitsch 1995, 31). Fourth grade and younger boys making hostile, obscene, taunting remarks and unwelcomely touching girls of the same ages on a school bus led to the school being charged with a Title IX violation (Letter of finding by Office for Civil Rights at the U.S. Department of Education, 1993, cited in About Women 1993, 8). Pictures of nude or partly nude women in the workplace can make those posting them and their employer liable for sexual harassment. (Ruling by a U.S. District judge in Florida, cited in About Women 1991). In a case where a female special education teacher's sexual harassment suit against a male principal involved "starkly different accounts of what actually occurred between plaintiff and defendant," the court resolved the issue based on the credibility of the parties involved. It found against the plaintiff because the defendant presented evidence that the plaintiff had lied about her temporary teaching certification, about a physical examination required by school policy as condition of employment, and about reasons for lateness to work, which cast significant doubt on the plaintiff's credibility. (Jury trial in State of New York: Locastro v. East Syracuse-Minoa Central School District.)

**RESOURCES:**

American Association of University Women. 1993. *Hostile Hallways*.[national survey of sexual harassment in grades 8-11]. AAUW sales office, P.O. Box 261, Annapolis Junction, MD 20701; (800) 225-9998. The fullest information currently available on the nature and dimensions of the problem.

*CWIS Newsletter*, Winter 1994. Issue on homophobia, gays and lesbians in independent schools, with resources. **Available from** NAIS, 1620 L Street NW Washington, D.C. 20036; (202) 973-9700.

Katz, Montana and Veronica Vieland. 1988. *Get Smart ! What You Should Know (But Won't Learn in Class) about Sexual Harassment and Sex Discrimination.* Second Edition. New York: The Feminist Press. Using case studies, it outlines problems and disadvantages faced by women in college, and offers realistic and practical solutions. Covers changes in civil rights and discrimination law. Bibliography.

Morris, Barbra, Jacquie Terpstra, Bob Croninger and Eleanor Linn. 1985. *Tune In to Your Rights: A Guide for Teenagers About Turning Off Sexual Harassment.* From: Director, Programs for Educational Opportunity, 1033 School of Education Bldg., The University of Michigan, Ann Arbor MI 48109; (313)763-9910. Most useful for junior high and up. Sensible and sensitive suggestions for the harassed, friends, bystanders, and even the harassers.

*Independent School* magazine, winter 1989, and spring 1996. Articles on homosexuality and homophobia, with resources on lesbian and gay youth: literature, AV materials, and organizations. **Available from the National Association of Independent** Schools, 1620 L Street NW, Washington D.C.; (202) 973-9700.

National Association of Independent Schools. Council for Women in Independent Education. Packet on sexual harassment, including information, sample policies, and case studies. **From NAIS, 1620 L Street NW, Washington, D.C. 20036;** (202) 973-9700.

Sex Information and Education Council of the U.S. (SIECUS). New York University, 32 Washington Place, New York, N.Y. 10003; (212) 673-3850. Publishes annotated bibliographies on sexuality and family life education.

Stein, Nan and Lisa Sjorstrom. 1994. *Flirting or Hurting? A Teacher's Guide on Student-To-Student Sexual Harassment in Schools* (grades 6 through 12). Wellesley, MA: Center for Research on Women, 106 Central Street, Wellesley, MA 02181, or from NEA Professional Library, Box 509, West Haven, CT 06515 (800) 229-4200. Classroom lessons suitable for social studies, English, psychology or health classes, with student handouts and quizzes, and teacher background notes.

Stringer, Gayle M. and Deanna Rants-Rodriguez. 1987. *So What's It to Me? Sexual Assault Information for Guys.* From: King County Rape Relief 1025 S. 3d, Renton, WA 98055; (206) 226-5062. Most useful junior high and up. Deals with verbal harassment as well as physical assault both by and towards boys in low-key way.

**PROBLEM EATING BEHAVIOR: NO TEMPEST IN A TEACUP**

*I*t has been said that we are what we eat. What we *don't* eat also shapes us — and not just physically. Consistent food deprivation among growing young people does not make for health or a happy atmosphere, and is cause for serious concern.

Unhealthy eating patterns are extremely common among adolescents and are filtering down to early grade-school levels. They differ substantially by gender and more commonly affect girls.

Part of the hidden, and perhaps of the null, curriculum in school and home are the unwritten agreements and actual policies about meals and food: snacks that are, or are not, made available, and what they are; what choices are provided at meals, and adults' reactions to what and how much of the provided food is eaten; what is considered under or overeating; how food choices adults do not approve of are handled; eating hurriedly or at leisure; and how those genuinely overweight, of both sexes, and those who fret unrealistically about being under or overweight, are treated.

Among girls, eating problems afflict half or more of the teenage population. The more serious cases are still substantial: a study conducted in four independent schools found that about 15 percent of girls in grades ten through twelve "frequently engaged in drastic and dangerous eating and dieting behavior. . . [and] about half of normal weight teenage girls are actively involved in dieting at any given time." The problems seemed to be more prevalent in boarding than in day schools (Timmerman 1992, 104). The order of magnitude of these figures is borne out by considerable other research (Graber et al. 1994; Striegel-Moore et al. 1990).

A large national sample of students in grade nine through twelve, conducted in 1991, found that 34 percent of the girls as opposed to 15 percent of boys felt they were overweight; about 40 percent of even those girls who thought they were the right size said they had skipped a meal during the past week, almost 15 percent had used diet pills, and nearly 10 percent had forced themselves to vomit. About half the girls said they had exercised during the past week in order to lose weight. White and Hispanic girls were more likely than African Americans to consider themselves overweight (U.S. Centers for Disease Control Youth Risk Behavior Survey, reported in *Education Week* 1991, 11).

Adolescent girls are increasingly concerned with weight and thinness. In a recent large-scale study of normal weight teenage girls, "69 percent claimed to be constantly concerned about being overweight, and 40 percent were actively dieting to lose weight" (Cited in Timmerman 1992a, 1). Among Minnesotan and Alaskan eleventh-and twelfth-grade girls, a recent survey found their appearance was their "most pressing concern."

The preoccupation with weight is showing up at ever-earlier ages. Both anecdotal information from independent schools, and local surveys (Kilbourne 1994, 396), have shown high proportions of girls as young as fourth grade watching their weight. There is some research that suggests that females' body image is affected by what they see (Richins 1991) — and what girls see is that "thin is in." A traceable historical change has resulted in a cultural ideal of feminine attractiveness that is almost unattainable after puberty. Since the 1960s, the emphasis in advertising has been on thin models. A long-range analysis of ads in *Vogue* and *Ladies' Home Journal* shows a waist-to-bust ratio that ranged from 1.8 to 2.1 in 1901-1910; hit a low of 1.2 for the single year of 1925 (the flapper); and thereafter ranged between 1.4 and 1.6 to the 1960s. Since then, the range has been 1.2 to 1.3 (Lazier and Kendrick 1993, 208). A generation ago, the average model weighed 8 percent less than the average weight of American women in general. By 1990, she weighed 23 percent less (Wolf 1991, 184). Similar slimming has been found on TV.

There is also greater emphasis on women's bodies in advertising. For instance, in *Seventeen*, a fashion magazine for adolescents with an annual circulation of almost two million, advertisements focusing on the body were 17 percent of all ads in 1951, and 68 percent in 1991 (Budgeon and Currie 1995, 175).

Learning from this cultural curriculum, a frightening number of young women engage in the hopeless pursuit of a mass-media promoted ideal that leads them to fad diets, diet and diuretic pills, and purging behaviors such as self-induced vomiting and the use of laxatives. The American Anorexia and Bulimia Association estimates 150,000 deaths a year for (mostly middle-class white) American women due to anorexia: they have literally starved themselves to death (Quoted in Wolf 1991, 182, 183).

A negative body image, strongly associated with weight for adolescent girls, is predictive of eating disorders; and it is significant that onset of these disorders is associated both with increases in body fat due to onset of puberty, and with the timing of the loss of white middle-class girls' self-esteem. African-American girls of the same class, whose loss of self-esteem is not as dramatic, also do not suffer from eating disorders at the same rates as the middle-class whites (AAUW 1992, 11-13; Graber et al. 1994, 824, 831). The problem is compounded for girls who are athletes, partly because some of their activities such as dance and gymnastics emphasize a slim, slight body even further, partly because the increased caloric demand makes diet-induced deficiency even more unhealthy and potentially dangerous.

While girls strive to be thin, boys strive for heft.

Paradoxically, recent studies suggest that about the same proportion of boys abuse anabolic steroids trying to become bulkier as girls develop serious eating disorders trying to get thinner; and that, whereas post-adolescent white girls' body-image is distorted towards inaccurate perceptions of overweight, exactly the opposite is the case for white boys, who misperceive themselves as being underweight. Actually, among those 20 percent or more overweight in the adult population, men (30 percent thus overweight) outnumber women (26 percent) (Betz, Mintz, and Speakmon 1994, 551; Statistical Abstract 1994, 146; Timmerman 1992, 104). With boys, problem eating focuses more on the nature of what is eaten, with stereotypically "masculine" foods (steak, French fries, greasy everything, bacon-and-eggs, rib-sticking fare) being virtually a prescription for heart trouble; and healthy eating looked down on as "sissy."

With both boys and girls, unhealthy snacking is a problem. According to one estimate, adolescents consume almost a third of their calories from snacks (Timmerman 1992, 105), most typically, sodas, candy, chips and pizza, the latter often a late-night addition to a hearty dinner for boys, and to make up for the solo salad consumed as "dinner" for girls.

### Schools and parents might consider educating boys and girls about:

- alternative sources of control over one's life that might make attempts to at least being able to control one's own body less important
- the results of eating unhealthy food in unhealthy amounts
- the realities of inherited body type, which cannot be significantly changed
- the fact that girls typically have twice the fat and two thirds the muscle mass as boys by about age twenty, and that this is okay
- that while the mass media create the perception that to be attractive to men, women must be thin, individual men's standards of attractiveness vary more than do the mass media's
- the commercial interests (the diet industry is a $33 billion a year business) behind the promotion of specific body-types as the only desirable ones (Wolf 1991, 66)
- the historical changes in the culturally approved type of female attractiveness
- the artifice that goes into making the models look the way they do

Schools might consider educating the faculty about symptoms of eating disorders, with a plan in place for dealing with them when identified. They might hold discussion groups and workshops for those concerned with body-image, and offer a school-sponsored weight-loss diet for those who actually need it. They could also make healthy snacks available, substituting other options for the midnight pizza aficionados in dormitories.

**RESOURCES:**

There is an extensive list of readings, films, organization, and high school curricula in the *CWIS Newsletter* (Winter 1992), which concerns eating disorders. Available from the National Association of Independent Schools, 1620 L Street NW, Washington D.C. 20036-5605; (202) 973-9700.

## DORMITORIES

Gender is an important variable to be taken into account in the rules made for dormitory behavior, in the style of interaction between adults and students in the dormitory, and in the kinds of problems that people in the dormitories need to be alert to.

If dormitories, regardless of gender, set their own rules (whether as a result of adult-only decisions, or of discussions with students as well), it is likely that there will be gender-related differences in some of the rules: keeping rooms and public areas clean and tidy; degree of quiet to be maintained; sports, audiovisual, and recreational equipment that may be kept and/or used, in dorms; TV viewing; checking in and bedtime; and the maintenance and use of laundry and food-related facilities. Schools need to make some decisions about the degree of divergence in dormitory rules they are willing to accept. Alternatively, in cases where rules are entirely uniform in all dormitories, they might ask whether some differences might not be tolerable if they improve the quality of life for inhabitants of dorms who may have different priorities.

If rules for dorms are intentionally made different by gender (for instance, closer supervision for girls, on the assumption that they are more vulnerable, and seek help and advice more often; or for boys, on the assumption that that they are less well behaved and more likely to get into trouble), it is worth discussing what message the differential treatment sends, whether the assumptions are borne out by experience, and whether continuing the different policy is in fact the best move.

Rules for parietals, and the ways parietals are used, are worth an extra look. Even when they are the same in both girls' and boys' dormitories, because of gender-stereotypic expectations or attitudes boys and girls may have different degrees of reluctance to take advantage of them. Girls visiting boys may be labeled "sluts," boys visiting girls, "studs"; both are undesirable, but the harm, and the inhibitory effect, is greater for girls. Ideally, both should be able comfortably to visit opposite-sex friends without fearing they will be put down for it.

The flavor and style of boys' and girls' dorms tends to differ, even though the differences between two boys' or two girls' dorms may be as great. It is worth considering whether, and to what extent, gender-stereotypic expectations (which have a tendency to become self-fulfilling) might be influencing gender differences between dorms; and what the pros and cons are of whatever differences do exist.

Faculty members' service in a dormitory will inevitably be affected by their gender, and that of the students they deal with (as well, of course, by many other factors). It is to both girls' and boys' benefit to have both women and men as supervising faculty in their dorms.

**In both boys' and girls' dorms, faculty need to be alert to privacy issues. Guidelines established at the start of the year are a good idea, such as:**

- always knocking and waiting a little before entering a student room
- considering asking that, when not in street clothes, students wear robes in corridors (even when both students and faculty claim that they are perfectly comfortable with boys in towels, or girls in nightgowns)
- avoiding being alone with a student in a room with the door closed

- recognizing that girls generally start feeling vulnerable, anxious, and uncomfortable in a state of considerably less "undress" than do boys

Sensitivity to privacy, however, should not lead to abdication of supervisory responsibility (for instance, there is no reason why checking that students are in bed when they should be, or running room inspections, should be delegated to same-gender faculty only).

**All faculty in both girls' and boys' dorms might want to:**

- consider the level and quality of cooperation and "togetherness" in the dorm
- consider the level and quality of competitiveness in the dorm
- consider formally and/or informally teaching conflict management techniques, and helping students to see that conflicts can, and should, neither be avoided nor allowed to get out of control (A very useful brief reading for faculty on issues to consider, and ideas to use, both in teaching students about conflict, and in their own coping with student conflict is Northrup 1989.)
- be alert to the need for making faculty of the opposite sex welcome in the dorm, so that no one feels either an intruder or an outsider
- have both women and men participate both in discipline keeping and nurturing behaviors
- examine their own beliefs and values, and decide what they consider inappropriate attitudes, comments, jokes, stories or behavior in boys about and towards girls, and vice versa
- discuss with each other and jointly with students, the issue of "pin-ups," male and female, in both girls' and boys' dorms; and, preferably in collaboration with students, establish some guidelines for acceptability
- compare information and ideas about any bullying and harassing behaviors within their dorms, and discuss what action to take (see **HARASSMENT**, page 27)
- have joint meetings for prefects from female and male dorms, so they can see, and discuss, both the similarities and differences in the problems they encounter, benefit from each others' experience, and help each other come up with imaginative solutions
- work to develop the leadership potential of prefects, seniors, upperclass students, and indeed all students, giving them increasing responsibility, in small increments and with decreasing supervision, and cooperate with them to increase students' sense of responsibility for each other in the dorm (see **LEADERSHIP**, page 131)

*T*aking the initiative to create opportunities for common dormitory activities can substantially add to morale. Taking part together in activities that call on varied skills, styles, and abilities can promote increased respect and healthy friendships between boys and girls. Such activities can be seasonal (building the biggest snowman possible; having a dorm-wide pumpkin-carving contest); or initiated at any time for a change of pace: Frisbee and board games; producing a quilt (why not try it even in boys' dorms?) to raise money for the dorm; showcasing stories, songs, and dances from students' home regions, countries, cultures; celebrating ethnic festivals and holidays, perhaps with appropriate food; inviting parents with special interests or areas of expertise, both male and female, for "fireside chats."

A potential bonding activity with several advantages is the one-day or one-evening cooperative work crew. All inhabitants of the dorm as well as out-of-dorm faculty who work at the school turn out to oil squeaky doors and windows, fill holes, tighten screws in doorknobs, replace defaced nameplates, touch up paint, and generally refurbish the place. It's an opportunity to help each other in a meaningful way. The event can be accompanied by singing together, or making up silly rhymes, and be followed by a more than usually lavish dorm feed.

Boys and girls may benefit differently, but advantages for all are when students gain greater appreciation for living comfortably in pleasant surroundings; subject property they consistently keep up themselves to less careless wear and tear, or deliberate abuse; and learn skills and habits that will stand them in good stead when they have homes of their own.

If it is possible to estimate the savings to the school by such ongoing repair, a part — or all — of what is saved might be turned over to the students for their joint decision on how to spend it for the benefit of the dorm, the school, or some other worthy cause.

After a tradition of dorm-bonding activities is established, consider having boys and girls work jointly on repairs, taking female and male dorms in turn, with gender rotation of student leadership; collaborate to produce skits and celebrations of festivals; and invite each other to mixed-team Frisbee matches followed by jointly run cook-outs.

These activities are more than fun; research suggests that cooperation in an activity that benefits both is one of the most effective ways to establish positive relationships between girls and boys.

(The above information on dormitories draws on Jordan 1992, and Crosier 1992.)

■ ■ ■ ■

## CHAPTER THREE

## WAYS OF KNOWING: GIRLS AND BOYS COMING INTO THEIR OWN

*…the most difficult instructional moment for the students —
and perhaps therefore for the teacher as well —
seems to occur at the transition from the conception
of knowledge as a quantitative accretion of discrete rightnesses
(including the discrete rightnesses of Multiplicity in
which everyone has a right to his [or her] opinion)
to the conception of knowledge as the qualitative assessment
of contextual observations and relationships.*

*—William G. Perry, 1970*

Boys and girls think, feel, and behave as potential "knowers" in various ways at various times and circumstances of their lives. Both what they are able to know (rather than memorize) and how they can best be helped to knowledge are profoundly influenced by how they envisage learning, themselves as learners, and the nature of authority and life.

The schematic overview below is based on two major studies (Perry 1970 and Belenky et al. 1986 and their extension in King and Kitchener 1994) and information drawn from a wide variety of other sources. Anecdotal evidence suggests that it agrees broadly with the observations of a great many teachers. It should be noted however that individuals will not always tidily operate within the parameters of any one of the five modes described, each of which is a characteristic "way of knowing." Moreover, other things besides gender are likely to influence what mode, or combination, will be used by an individual at any particular time.

While maturation is obviously related to the developmental progress of the modes outlined, there is no particular age when any one student may be expected to, let alone "should have," progressed to a "higher" mode. All five modes are found among adults; and it would not be a safe assumption to assign a definite limit to elementary school-age students' development.

Maturation in and of itself, then, does not necessarily result in a student outgrowing a mode; but, while appropriate pedagogies help them to get beyond earlier modes, they may progress extremely slowly, may fluctuate between modes, and may skip modes.

Since any one classroom is likely to have a mix of students operating in different modes, using a mixture of pedagogies in class, their frequency adjusted to what predominates or is rare in the mix, and tailored as far as possible to individuals, is probably the safest bet for teachers.

In the naming of the modes, the first term is derived from Belenky 1986, the second from Perry 1970. The student metaphors for mathematics that serve as epigraphs for each mode are intended to give a feel for student attitudes associated with the various modes. They come from boys and girls in math courses in grades eleven and twelve and were collected in 1988.(Buerk 1992, 94-97). That it was mathematics the quotations refer to, and that there was a quotation evocative of each of the modes, is entirely happenstance.

The quotations by students under "students see" are from the four-year study of the impact on Harvard undergraduates of the pluralism of thought and values encountered in college in the late 1950s and early 1960s. All emphases are as in the original (Perry 1970, 61, 63, 64, 67, 98, 103, 126, 148,161).

**MODE ONE: SILENCE/DUALISM**

*"For me math is like an abusive parent. If you do not stay on guard, your parent will strike you when you least expect it. It's not rational, and it's difficult to understand why things are the way they are. Parents and math are supposed to help you through life, not screw you up and hinder you. I hide from the parent, yet it always seems to find me. And that sense that math is out to get me, no matter what I do."*

In this mode, students see authority as external, absolute, unpredictable, and necessary. Without being constantly told what to do, they feel they cannot function. They experience learning as blind obedience. They have total belief in, and reliance on, personal authority. They see life as starkly dualistic; propositions and acts are right or wrong, without the possibility of better or worse. They see themselves as having no control over what is happening in their lives. They lack a sense of self, are unable to trust themselves consistently to remember and/or understand what they are told.

*"What the man said was just God's word, you know. I believed everything he said, because he was a professor."*
*—Harvard student, 1960s*

The teacher sees a student who does not comment or ask questions, overwhelmingly answers, if at all, with "I don't know." The student has a short attention span, is immature and impulsive, alternately acting withdrawn and acting out.

**Pedagogy for mode one involves:**

> providing confirmation that the student can be trusted to learn
> ensuring that she or he has opportunities to succeed
> lavishly praising success
> providing a learning environment that the student perceives as safe and unthreatening and where they can feel sure of exactly what they are being asked to do (see suggestions for reducing test anxiety in **MATHEMATICS**, page 99).
> providing concrete learning activities
> helping to develop the ability to speak out by facilitating inner dialogue (one of the things inhibiting this, which can be addressed, is perception of any conflict as dangerous, and perception of internal as well as external discussion as conflict)
> strengthening the student's sense of his or her own mind and personality (exercises such as "write yourself a recommendation" or "describe yourself as seen by . . . " are helpful)

Girls are somewhat more likely to operate according to mode one, and to stay with it for longer, than boys. Mode one boys are more likely to act out, girls to act withdrawn; the result is likely to be attention for boys, ignoring of girls. Both boys and girls are likely to return to this mode when they feel insecure.

**MODE TWO: RECEIVED KNOWLEDGE/DUALISM**

*"For me, math is like an earthquake. Seeing as if an earthquake was to hit, even just a tremor, it could knock down and ruin a lot of things. Just like in math, if you make one error in a problem — even a small one — it can ruin or tear down all of your work."*

*I*n this mode, students see authority as external and, if true authority, having the one right answer to every question or problem (those claiming otherwise are not true authorities). They experience learning as receiving, retaining, and returning the words of authority unchanged: knowledge as quantitative, additive, and absolute; and life as endemic conflict, a win/lose proposition. They see absolute division between facts, which must be true, and opinions, which don't count. The partly wrong is worthless; paradox, impossible. They experience themselves as static, vessels to be filled; as discrete thinkers, it is hard for them to conceptualize themselves as growing, as becoming.

> *"I didn't think any question could have more than one answer."*
> *—Harvard student, 1960s*

The teacher sees a student who is a literal-minded, dualistic thinker; has a strong need for predictability and clarity; and who may feel betrayed if asked for application or transformation of material, or for her or his own thoughts.

**Pedagogy for mode two involves:**

> ➤ giving students responsibility for helping others learn, both to distance them from constant reliance on external authority and to help them develop a sense of having some authority of their own
> ➤ modeling for them, by thinking out loud, ways of arriving at an answer other than by remembering it; and getting them to try "think-alouds" themselves, prompting them as necessary and praising every instance of independence or initiative (for specifics on promoting personal construction of knowledge in the classroom, see Chapman 1993)
> ➤ marking for them stages in their own intellectual development, to help them see their own growth (have them keep all their work, and compare later with earlier)
> ➤ pointing out to them the existence of multiple perspectives; the intertwining of facts and interpretations; the assumptions that underlie the acceptance of anything as a "fact"

Girls are somewhat more likely to operate in this mode two, and to stay with it longer, than boys. Both boys and girls are likely to use this mode when insecure.

### MODE THREE: SUBJECTIVE KNOWLEDGE/MULTIPLICITY

> *"I feel like I'm falling off a cliff sometimes. It's free falling."*

*S*tudents in mode three see authority as internal. They rely on gut feelings and intuition. They see external authorities as not having answers that are any more "right," yet insisting on factual/logical support (which the students may perceive as irrelevant) for feelings and opinions. They experience learning as derived from first-hand, unique experience; truth as relative and diverse; and knowledge as relevant only to self, which takes a stand in chaos. They see life split between ideas and facts from outside authority and their own more important inner feelings. They feel that in the absence of absolute truth each person's opinion is valid for them and not negotiable. They are shifting, fluid, without anchor, and experience themselves as conduits through which a felt personal truth emerges. They have an unsettled sense of self, fearful of isolation and of the need to defend their views.

*"…no way to, ah, really prove anything, anyway — logic is really meaningless.*
*I'm a great believer in intuition rather than science or logic."*
—Harvard student, 1960s

The teacher sees a student who is overly personal, emotional, arbitrary, and concrete. He or she distrusts and is uncomfortable with abstraction, logic, and analysis. The student may be hostile or withdrawn, perceiving academic learning as irrelevant.

**Pedagogy for mode three involves:**

> ➤ providing means for validating, reinforcing, and making convincing to others the student's "inner voice" rather than questioning or suppressing it
> ➤ helping students to connect the subjective with the objective by getting them to ferret out the sources of their opinions and feelings ("What triggered this feeling for you?" "How did you arrive at this opinion?" Note: much patience and ingenuity may be needed.)
> ➤ offering techniques for constructing answers that, if at all possible, include or at least do not run counter to feelings, rather than providing alternative, unconnected answers
> ➤ respecting concrete, unique experience, but helping to set it into the wider context of the appropriate abstractions, generalizations, and theories, and pointing out ways it is shared
> ➤ evaluating student performance in terms of procedures used to substantiate opinions and feelings rather than of the opinions and feelings themselves

Girls are more likely to verbalize their operation in mode three as "It's only my opinion," and may be more fearful of isolation than concerned about defending their opinion. Girls may be better motivated with techniques for validation and reinforcing, and with recognizing how their opinion is shared with others. They may be more willing to accept the role of abstraction, generalization, and theory in their construction of knowledge if the steps leading from the personal to the abstract, and the relationship to others' experience, are made clear.

Mode three boys are more likely to verbalize their operation in this mode as "I have a right to my opinion." They may be more anxious to defend their opinion than to fear isolation because of it, and may be better motivated by being given means to convince others. They are more likely to accept the role of abstraction, generalization, and theory if it helps them to defend their own opinion and feelings against potential criticism or attack.

Those who emerge late from the "silence" mode (who are somewhat more likely girls) may skip the "received knowledge" mode. Girls in this case may need extra doses of help in overcoming their fear that the autonomy of their own opinion will lead to their isolation, boys the fear that their claim to their own opinion will invite attack.

### MODE FOUR: PROCEDURAL KNOWLEDGE/RELATIVISM

*"With math, things don't always work out right. I don't know how many times I've screamed,*
*pulled my hair out, trying to fix a math problem, but when I finally figure it out, I feel fantastic,*
*like I've accomplished something. Sometimes you break down, in a car or during a math problem,*
*but if you work at it, you'll get to where you're going."*

*I*n mode four, students see authority as expertise that can be respected and useful; truth as shareable, with some truths truer than others; and neither facts nor feelings as infallible. They experience learning as a following of objective procedures leading to valid knowledge, as the use of techniques to generate and evaluate different perspectives and interpretations, which leads to fuller understanding. To them, learning is a system that can be analyzed and criticized, but only in terms of its own standards. They see knowledge as qualitative as well as quantitative, depending on context. They see life as diverse, but orderly and manageable, and themselves as "separate" or "connected" knowers.

| Separate | Connected |
|---|---|
| • doubter/skeptic | • believer |
| • adversarial | • empathetic |
| • asks of other's stance: "what steps in reasoning led to ...?" | • asks of other's stance: "what experience led to ...?" |
| • assails other's logic | • seeks to share other's experience |
| • brings to group polished argument, tries to get others to accept it | • brings to group incomplete ideas, tries to get help to develop them |
| • sees personalities as distraction | • sees personalities as enrichment to perception |
| • feels that, in discussion, knowing other participants is unimportant | • feels that, in discussion, knowing others is important |
| • understanding seen as gained by detachment, control over others | • understanding seen as gained by closeness, opening self to others |
| • arguments are for trying to prove/disprove/convince | • arguments are for trying to understand/be understood |
| • strives for certainty | • can tolerate uncertainty |
| • insists on closure, clarity | • willing to leave things open-ended, undefined |
| • typical stance: only one can win: I want it to be me | • typical stance: perhaps all can win: I don't want others to lose |

*"...what I'm trying to do is, ah, become...one who can, to the utmost of his ability, detach himself, ah, emotionally from the problems, in an objective, empirical type of way — look at the pros and cons of a situation and then try to ...analyze and formulate a judgment... bringing into consideration in this judgment, ah, well, what the other person would feel and why he should feel so."*
*—Harvard student, 1960s*

The teacher sees the mode four student as one who has a stake in the academic enterprise; has embarked on higher-order thinking; approaches learning consciously, deliberately, and systematically; is likely to value form over content; and is willing to think about thinking.

**Pedagogy for mode four involves:**

> ➤ modeling the construction of knowledge by thinking out loud (for specific suggestions about "think-alouds" and knowledge construction in the classroom, see Chapman 1993)
> ➤ demonstrating the process as a struggle, the end as attainable though imperfect
> ➤ showing students that their struggle with academic work is of the same kind as that of the teacher in putting together a course, a scholar in producing a book (emphasizing both the community of scholarship and the need to critique and counter the critiques in order to hone scholarship)

> - playing down the "right" answer in favor of the "best answer we now have, because..."
> - helping to build on/incorporate the personal
> - validating both striving for individual excellence and collaboration — with hints about when each might be most productive
> - alerting students to the existence of different styles in approaching the construction of knowledge; helping them to choose, or to combine, appropriately for the task at hand, and helping to maximize advantages and minimize disadvantages of each style in a given context
> - exposing them to open-ended problems that may have no answer, to "fuzzy sets," to paradox, uncertainty, and the need for commitment even in the face of uncertainty

While all mode four students are capable of operating as either separate or connected knowers, and while most students use parts of each style selectively, depending on circumstances, all tend to favor one or the other; and some use one virtually exclusively. Boys are more likely to be markedly separate, girls markedly connected knowers.

These styles of knowing are along the same lines as the well-documented gender difference in the extent to which an individual's perception of an item is influenced by the context (field) in which it appears. The ability to decontextualize, to ignore the effects of background, to find simple figures embedded in a complex pattern is more characteristic of males — and of whites. Females, Mexican Americans, Native Americans and African Americans are more alert to, influenced/distracted by, and responsive to context. There seem to be generational differences, however: first-generation Mexican Americans tend to be more field-sensitive than third-generation ones.

The former style has been labeled field-independent, has been linked to analytic thinking, and has been seen as an advantage — the ability to separate the important from the unimportant. Some posit a relationship between the ability to decontextualize and high spatial ability. Field-independent students like to work on their own and respond well to impersonal abstractions. They find it relatively easy to extract nuggets of information from a text, but tend to retain it piecemeal. They are comfortable with linear relationships. Metaphorically, they concentrate on individual trees, if necessary at the expense of forest ecology. Another way to think of this style is as "field-insensitive" or "context-deprived."

The opposite style, labeled "field-dependent," used to be considered a deficiency (and still is by some). Students using this style respond well to group-work and close personal interactions. They are globally rather than analytically oriented and are often adept at finding meaning, but less so at finding specific information, in a text. They bring emotion to learning. Metaphorically, they concentrate on forest ecology, finding it hard to focus attention on individual trees. Another way to think of this style is as "field-sensitive" or "context-aware."

Cognitively focused analytical thinkers who do well at memorizing facts are those most commonly rewarded in most classroom situations, especially at the pre-college level. Those with the "field-sensitive" style are disadvantaged, though their bent is valuable in many higher-level intellectual contexts.

The association of males with the "ethic of justice," the more habitual judging by abstract right and wrong regardless of circumstances; and of females with the "ethic of care," which more habitually judges the morality of an action while taking circumstances into account, is congruent here.

Both styles have advantages and disadvantages, depending on circumstances. It is to teachers', and students', advantage if all are alert to the difference the use of one rather than the other style makes in student performance in any particular context. The benefits of encouraging greater versatility in the use of both styles, with information on contexts when one or the other is more appropriate, might be considered. Whether classroom expectations and ways of presenting and testing material favor one style over the other, and if so, whether anything should be done about it — and if so, what — might also be considered.

*"For me, math is like a good hiding place that I can escape to, think in and be comforted by . . .
I have all the time in the world in this place, trying to unravel its mysteries and trying to find out
what they really consist of. Some are easy to discover; others are very difficult, almost impossible.
When I've had no luck with these more difficult objects, I wander back into the cave, the center of
this secret place . . . . Here lie all the basic truths. The foundations upon which everything is based.
And then I go back out again, renewed with strength."*

*I*n mode five, students see authority as expertise to be evaluated, and used when helpful, rather than to be either followed or rejected. They experience learning as questioning and problem posing, making connections, and caring attentiveness. They see learning as a sharing of the process of thinking as well as thoughts, as "real talk" that is collaborative rather than adversarial, but not uncritical, a dialogue important to the nurturing of emergent ideas. They recognize that not only a system, but its standards and values, can, may, and perhaps should, be questioned. They see learning as leading to responsibility for personal choice, having moved through detachment, doubt, and the awareness of alternatives. They see life as interconnected, that separation between knower and known are artificial, and that values are to be wholeheartedly but tentatively held. They are passionate about knowledge, committed to the development of all parts of their lives, and recognize the need to balance commitments.

*"And so you have to operate within a certain set of rules, a certain set of principles, or you're going
to lose your self-respect. You still have to recognize that all these things that you learn, all these odd
things about yourself and other people, are potential tools for destruction or construction . . . you've
got to be able to see the effects you're having on other people, and the effect other people have on
you. And you've got to be careful how you use all these things you've developed."*
*—Harvard student, 1960s*

The teacher sees a mode five student as one whose questioning may pose intellectual challenges, and whose concerns may raise difficult ethical questions. There is a need for the teacher to model tolerance, appreciation, joy in discovery, intellectual integrity, and new horizons for mind and spirit. The potential of mode five students for collegiality with the teacher in the inquiry process is manifest.

**Pedagogy for mode five involves:**

> ➤ providing opportunities for both independent work and collaboration; for students to deal with amorphous or ambiguous situations, and with having to establish priorities; for dabbling, tinkering, going down blind alleys, and muddling through
> ➤ allowing whatever time is needed for knowledge to emerge and be constructed, recognizing it as a powerful but not efficient process
> ➤ supporting and validating students in their efforts to construct knowledge when they have sudden accesses of self-doubt; difficulties with accepting their own authority; discomfort with uncertainty; and feelings of being overwhelmed

Boys, girls, and teachers are all likely to benefit from developing an understanding of the ways that knowledge, the paths toward it, and its structuring, are gendered (see chapters on the academic disciplines for explanations and examples). They should take this information into account in their own construction of knowledge, and in helping others to do so. They should consider the possibility that any particular way of knowledge's gendering, and perhaps its gendering at all, may be altered — and that such alteration might be salutary.

(The information presented above draws most heavily on King and Kitchener 1994, Belenky et al. 1986 and Perry 1970; and is also influenced by Sizer 1992, Crawford 1989, Resnick 1987, Kratwohl, Bloom and Masia 1964, Bloom ed. 1956. Field dependence/independence information from Cushner, McClelland and Safford 1992, 108-114; Ramirez and Castaneda 1974 quoted in Banks 1994, 86 (Mexican-Americans), 87 (Native Americans); Haaken 1988; Halpern 1986, Chapter 3 (spatial relationship); Shade 1982 (African Americans); Witkin and Asch 1948; Witkin et al. 1977. Ethic of justice and care from Gilligan 1982).

■ ■ ■ ■

## CHAPTER FOUR

## THE FORMAL CURRICULUM: BECOMING INCLUSIVE

*What. In what. Way. Do they differ.*

*And. In what. Way. Are they. The same.*

*Those of them that have. Fame. From those of them.*

*That do not. Have. Fame. In what way.*

*Are they. The same. Those. Of them. That do not. Have fame.*

*What is. Fame. That they. Have.*

*And what. Is different. In them. That gives to them. This. Fame.*

*From those of them. That do not have.*

*Given to them. Fame. Or is it. Not the same.*

*Not. To have fame. As to. Have fame.*

*And are they. Who have fame. The same.*

*As those. Who do not have. Fame.*

*This is why. It is. The same.*

*—Gertrude Stein, 1931*

The formal curriculum taught in the classroom is the guts of any school. It is the most important of the messages we send to students, parents, and ourselves about what reality is like, and about what is truly worth teaching and learning. In the last couple of decades, both scholars and teachers have become increasingly dissatisfied with messages sent concerning the nature of reality and about worth by a curriculum that largely turned a blind eye to those who were by elite definitions non-elite.

The outline below can serve as an aid to navigating the sometimes rough waters of curriculum reform with women, gender, and non-elite men in view.

In rethinking the curriculum with a view to including the perspectives and experience of groups other than elite men, the thousands who have by now done so have found their experience roughly followed the path outlined below. Based on that experience, those currently engaged in the process of examining their own curriculum need to note that:

- teachers and students benefit when they become informed and versatile enough to be able to make use of elements of all the various "stages," as appropriate, in the sciences and mathematics, as well as in history, literature, and the arts
- reality is far less tidy than the models below suggest; more than one "stage," and/or the features of more than one, may coexist in various parts of any one course during any particular time period
- different levels of student maturity, different courses, and different parts of any particular course more appropriately or readily accommodate some "stages" than others
- in planning to put ideas from this model into effect, taking the information in Chapter Three and its applicability to one's own students into account is likely to be helpful

"Elite" and "non-elite" are unsatisfactory terms, but the best available to serve as shorthand for groups that had to be frequently identified in the discussion below. "Elite" is a shorthand term summing up the characteristics of those people who historically created, defined, used, and were the gatekeepers to knowledge; were themselves the norm, relative to whom others were judged; held most authority, physical, mental, and moral, over others; were, in the last 500 years or so, usually Western white, upper, or middle class men.

"Non-elite" is a shorthand term intended to include usually all, and at least several, of the following (though of course any one individual could be "elite" relative to some people, or some contexts, "non-elite" relative to, and in, others). These descriptors are only valid statistically:

- ➤ women
- ➤ racial, ethnic, religious, and other minorities in the United States and elsewhere
- ➤ working-class men
- ➤ non-Western peoples worldwide

The information that follows is intended to serve as background to the more detailed treatment of individual disciplines that follows.

## ➤ I. THE PRE-1960S "CANONICAL" CURRICULUM

### 1. Characteristics
- Deals with elites and the publicly validated (people in official positions; art in museums/performance; literature published/critically acclaimed; scientific research funded/published)
- Slights "invisible" women, minorities, working classes, non-elite people
- Uses a "win-lose" style of thinking with a relatively narrow definition of "winners"

### 2. Typical questions
- Who were the truly great thinkers/actors in history?
- Who were the great creators/innovators in the arts and sciences?

### 3. Incentives/justification
- Providing fixed principles of value
- Maintaining standards of excellence
- Fulfilling need for passing on accumulated wisdom and world view of past

### 4. Means
- Covers the material
- Drills in important facts
- Tests mostly for recall
- Back to basics

### 5. Typical assumptions/concerns about pedagogy
- Student is vessel
- Teacher is conduit
- How teacher can best pour information into students' minds

### 6. Advantages
- Fulfills need for passing on accumulated wisdom/world view of past
- Provides justification by appeal to fixed principles of value: avoids fragmentation, confusion, and uncertainty
- Gives student a touchstone for excellence
- Comfortable; allows us to teach what we know because we have been taught it ourselves

### 7. Problems
- Equity/justice: If indeed there have been some female/minority "greats," are they unfairly neglected?
- Knowledge: How can we teach about reality if we leave large chunks of reality out?
- Accuracy: Was there really one person who was the creator/innovator? What about those shoulders the "giants," according to Newton, have stood on?
- Role models: Might their absence be damaging?

## ➤ II. SEARCH FOR THE MISSING WOMEN AND NON-ELITE MEN

### 1. Characteristics

- Rescues from obscurity non-elite people who meet elite standards of greatness
- Adds contributions of the non-elite to mainstream elite activity/ideas
- Casts a wider net for "winners"

### 2. Typical questions

- Who are the non-white Jeffersons, Shakespeares, Einsteins, and Rembrandts?
- Who are the left-out "greats" who may justifiably be added? (W.E.B. DuBois? Spartacus? Marie Curie?)
- What did women/minorities contribute to the institutions and ideas of the dominant culture?

### 3. Incentives/justification

- Affirmative action
- Compensatory

### 4. Means

- Adds new information to existing information, within existing frameworks

### 5. Typical assumptions/concerns about pedagogy

- Recognition that female and minority students may need help to fit the traditional educational mold
- Effort to remedy student deficiencies so that eventually all groups approximate normative group's performance
- Conscious striving for tolerance and for reduction/avoidance of negative stereotyping

### 6. Advantages

- Demonstrates that non-elites have been capable of elite behavior/achievements
- Gives non-elite learners role-models they can more readily identify with

### 7. Problems

- Difficulty identifying a female Jefferson, African-American Einstein or working-class Shakespeare reinforces perception of inferiority
- Giving visibility to some non-elite people makes their dearth in the limelight more obvious

## ➤ III. WOMEN AND NON-ELITE MEN AS A DISADVANTAGED, SUBORDINATE GROUP

### 1. Characteristics

- Questions and tries to explain the causes and results of the exclusion of non-elites from public-sphere access, and of the devaluation of non-elite people not only in history and literature, but in math, science, and arts
- Examines the multiple structures and ideologies that defined women and non-elite men as subordinate or disadvantaged groups
- Looks at the ways "losers" were handicapped, and/or kept out of the competition altogether

### 2. Typical questions

- Given that some of the non-elite did succeed, why did not more do so?
- Why were the experiences and activities of the non-elite devalued?
- Why were there so few women leaders?
- Why was female performance in math/sciences/athletics inferior? Why do women feel at a disadvantage in these areas ?

### 3. Incentives/justification

- Social justice
- Intellectual curiosity
- Activism

### 4. Means

- Continues to use perspective of dominant group, but begins to question its premises and assumptions
- Encourages student questioning; tentatively adds experiential opportunities for learning
- Increased testing for understanding necessitated by the nature of the new material and its focus on processes, conditions, ideas, relationships

### 5. Typical assumptions/concerns about pedagogy

- Recognition that sensitive ways need to be developed to deal with student behavior that may occur in this stage, such as fervent student questioning, sometimes militantly adversarial, though not always knowledge-grounded
- Resistance to information about gender asymmetry and its cultural supports, which may suggest to them that their behavior is either constrained (females) or culpable (males). This and a similar dynamic in the case of non-white/white students may give rise to strong emotions.

### 6. Advantages

- Begins to uncover the invisible paradigms, unconscious assumptions, implicit judgments, and unspoken conventions that structure both fields of knowledge and the content and process of education
- Identifies what images of the "other" have been current in the dominant culture, some of their historical roots, and the changes they have undergone

### 7. Problems

- Sees the non-elite through elite lenses, not on their own terms
- Sees the non-elite as passive victims
- Tends to ignore/neglect differences within non-elite groups
- Tends to the adversarial, and may create resentment, anger, guilt
- Sees the problem primarily as getting the non-elite to fit more successfully into elite culture, society, and ideas

## ➤ IV. WOMEN AND NON-ELITE MEN ON THEIR OWN TERMS

### 1. Characteristics

- Studies "others" in depth
- Uses women's and non-elites' own perspectives
- Tries to avoid assumptions rooted in the experience of the dominant culture
- Need not be constrained by existing paradigms
- Focuses on the lateral values of relationship and of collaboration to ensure the decent survival of all

### 2. Typical questions

- What was/is women's and non-elite men's experience? What did they do, how did they live?
- How did women use the written word/creative expression, and to what extent/in what ways did their experience as women influence this use?
- How do women approach mathematics and science? What is their experience in these fields?
- How did/do the experiences and activities of women differ due to race, class, culture? What are the commonalities?

### 3. Incentives/justification

- Intellectual: broaden and deepen knowledge of reality
- Emotional: empathy
- Pedagogical: provide a mirror for some students in which they can see experiences of people like themselves; a window for others through which they can look into the experience of people unlike themselves

### 4. Means

- Uses exclusively, or primarily, what women and other non-elite groups have said about themselves, and have expressed in nonverbal ways (music, art), and what they now say about their own experience
- Is interdisciplinary

### 5. Typical assumptions/concerns about pedagogy

- Student-centered teaching; teacher as facilitator rather than authority
- Seeks opportunities for group work, cooperative learning, experiential learning
- Recognition of women's ways of learning
- De-emphasis of formal testing and memorization
- Focus on understanding, with use of journals, projects, portfolios, oral examinations; students given some choices about timing, and perhaps also nature, of tests
- Aims to create shared meanings through collaborative problem-solving, rather than learning the right answer
- Emotions seen as potentially contributing to, rather than distracting from, learning
- Sees teaching by a member of the group studied, and/or of the group that does the studying, as an asset

### 6. Advantages

- Sheds light on what is distinctive in the experience and activities of groups other than the normative culture, thereby giving a more accurate view of reality
- Gives more opportunity for non-elite students to learn every kind of subject matter in their own preferred styles
- Gives all students better insight into ways of living and thinking about "other" peoples, to whom they will be relating in an increasingly diverse and global world
- Gives members of the dominant culture the experience of seeing themselves as the "other," thus aiding empathy
- Validates the experience and activities of non-elite groups as worth teaching and learning about
- Validates students' own experience as relevant to learning, and learning as relevant to personal experience

### 7. Problems

- Fragmentation: difficulty in avoiding presentation of a series of unconnected parallel, and perhaps conflicting, accounts
- Superficiality: including the experiences of many, let alone the full spectrum, of the non-elite means that none can be covered in depth
- Distortion: just as any account of the elite that leaves out the non-elite distorts the account of the former, so is any account of the non-elite distorted without inclusion of the elite
- Inaccessibility: while a great many voices thought in the past to have been silenced, lost, or suppressed have by now been recovered, much of what the non-elite said about themselves is not readily accessible — especially to pre-college teachers
- Balance: some students may come to overvalue and rely too heavily on personal opinion, feelings, and relevance

## ➤ V. WOMEN AND THE NON-ELITE AS CHALLENGE TO THE DISCIPLINES

### 1. Characteristics

- Asks not only what is important, but by what yardstick importance is measured; on what basis priorities are assigned and value judgments made
- Asks not only what we know, but how we came to know it
- Reexamines and reevaluates, with the diversity introduced by women and non-elites in view, the ways knowledge, and its acquisition, is structured and conceptualized

- Questions the ways that definitions of "winners" and "losers," and the concepts of "winning" and "losing," are constructed

2. **Typical questions**
   - In what ways and to what extent are specifications of greatness, norms of behavior, definitions of historical periods, characterizations of excellence in creative work and science, universal? In what ways and to what extent are they culture-bound?
   - How might some of the specifications, definitions, and characterizations have to change when no longer viewed from the single perspective of a dominant, normative elite?
   - How must the questions we ask about the subject matter, methods, and means of attaining knowledge have to change to account for women's experience, diversity, difference — and that of other non-elite groups?

3. **Incentives/justification**
   - Epistemology: the need to know what influences the way we generate, validate, structure, and think about knowing and knowledge
   - Practicality: learning from, as well as accepting and validating, the perspectives and experience of the "other"

4. **Means**
   - Using diversity as a category of analysis in dealing with knowledge and knowing, always asking whether diversity makes a difference in the specific instance considered
   - Testing the paradigms, both of the nature and structure of knowledge, and how it is arrived at
   - Watching for: faulty generalizations; partial knowledge, assumed and unquestioned neutrality and objectivity; circular reasoning

5. **Typical assumptions/concerns about pedagogy**
   - Giving students responsibility for their own learning; teacher more like the conductor of an orchestra than an authority
   - Favoring of interdisciplinary approaches
   - Recognizing that students need to see that more than one valid approach to arriving at knowledge may exist
   - Testing by multiple methods, understanding and problem-solving-oriented, with links to "real-world" applications
   - Giving students choices in ways of testing, including invitations on occasion to design their own demonstrations of competence
   - Viewing knowledge as a process rather than a product; as constructed not discovered; as potentially contingent, context-influenced, complex multiple, conflicting, incomplete, and tentative
   - Seeing interpersonal relationships and respect for each others' experiences and opinions in the classroom as an important component of knowledge-acquisition

6. **Advantages**
   - Contributes to increased accuracy of knowledge and better understanding of the nature of knowledge
   - Is genuinely inclusive of the experiences and activities of all
   - Enriches perspective on own culture for all groups
   - Increases student involvement in their own learning
   - Develops critical thinking/higher-order thinking skills
   - Enhances, in a rapidly changing world, the ability to handle multiplicity, listen to all the voices, and see that versatility is of practical importance
   - Redefines "winning" and "losing" in global contexts

## 7. Problems

- Fear that if the concept of the normative culture's single, dominant standard of value and excellence is abandoned, then there will be no standard to judge by at all
- Questioning whether the work of this stage is accessible to students in high and elementary school, and is important enough to teach
- Fear of fragmentation, and of conflicting and idiosyncratically conceived presentations of subjective realities, since the existence of multiple perspectives challenges the universality of any one

## ➤ VI. THE TRANSFORMED, BALANCED CURRICULUM

### 1. Characteristics

- Experience of elites and non-elites, of women and men, understood together, as both inter-dependent and in some ways independent of each other; and with due accounting for the intersections of class, race, and ethnicity with gender
- Differences positively valued, and learned from, without loss of identification with and pride in one's own group

### 2. Typical questions

- How can we best balance uniformities and diversities?
- How do we teach those aspects within our own and other groups' culture that run counter to strongly held values of our own?

### 3. Incentives/justification

- Inclusive vision of human experience, based on recognition both of diversity and difference, and on the commonalities and shared characteristics/experiences of diverse human beings
- Vision of the kind of knowledge that this would give rise to
- Increased social equality

### 4. Means

- Transformation of paradigms of knowledge: of its nature, structure, and how it is arrived at

### 5. Assumptions about pedagogy

- Multiple paths toward student empowerment
- Variety of teaching styles

This final stage is necessarily sketchy, since it exists nowhere as yet. Its advantages and problems are yet to be identified.

(The information presented above was influenced by the following: McIntosh, Peggy. 1983. *Interactive phases of curricular re-vision.* Working paper #124. Wellesley, MA: Wellesley Center for Research on Women; Banks, J. 1984. *Multiethnic education in the U.S.A.* In Corner, T. ed. 1984. Education in multicultural societies. New York: St. Martin's Press; Schuster, Marilyn R. and Susan R. Van Dyne eds. 1985. *Women's place in the academy.* Totowa, N.J.: Rowman & Allanheld; Maher, Frances. 1985. *Pedagogies for the gender-balanced classroom.* Journal of Thought 20 (3), Fall; Minnich, Elizabeth. 1990. *Transforming knowledge.* Philadelphia: Temple University Press; Van Dyne, Susan. 1990. *Notes on a decade of change.* NWSA Journal 2 (2), Spring; Tetreault. Mary Kay Thompson. 1993. *Classrooms for diversity: rethinking curriculum and pedagogy.* In Banks, James A. and Cherry S. McGee Banks eds. 1993. *Multicultural education: issues and perspectives.* Second edition. Boston: Allyn and Bacon; Banks, James A. 1994. *Multiethnic education: theory and practice.* Boston: Allyn and Bacon.)

■ ■ ■ ■

## CHAPTER FIVE

# HISTORY

*When abstractions about "mankind" have been made in the dominant tradition,
they have far too often been distilled not from knowledge gathered from the
study of humankind but from knowledge about one group within it.
This is faulty abstraction; it is rather like creating
"abstract of vanilla" but labeling it "flavor."*

*—Elizabeth Minnich, 1990*

We cannot do a satisfactory job of teaching about past reality if we leave large chunks of it out. Giving as accurate a picture of the past as possible requires including the past of majorities as well as that of the minority elite. Keeping silent about the experiences and achievements of the major part of humanity — women and non-elite men — gives our students an incorrect picture of the past.

Rethinking the history curriculum in light of the last twenty-plus years of women's studies scholarship means opening up to the consideration of new information, new ideas, and new ways of looking at traditional subject matter.

The arguments in favor of teaching a revised, more inclusive, history are based both on the integrity of the historical discipline itself, and on the needs of the students who are intended to benefit from learning history.

A broader and more accurate assessment of the part played by the elite itself becomes possible when women and non-elite men are an integral part of the story. An account of leaders is incomplete and distorted if their relationship to followers, and to those whose unsung work they needed to achieve the top, is lacking.

Using the new information uncovered by women's studies scholarship we can build a sounder and more complete image of the past. A major obstacle to telling the story of those once called the "voiceless masses," lack of records that tell their stories, has been found less limiting than used to be thought. When the historical record is examined with women in view, scholars find women who were outstanding in public ways, and participants in institutions important according to traditional standards. To consistently exclude them is inequitable as well as inaccurate.

*"We did found and run institutions that cared for the sick and old and wounded outside the home.
We did found and run schools that provided for newly freed black people and for children. We did
struggle for goodness in the church, the synagogue, the community — and we did so politically.
We were active in the abolition movement and the civil rights movement. We outsiders did our
work, work of all kind, and whatever we did remained obscured from the light."*
*— Elizabeth Minnich, 1982*

To help young people construct their own identities, know their own roots, and to understand "others" well enough to neither look down on nor fear those different from themselves, they need exposure to diversity in history. Knowing about one's own past, that of people most like oneself, is important for individuals. Therefore, women, people of color, and people who are not middle-class, need to be able to see themselves in history.

Our students will live in a world where they will have to work, play, and negotiate, on equal terms, with far more diverse people than has been the case in the past. Middle class white boys, therefore, also need the history of women, people of color, and those who are not middle class, so they can have an accurate understanding of, and empathy with, the "others" to whom they will be relating.

*"All students deserve a curriculum which* Mirrors *their own experience back to them, upon occasion. But curriculum must also insist upon the fresh air of* Windows *into the experience of others — who also need and deserve the public validation of the school curriculum.*
*—Emily Style, 1988 (emphases in original)*

Research shows that students' values are affected by what they read and are taught. The messages being sent, and the values taught, both by what is included in history and what is excluded, is worth serious examination. (For studies that document the favorable impact of a gender-inclusive history curriculum, see Bernard-Powers 1995, 199.)

Caretaking, both personal and cultural, and the maintenance of production and reproduction, are virtually invisible in history textbooks and history courses. Little if any time or attention is given to the experiences and accomplishments of people who weave and maintain the social fabric, and much to those who disrupt it. Whether or not there might be an over-emphasis on male-identified war and violence, and what message this sends to boys as well as girls, could use scrutiny.

Girls do substantially less well than boys overall on standard history tests; but boys do substantially less well in some indispensable areas. While the same or larger number of girls than boys takes the U.S. and European History Advanced Placement tests, the boys' mean grades are significantly higher among all racial and ethnic groups. In U.S. history the disparity is especially marked; a third of the boys, but only a quarter of the girls, scored at the top two (4 and 5) levels (Advanced Placement AP 1994, 4-5).

In the second half of the 1980s, both the California statewide assessment test of eighth graders in history/social science, and the National Assessment of Educational Progress in History of eleventh graders, found boys outperforming girls. On the California test, boys did better on two thirds of the questions. Their superiority was especially marked on questions dealing with political events and documents such as the U.S. Constitution; all questions associated with military conflict; and questions involving maps. Girls did better on questions about rights and responsibilities, voter decision-making, desirable citizenship behavior, democratic participation values, and humanitarian concerns (Kneedler 1988, 119-120). These findings were in accord with those of the national assessment (Ravitch and Finn 1987, 130-131). One explanation for boys' overall higher performance is that so much of the information learned, and tested, in history is associated with military conflict and politics.

These results fit well with the evidence that gender stereotyping affects student learning ability. Children have difficulty remembering materials that are counter-stereotypic, or that are associated more strongly with the other sex (Liben and Signorella 1993). Evidently, in the field of history, both boys and girls are disadvantaged, though differently so; and it is a problem that will not be solved simply by introducing more women's history. As future responsible citizens, girls need to become knowledgeable about military issues and maps, and boys about democratic values and humanitarian concerns. Teachers need to stay alert to the different areas in which they might need extra support.

There is no one best way to bring women and previously underrepresented groups into the history taught in school. Whatever choices are made have both advantages and disadvantages. The appropriateness of any choice will be influenced by teachers' knowledge, values, and goals, by student age, by the nature of the class, and by many other variables.

There are two main conceptual possibilities. One is to add the new information about women and women's issues to traditional history, leaving the traditional subject matter basically unchanged, except perhaps for some compression.

The other is to use the new information in ways that not only supplement, but shed new light on, promote rethinking of, and may very likely lead to changed organization and emphases in traditional subject matter. It usually involves conceptual change, rearrangement of frameworks, and asking new questions.

These changes represent stations on a journey of discovery which has a beginning but no end. We may start from different places, and forge ahead in the same general direction suggested by others' efforts, without the need to follow their steps exactly. Having set foot on the path, however, while recognizing that a fixed destination is not to be had, stopping too soon means missing out on the full benefits of being along for the while trip.

To borrow from Gertrude Stein, there is no "there" there for us to get to on this journey; no single "right" gender-balanced curriculum to aim for. It is the journey itself that is energizing, intellectually challenging, and growth-producing for teachers and students alike. The value lies in the open-mindedness, sensitivity, and intellectual integrity brought to the curriculum transformation that tenacious involvement with women's history leads to.

In the process of integrating women into the curriculum, students need to become aware of the differences between culturally dictated ideologies about women's nature and proper role on the one hand, and the realities of women's lives on the other. A balance also needs to be struck between the diversity of womens experiences according to time, place, class, race, ethnicity, religion, age, and stage of life-cycle, on the one hand, and the uniformities of their experiences as a group, sharing as they do female socialization patterns, potential for motherhood, responsibility for childrearing and housekeeping, and culturally decreed subordination to men.

For any changes that are undertaken to be meaningful, it is essential that the information and ideas newly included be tested in the same ways that all other information and ideas are tested. The new needs to be included as the topic, or the right answer, as well as among the wrong answers, on multiple choice tests, on essay-questions, identifications, and all other kinds of tests, at least often enough not to be token. It needs to be the subject of questions asked about homework in class, among topics covered in class discussions or assigned for papers, and part of research assignments.

The following ways of dealing with the new scholarship on women and non-elite peoples have all by now been used by a great many teachers at all levels. All are worthwhile and appropriate, depending on circumstances; but, for the sake of both history as a discipline and the students whom we teach, willingness to explore them all as part of a short or long-range plan is needed. They are presented in order of increasing complexity, demand for knowledge and flexibility, and length of time it is likely to take to put them into practice.

> **1. HOLDING ON WITH ONE HAND, REACHING OUT WITH THE OTHER**

I t is possible to bring hitherto invisible/underrepresented people into students' view on the basis of their notable participation in the public sphere (the traditional criterion for inclusion), while continuing to teach pretty much the same course. It is important, however, not to isolate those included ("Before tomorrow's test on the middle ages, we'll finish the unit with an overview of women's life… ") and to make the inclusion an integral part of the existing story. (Anne Hutchinson is better presented in the context of structures of authority and dissent, or of colonial religion, than mentioned as "one of the few women who achieved importance.")

**Turn on more spotlights:** "Great women" and "great men" of non-elite backgrounds have begun to make their way into the more recent textbooks; teachers can supplement and expand text coverage. Take care to stitch those included to the fabric of the rest of history as firmly as possible. This approach fits in especially well with biographically oriented courses and sparks interest in younger students.

**Widen the beam:** Those more numerous women who participated, albeit without earning fame, in the public events and institutions embodied in the historical canon, can be talked about and read about in the context of covering the canonical subject matter. Women as fief holders and abbesses in the early Middle Ages controlled land, wealth, power, and men. They were members of guilds, craft and labor unions. In America, they went west on their own as well as with husbands and fathers. They played a part in anarchist, socialist, literary, artistic, and reform movements; served unofficially and sometimes officially in armies at various times and places; held down the home front in World War I, and were key to the productivity that kept belligerents going in World War II. One way to approach integration of women is by including them in all those traditional topics in which they genuinely played a part.

When did they genuinely play a part? The answer, of course, is "always," since they were always half the total population and therefore half of history. But their presence in the public sphere, to which most history continues to devote itself, varied in scope in different contexts.

**Choose focus carefully:** The teacher's choice of how to focus any particular topic may well be decisive in whether inclusion of women is more, or less, easy, comfortable, and appropriate. "The American War of Independence" conceptualizes a topic very differently from "Formation of the Republic." World War I can be taught as the battles or as the war effort (the battles and the home front both). Either is a canonical choice; the latter favors inclusion of women, the former does not. The choice, however, is rarely either-or; it is a matter of difference in emphasis.

Those who have used these ways of bringing greater diversity into the history curriculum have found both advantages and disadvantages.

**Experience suggests that these ways are useful in that they do:**

- provide a somewhat more accurate picture of the past
- show that the non-elite are capable of being like the elite, and that some of them "made it" in elite terms
- give groups that had been ignored, and thereby devalued, the stamp of historical validation: they are worth knowing about
- highlight shared experience, and emphasize unity, with the tacit assumption that all were part of the same normative history, albeit some less completely than others

**Disadvantages are that they do not:**

- allow the inclusion of non-elites unless they proved acceptable as, as it were, "honorary males" and "honorary whites"
- explain why so few of the non-elite participated, let alone "made it"
- account for why their participation was qualitatively, as well as quantitatively, different from that of the elite
- convey the flavor, the distinctive character, of various non-elite peoples' experiences
- do justice to the *pluribus* part of E *pluribus unum*, though they may do a good job with the *unum*
- get at the experience of women *as women* (or of the non-elite men as blue-collar workers, Hispanics, African or Asian or Native Americans), because that experience is not considered historically significant

*T*here are potential pedagogical problems also. Gender and minority stereotyping may actually be reinforced by student perception of women and non-elite men as marginal, and visible or important only to the extent that their experience, exceptionally, approached that of elite men's. Teachers can address this problem by giving some attention to the ideas and social arrangements that served to maintain the exclusivity of the elite. (An excellent short text to use with students, even in junior high, is Virginia Woolf's "Shakespeare's Sister," in her book, *A Room of One's Own*.)

Teachers also need to watch out for, and be prepared to deal with, anger and frustration on the part of some non-elite, and guilt and resentment on the part of some elite students. They may experience some of these feelings themselves. Examination of the ideologies, institutional arrangements, and social structures that were responsible for the systematic exclusion of women and other non-elite groups from avenues of access to power in the past can, however, in addition to being intellectually explanatory, help defuse some of the problem of felt injustice, as being due to more than only individual malice.

It also helps to set this in the wider context of a look at the distribution, legitimization, and maintenance of power in general in the society studied. Who held the power, and how did they get it? What kinds of power were recognized? Who were the powerless? What gradations were there? How did those in power justify being so? What mechanisms did they use to maintain unequal distributions of power? What actions did the powerless take to limit those in power, or gain more power themselves? What part was played by ideologies (religious and other), institutions, education, economics, physical force? On the power/powerlessness continuum, what were the intersections of class, gender, age, race, religion and other factors? Most students respond with interest to finding out about, and discussing, such issues.

## ➤ 2. TAKING HOLD WITH THE OTHER HAND

Not only does this approach involve grasping and handing on new subject matter, but new and different kind of information as well. The emphasis is not on events, but on conditions, processes, experiences, ways of being. It is less about what people had done, but about how they lived. What was it like to live in America as a Navajo, a Southern rural woman, a first-generation Asian-American woman? What did their differentness mean to them?

**Create a mirror and a window simultaneously, while listening to different voices:** Teach about those experiences of non-elite groups that they did not share with the elite. The former will be able to see, and to recognize, themselves as in a mirror; for the latter, a window will be opened on that which differs from them; all will get to hear, and benefit from, previously silent voices.

> *"Having taken for granted 'American history as usual — Puritans, thirteen colonies, a nation of immigrants, westward expansion, new frontiers, hearing new voices may mean hearing Asian-American students say that their ancestors came eastward, not westward. African-American students explain that being shackled in a slave galley cannot fruitfully be called an immigrant experience. Native American and Chicano students affirm that, rather than immigrating, they stood still and the border moved."*
> —quoted in Maher and Tetreault, 1995

Examples of this approach would be dealing with:

> ➤ inter- and intra-tribal relations of Native Americans apart from their contact with Europeans or the U.S. government
> ➤ the nature of shifts in African-American cultural expressions
> ➤ the system of middle-class women's friendships and support groups in the nineteenth century
> ➤ the degrees of women's control in the area of productive work within the family

**A key part here is using what the non-elite said about themselves, rather than what was said about them by others. It lends itself particularly well to:**

> ➤ integration with role-playing and art projects in the early grades
> ➤ courses using primary source documents

> ➤ the development of units about a particular group, or topic, of special interest (Asian American groups on the west coast, women factory workers in Massachusetts, Chicanas in the southwest)
> ➤ creation of elective courses — full year, semester, or intersession — on topics such as "Turning Points in American Women's History," "Black Women and Religion in America," "Did Women Have a Renaissance?" (Stevenson 1993; Kelly-Gadol 1987)

While far from a preferred choice, this kind of information can be inserted into traditional curricular frameworks. The problem is that it will stick out like buttons on cloth, will be hard to stitch to the main fabric of traditional information, and will perforce remain discontinuous. If it has to be done this way (one hopes temporarily), it is particularly important that the presentation of non-elite experience does not become too fragmented. For both understanding and impact, it helps to restrict the number of both themes and groups dealt with, but to touch on those chosen consistently through time. (Examples of themes might be changing relations of mothers to their children; redefinitions of what properly belongs in "women's sphere"; women's power, and its lack, in the family economy; or relationships of dominance and subordination between women.)

Those who have used this approach have found the following advantages and disadvantages.

**In favor of this approach is that:**

> ➤ it presents the other side of a coin we are familiar with — non-elite history as history in its own right, not as a supplement to that of the elite
> ➤ it sheds light on the *pluribus* — on what is distinctive — and gives a hearing to different voices
> ➤ it has very strong appeal for some students

**Some disadvantages:**

A basic problem is conceptual. You now have the other side of the coin, but it's still only one side. This approach tends to produce what you might call "parallel histories." The network of relationships between the groups, that would allow a disparate collection of histories to become the interrelated seamless web in which all strands are connected to all, and none can be touched or broken without affecting others, is missing. Yet it is this vision that more closely resembles reality.

There are also pedagogical problems. Without considerable teacher guidance, the differentness of the material may lead students to perceive it as quaint, or weird, or pointless, and, because it is not easily linked to the familiar, to what is in the textbook, to dismiss it as unimportant.

## ➤ 3. USING BOTH HANDS TO SHAPE BOTH OLD KNOWLEDGE AND NEW

*I*ncorporating women fully into history means both understanding the history of gender itself, how, why, and with what results its parameters varied in different historical circumstances, and taking into account both gender-shared and gender-specific historical experience.

The first of these means staying alert to the fact that gender, class, and race are the main "givens" that inevitably affect both what happens to people and what they do. Gender definitions themselves have a history, and male as well as female roles have undergone significant changes. It means understanding the gender messages sent by ideologies and institutions, the ways gender is used to construct, preserve, and subvert relations of power. It means being aware of the ways gender itself is shaped by, and in turn shapes, ideologies and institutions.

In the context of the Industrial Revolution, it would be seen as relevant that workmen articulated their relations to their employers in gendered terms, feeling "unmanned," "unsexed," and "impotent" in relation to the latter; and that this and other gender concerns had repercussions on unionization (hostility to women's admission to unions) and wage issues for both women and men (Baron 1994).

This approach depends on acquaintance with a body of information about which the scholarship is only a decade or two old. Because its impact depends on tracing relationships that are wide-ranging and relatively complex, and because it deals with conditions, experiences, and ideologies rather than events, it is difficult to sum up concisely.

**Develop stereoscopic vision:** This approach looks at both men's and women's experience (not at how women's experience differed from men's, which assumes that men's experience is the norm, and women's the divergence from the norm) and also at the experience they share. It works well, and is easily introduced, in the context of family and oral history with all age groups (see **What Schools and Teachers Can Do** for suggestions). It can also work well, but requires more research, and rethinking, in upper-level conventional history courses.

It involves:

> ➤ seeing from both female and male perspectives
> ➤ focusing on both male and female experience and activities
> ➤ recognizing, and teaching, history as both gender-shared and gender-specific
> ➤ Taking into account that not only women, but men as well, are gendered beings, and dealing, when occasion warrants, with their specifically male experience: "Examined through the lenses of masculine and feminine experience, the Overland Trail acquires a new historical shape. ... Men as well as women were full of aesthetic appreciation; women as well as men were practical and economy-minded." (Faragher 1979, 5, 15)

*T*he "doubled vision" created by women's history (and the history of other non-elite groups) sensitizes learners to multiple viewpoints. Therefore, in this phase of re-vision, historiography becomes particularly salient. First, it raises questions of balance, objectivity, validity, and historical significance that students need to learn how to tackle for their proper understanding of history. Students need to find out how what is in the textbook was arrived at, and on what basis judgments about what is "important enough" to include were made.

According to what criteria, and through what mechanisms, is evidence selected and preserved? How, and on what terms, are claims of historical "truth" validated and authorized, and what is occluded in the historian's assertion of objectivity? How are assumptions about gender [and other things] written into the historical record? And how can presumptions preserved in the historian's very categories of analysis be unpacked, interrogated, and transformed? (Shapiro 1994, vii)

Second is the question of the historiography of women's history itself. Understanding the historical roots of concern with gender balancing and diversity — which are usually thought of as new concepts in history writing and teaching — contributes to defusing attempts at politicizing the history of women and minorities at the expense of scholarship both from those who want history to serve the goals of each day's activism and from those who deny these histories' academic integrity.

In fact, there are substantial links between the ideas and methods of women's and minority historians and those of historians with much longer pedigrees who were also seen as maverick innovators in their time: social historians, demographers, historians of the working classes, and of ways of thinking (*mentalitiés*). Nor is evidence lacking of traditional historians unabashedly writing histories for political purposes. (Ranke himself, that pillar of objectivity, who insisted on "telling it like it was" (*wie es eigentlich gewesen*), said, "History is not simply an academic subject; [it] should above all benefit our own nation... ." (Quoted in Stern, 1956, 62)

More telling, however, is the recognition that all history, and all teaching, is inevitably colored by the background, training, culture, life-experiences of the historian and the teacher, a concept articulated very clearly by women's historians. The historian's values determine what, of all the evidence available about the past, he or she will choose to include, emphasize, minimize, dismiss as unimportant or irrelevant. The teacher's values determine what, of all that is included in the textbook, she or he will highlight, spend class time on, mention in passing, drop when there's a snow day, or put on the test.

Some of the same concerns as those fueling the movement to make history more inclusive are, moreover, appearing in overall reform efforts, such as the Bradley Commission (Quoted in National Council 1994), which recommended that history education should help students to:

> ➤ perceive past events and issues as they were experienced by people at the time, to develop historical empathy
> ➤ acquire at one and the same time a comprehension of diverse cultures and of shared humanity
> ➤ appreciate the often tentative nature of judgments about the past

(The above information, on ways of bringing women and previously underrepresented groups into the history taught in schools, is based on Bernard-Powers 1995; Rosenfelt 1994; Zinsser 1993, Chapter 8; Ravitch 1991; Higginbotham 1990, 3-15; Neuschel 1989, passim.; Scott 1987; Brod ed. 1987, Chapters. 2, 4, and 5; Schuster and Van Dyne 1985, Chapters 1 and 2; McIntosh 1983; Lerner 1981.)

History textbooks still do not help teachers much in an attempt to make history more inclusive and accurate, although some are better than others. Reliance on textbooks by teachers is very high, and this is unlikely to change. It is necessary however to be alert to, and compensate for, those aspects of textbooks that fall short in ways teachers consider important. If women are to become an integral part of history teaching, there is a severe shortfall of texts to model how to do so fully. Regular analysis of textbooks over the last two decades for whether, and how, they include women, shows that in the 1960s and 1970s, twenty-seven U.S. history texts mentioned women on a total of 137 of their combined 29,000 pages (Zinsser 1993, 121). By 1986, there were some changes. The percentage of women in the pictures increased dramatically, from virtual absence to virtual parity. However, text about women and their experience was still under 5 percent of the total in half of the twelve popular high school U.S. history texts analyzed in the mid-1980s, and did not exceed 8 percent in any. In all, the conventional framework of history was retained, with women tacked idiosyncratically here and there on to the unaltered structure (Tetreault 1986).

*"Install your favorite textbook, the one you are now assigning, on a computer. Go through the text, and select every passage mentioning Indians, Hispanics, women, African Americans, workers, etc. Finished ? Now press Command-X. You have just deleted all the underrepresented groups from American history. Read the edited text. Leaving the outsiders entirely out, we still have a coherent narrative of discovery, exploration, settlement, expansion, progress. You can read for scores, maybe hundreds, of pages without any sense that something is missing.*
*—James A. Hijiya, 1995*

Textbooks of the 1990s mostly continue to reproduce the exclusionist traditional histories. A few lumps of women's experience, in a separate paragraph or subsection but very rarely more, are sprinkled into the inert dough of the "regular" text in those books that are making an effort; what has been called the "add women and stir" approach, but without much stirring. The assumption seems to be that separate readings, specifically about women, will be used to "supplement" what is lacking in the text; this, unfortunately, tends to strengthen perceptions of women's' marginalization, segregation, and lesser importance (Sadker and Sadker 1994, 130-131; Zinsser 1993, 121-122).

The College Board's Advanced Placement tests in history are based on examination of current textbooks; they are intended to test what is taught. That some change in favor of women has taken place is suggested by the fact that, since the late 1980s, the AP tests and their Graduate Record Examination have begun to include among document question selections writing by women, and to have women-related questions on the multiple choice and essay parts of tests. That the change is very limited is suggested by the paucity of women-related questions, and the fact that they focus on conventional topics such as women's suffrage and reform movements participation (Zinsser 1993, 124-125).

For suggestions on how to counteract the deficiencies of textbooks, see below.

## ➤ What Schools and Teachers Can Do

Most of the curricular suggestions below will work, some with adaptation, at most if not all grade levels. Some will work for non-elite groups other than women. For suggestions on gender-related issues in pedagogy, testing, and classroom interactions, see the **What Schools and Teachers Can Do** sections in **ENGLISH** ("to improve students' ability to communicate effectively . . . " page 89); **MATHEMATICS** ("build on known connection between discussion and deepening understanding." page 107), and **SCIENCE** ("promote more in-depth understanding, reduce anxiety, and build student confidence," page 79. A few of these are science-specific; but most apply just as much in history).

**Take opportunites for professional development:**

- As administrator, provide, or as teacher, ask for and take, opportunities for professional development in the new women's history scholarship.
- Talk with people teaching women's history in local colleges and universities.
- Write or call those who offer help or resource people in the catalogs available from organizations listed in the **Resources** section, page 69.
- Invite speakers and workshop leaders on women's history.
- Choose one or more books relevant to courses you, or preferably several of you, now teach, from the catalogs available from publishers listed in the **Resources** section, page 69. Discuss how you might be able to integrate the information presented into your teaching. (Brown-bag lunches are one way to generate time for collegial discussion).
- Attend meetings and workshops of professional organizations dealing with women's history; share the information gained with colleagues at all grade levels.
- Target one major theme or period (industrialization, totalitarian governments, the Progressive Era, the French Revolution of 1789) with a view to in-depth reading about women in that context, and changing your teaching of it with women in view. The experience gained can then be used to go further.
- Hold an intensive summer curriculum review workshop with schoolwide inclusion of women's history in view (several local schools may want to collaborate on this).
- Having become acquainted with women's history content in your teaching field, use the "find the time" activities below, preferably with colleagues, sometimes in mixed grade levels, to help decide what and how to include.
- Participate in the SEED program listed in the **Resources**, section page 69.

**Find the time:**

- Start with the "fire drill and snow day" approach. Think about what you would not teach when time is unavoidably lost out of the total available to "cover the syllabus." Identify those things that you are now teaching that you are most willing to let go, and those things that you could bear to condense. Do so, and you have created time in which you can include new material. Every little bit helps!

- Do more intensive "post-holing." Use the metaphor of thick, solid, well-dug-in fence posts serving as supports for the thin but strong wire strung between them, and consider some events, periods, or themes in depth; connect them with a narrative that touches on the main points, issues, and developments. (We all already spend more time with some events/themes than others; we can more consciously choose how much we do so.) Merely changing which events, periods, or themes are chosen as posts will make it possible to include women's history.

- Use the "stacked timeline" exercise in Chapman 1980 to help alert yourself to what you consider important in what you teach and why. Reconsider: how important is it for students to know (whatever)? Do you want them to remember it five years from now? What are the chances that they will do so? What is indispensable, what so-so? Why is it important/indispensable? Most people will, on examination, find things they feel they can emphasize less, or even drop altogether, freeing up time.

**Do noteworthy women activities:**

- Ask students to list ten important women (excluding actresses and writers), and/or ten events important to women, before 1950, and do the same for men. Discussion of various topics may follow, including the relative difficulty of the two tasks, and possible reasons, the implications of the kinds of people and events named, on what basis students made their judgments about "importance," and whether it differed for women and men.

- Have students find names of women not in their textbook who lived during the period under study, pick one they consider "important" and find out more about her. Ask them to share what they found, and explain their bases for assigning "importance." (Extension: What were the lives of men and women who were not noteworthy like during this period?)

- Assign students in pairs or groups to research the life of a notable woman you identify. You could use women of the same period, active in the same or different fields, or women with the same interests or in the same field at successive historical periods. (A look at the time period of your choice in Franck and Brownstone 1995 will suggest possibilities.)

Ask students to consider not only their subjects' achievement in the public sphere, but also in their private lives. Come up with a list of "core questions" in class discussion that each student should try to answer for his or her subject. Consider what is most worth knowing about the lives of people in the past. Discuss, having shared their information, connections between "their" women's lives and the canonical themes of history covered in their textbook for the same period. If she is mentioned in their textbook, in what way(s), if any, did their perception of her change as a result of their research?

A variation on this exercise is getting some posters of women of achievement for the classroom and have students, perhaps in groups, write a biography for each that can be posted under her picture. One source for posters is the Organization for Equal Education, listed in the Bibliography.

(Sources: For noteworthy women, James, James and Boyer, available in libraries, is helpful. For non-elite women: information on Southern white women, Spruill 1972 (repr.) is a teacher-resource gold mine: 11th and 12th graders could read selections for themselves, younger students brief excerpts. For African-American women, Lerner 1973 will have some documents for the period, most readable for junior high and up. Gutman 1977 is primarily a teacher resource, but could be used selectively in high school and adapted for earlier; for Native-American men and women from the east, Axtell 1981; for Chinese-American women, Yung 1986, for high school and earlier, with text based on oral history interviews and archival data and pictures a resource for young students.)

**Supplement textbooks:**

- Broaden, deepen, and correct information in, and messages sent by, the textbook, using short primary source documents for students to read and discuss, and/or passing on information from your own reading in context.
- Start working on incorporating women into events, periods, and institutions that you already spend some time on, such as the American Revolution; the French and Russian revolutions; both twentieth century world wars; industrialization. Draw on the "Teacher Background" works in the **Resources** section about women's part in the event, period, or institution to add to, and eventually reconceptualize, teaching about it.
- Browse the document collections in the Resources section, and elsewhere, for documents relevant to what is taught. Assign document(s) for students to read, and discuss with them ways in which the information in the document ties to, supplements, contradicts, or sheds new light on, textbook information. Occasionally, have a brief document read in class right after or right before discussing the textbook information; an immediate written reaction to the document is a variation. Note that, unless the new information is given equal treatment in terms of testing with the rest of what is taught, it will make little or no impact on the students, amounting to wasted effort.

(Sources: For the American Revolution, try DePauw for teachers of 7-12 students; Evans 1989, Chap. 3; Wilson 1982 (both good places to start, for teachers and for honors/AP students), Kerber 1980; Norton 1980 (both have many brief quotations from primary sources; some could be used with younger children; otherwise, both for teachers, good readers in upper high school years); Buel and Buel 1985 includes detail drawn from letters and diaries of one woman's life. For French Revolution, try Levy and Applewhite 1987 (for teachers and honors/AP students), Levy, Applewhite and Johnson 1982 (for teachers and selectively, high school students), Landes 1988 (teachers); For Russian Revolution: Stites 1987 (teachers and honors/AP students); a broader context for teachers is Stites 1978; Bingham and Gross 1980 (targets 8-10 grade students; teacher's guide). For industrialization: Frader 1987 Britain, France, Germany; Tilly 1993, U.S., England, France, China, Japan; Lerner 1982 U.S. (all three for teachers and honors/AP students). For World War I: Filene 1986, Chap. 4 (good starting place for teachers and 11-12 students); Greenwald, U.S.; Breen 1982 U.S. (both best as teacher background). For World War II, Evans 1989 Chap. 10, Filene 1986, Chap. 6 (both teachers and 11-12 students), Hartman 1982 (offers lots of statistics and brief quotes from sources that could be adapted for students, otherwise teacher background); Saywell 1985 (has first-hand accounts of experiences by women war veterans, over half WW II, and is selectively usable for student reading in grades 8-12). For all the topics, consult the document collections in the **Resources** section for primary sources, and introductions/essay backgrounds in them that may be relevant.)

**Using family and oral history:**

- Use family/oral history to introduce women's history, an exercise that also teaches students some of the basic methods and problems of historical research, works well with different ages, and can take very little or a lot of time. It can be tied more closely to "formal" history by the two suggestions at the end. Work with houseplans and architecture can make for some interdisciplinary approaches.

- Have students collect information about the past from people who have lived through it by interviewing them (family members are the most obvious choice, but other adults, including people in an old age home, are possibilities).
- Ask students to find and examine old letters, diaries, Bibles, photo albums, furniture, and heirlooms and try to discover what meanings they have/had for the people who used them, male and female. Local collectors or antique dealers may be willing to come to demonstrate and explain items from the past.
- Find additional information in the public domain: city directories, birth, marriage, and death records, and records of local historical societies about families of their own interviewees, or of people like them. Use the information uncovered to write a family, or oral, history paper, present a skit or report, or produce artwork that might focus on themes such as how the lives of women and men among the interviewees and their families were similar and different. Additional activities include: a comparison of their own life now with that of a parent, grandparent, or other interviewee at the same age, and a biography of someone interviewed who was especially interesting or important, taking into account what impact being male or female had on their life.
- Have students construct a timeline of what they consider to have been important public events during the time period they have data for (or provide one for them). Have them go over the events on the timeline with the people they are interviewing, asking both how they were affected by the events on the timeline, and where on the timeline events important to them fit. What differences are there between events interviewees consider to have been important to them, and the historically important public events? What gender differences, if any, are there?
- Assign students, or have them choose from a list, a particular kind of family to research and report on. For younger students, make available the information they need, such as photocopied primary source documents and books on reserve in library. (Document collections, some cited under **Resources**, provide good, brief, and mostly user-friendly material.) Assignments and materials should be chosen so that when the information collected is pooled students will be able to recognize diversity of family patterns in one particular historical period. (In connection with early-mid nineteenth century, possibilities include various Native-American cultures, perhaps the matrilineal and extended families of Hopi or Iroquois, those in utopian communities such as celibate Shakers, or Oneida Perfectionists with their "complex marriage" and communal childrearing, and frontier, urban, plantation (African American and white) and immigrant families.
- Trace the changes over time in one particular kind of family organization, lifestyle, and functions – for instance, those in Northeastern urban middle class family from the nineteenth century to the present.
- Become aware of the uniformities, diversities, and changes in women's and men's family life experiences. Within these, there is a lot of scope for discussion of issues such as: change in the American family from production to consumption unit, and from agent of to refuge from the wider society; changes in the kind and extent of influence their family life had on the overall pattern of women's and men's lives; and the relationship of husbands and wives to each other and to their children. Changes can be set in the context of discussions of industrialization, urbanization, demographic change, and other factors.

(Sources: For family and oral history, see Kolb, Swerdlow et al.1987, and Sitton, Mehaffy and Davis 1983, Scott and Wishy 1982 , Demos 1971. See also Genovese 1988; Gottlieb 1993, though not about the U.S., is recommended as a scholarly but readable teacher background on research-based views about family issues past and present; Clark 1986 and Hayden 1983 have lots of illustrations that would lend themselves to being made into "inquiry" exercises for younger elementary as well as older students. Strasser 1982 is a mine of information about the technology and tools of housework; lots of contemporary illustrations make it a resource for younger grades as well. Green and Perry 1983 has over a hundred nineteenth century illustrations showing styles in clothes, pictures of nursing bottles and kitchen tools, and advertisements. The text useful for a basis of nineteenth-century-to-today comparisons, and is selectively readable by 11th-12th grades. Primary source documents about women's work, of reading difficulty varying from 8th to 12th grade, is found in Baxandall 1976; about African-American women's lives, in Lerner 1973 (readable for 9th grade and up); Chinese American women, Yung 1986, with lots of pictures. For Appalachian families, see Agee 1971; for utopian communities: Swerdlow et al. 1987, and the bibliography in its Teaching Guide; for African-American women and family: Gutman 1976, Fox-Genovese 1988, Sobel 1987 ( teachers need to assess accessibility/adaptability of all three for student use), Lerner, 1973 useful for varied ages, some from elementary up; for Native American, several articles in Etienne and Leacock eds.1980 would need adapting for student reading, but quotations from primary sources might be used with different ages; Axtell 1981; Clifton is probably suitable for 11th and 12th or earlier, and has four chapters on women; several student-accessible autobiographies are listed in Field and Walker 1994. For urban families in the northeast U.S. Ulrich 1982, text of which is interwoven with quotes from primary sources, and which gives excellent insight into women's and men's lives. For all kinds of women in families, check the document collections in **Resources**. See also the family/oral history information in Chapman ed. 1979, 33-47)

### Using original sources:

- Have students do hands-on research in original sources, and use it to spin off into various history-related areas. (A non-print approaches work especially well with younger students.)
- Use print sources such as old newspapers, magazines, and journals in local library collections that can be studied for revealing gender related information in advertisements, classified ads, and sometimes articles/editorials (see the arts curriculum section for a more detailed suggestion on gender analysis of advertising).
- Use school archives with gender-related questions in view. The questions may be raised: What governed the survival of the particular evidence included in the collections and archives? Who would have decided what should be kept, and how?
- Investigate tombstones in cemeteries, which give access to gender-related demographic information, with possibilities for comparison across time.
- Conduct a room inventory for contemporary gender-role impact. Students may be asked to do a detailed inventory of the room of a same-sex and an opposite-sex peer, listing information such as presence, kind and number of plants, stuffed animals, pin-ups, sports and stereo equipment, curtains, color and kind of fabrics, nature of furniture, level of tidiness and cleanliness and so on. (Students could make their own list, hypothesizing both what differences the think they will find and what features they think will be the same.) Pool results, and allow it to lead into discussion of nature of gender expectations in current culture, how they may differ by age, class, race, ethnicity and geographical area, and how they might be maintained.
- Check the garbage. From an examination of a few days' trash, what conclusions can be drawn about the culture in which it was found? How much of what is produced and discarded today will survive to serve as evidence for future historians? Are products of some groups or individuals more likely to survive? Why or why not? (This connects well with study of archaeology.)

**Additional activities and approaches:**

- Address the issue of gender head-on. A fourth-grade teacher wrote this "letter" on the board: "Dear Advice Columnist, My seven-year-old son wants me to by him a doll. I don't know what to do. Should I go ahead and get it for him? Please help! Concerned." The teacher asked students to write replies. Discussion followed, then a reading of the book *William's Doll* (Zolotow 1985), and the opportunity to make final corrections to students' written advice — including, if they wished, changing the advice. A number of students changed to okaying the boy's doll. (Sadker and Sadker 1994, 224).

- Set women's history into broad contexts. For instance, consider women's suffrage in the context of the gradual broadening of political participation, from the days of restriction to the nobly born, to free and white and non-servant and owning (decreasing amounts of) property as qualification, to free males, to those of both sexes over age 21, to both sexes over age 18. Examine the part played in the granting and withholding of suffrage by the ideas of freedom (property ensured independence of judgment) and rationality (women were not considered rational enough to vote). Ask students: Are 18-year-olds rational enough? Would 15-year-olds be? In what other ways, besides being considered "not rational," did the stereotype of women resemble that of children?

- Examine built-in assumptions and messages. For instance, consider what overall proportion of a course, and of the history curriculum at all levels in the school, is devoted to violence, and what to life-enhancing activities such as more humane childrearing and educational practices; services created for, and extended to, those in need; medical breakthroughs of widespread application; and peacemaking. Consider whether or not there is an imbalance, and whether or not it would be a good idea to amend it by some, perhaps even minor, changes. Involve students in the consideration (Stomfay-Stitz 1993, listed in **Resources**, may be helpful here).

- Consider the position of what you teach for each dimension on the continuum between the two poles in the right- and left-hand column respectively. Of course, all history courses have both sides, but most lean towards one or the other, not necessarily consistently. Teaching consistently and markedly to the left will make integration of women's history more difficult.

| | |
|---|---|
| change | continuity |
| events | conditions |
| individual actions | collective experience |
| narrative | patterns |
| unique | comparative |
| uniformity | diversity |
| elites | masses |
| political/economic | social/intellectual |

- Consider the part played by what is easy to test in what is usually taught. Perhaps part of the reason subject matter that more obviously is nearer the right in the chart above (such as social history, and that of (*mentalitiés*) as well as women's history) is less often taught is because it lends itself less readily to testing.

- Make small changes in topics covered or assigned reading. Condense Rousseau's political theory advocating freedom and equality, in order to include some of his (equally influential) educational theory advocating different and unequal education for boys and girls; include passages from Nietzsche representative of his negative attitudes to women as well as his positive ones to Superman.

- Use statistics in class. In the context of twentieth century history, or of economics, provide students with figures such as births, marriages, and divorces, and changes in labor-force participation, earnings, kinds of jobs held by sex (easily available in *Historical Statistics* 1976, and *Statistical Abstracts* annually) and ask them to: identify changes, continuities and relationships in the statistics, consider what influenced women's decisions to take jobs and their opportunities to do so. Segue into discussion of the variables involved — labor supply (immigration), demand for labor (expanding economy, wars), ideology (the notion of women's proper "sphere," feminism, child-centered family), financial conditions (inflation, high interest rates, credit buying), demography (life expectancy, marriage, birth, and divorce rates) and other factors that tie to conventional history. (Further suggestions for building on such statistics are available in Chapman 1982, which this exercise is based on.)
- Use examples of differential historical impact according to sex and class. The industrial revolution is a good case study for differential impact (See Tilly 1993, 48-49).
- Treat the textbook as a primary source. Chapman 1980 has several exercises as examples of what can be done in class to help students view the textbook as a contemporary document, reflecting the currently accepted world-view with its interests, unstated assumptions, and biases. It suggests tie-ins with value clarification, research, historiography, and other areas.

## RESOURCES

*T*his list is intended to illustrate the wide range of information available and, for a few topics, to suggest the depth and variety of available sources. See **Resources** in other chapters for historical accounts and biographies of women in particular fields, and the **ENGLISH** chapter for collections of documents with some historical relevance and bibliographies with some historical content.

Adler, David A. *A Picture Book of Sojourner Truth*. National Women's History Project, 7738 Bell Road, Windsor, CA 95492.
Full-color illustrations, straightforward text for grades K-3.

Axtell, James, ed. *The Indian Peoples of Eastern America: A Documentary History of the Sexes*. New York: Oxford University Press, 1981.
A collection of primary source materials that provides descriptions of experiences connected with birth, coming of age, love and marriage, work, peace and war by both European observers and Native Americans themselves. Mostly colonial, some nineteenth century. Excellent introductions.

Baxandall, Rosalyn, and S. Reverby, eds. *America's Working Women: A Documentary History 1600 to the Present*. Rev. ed. New York: W.W. Norton, 1995.
Documents include letters, diaries, popular magazines, oral histories, formal histories, poetry and fiction. Different races, ethnic origins, and occupations represented. Reading difficulty varies, elementary on up. Recommended teacher resource, and source of student readings.

Bell, Susan Groag and Karen M. Offen, eds. *Women, the Family, and Freedom: The Debate in Documents*. Two volumes. Stanford, CA: Stanford University Press, 1983.
Explores the debate in Western nations over women, their relationship to the family, and their claims to freedom, 1750-1950. Statements of prevailing ideas, all published in their time, are juxtaposed with contemporary challenges to these ideas. Selections from the mostly multi-page documents can be made for able 12th, and perhaps 11th grade, student reading. Recommended teacher resource.

Bingham, Marjorie Wall. *Women and the Constitution.* 1983. Upper Midwest Women's History Center, Hamline University, 1536 Hewitt Avenue, St. Paul, MN 55104. (612) 644-1727.

Deals with topics such as the Declaration of Independence, the presidency, and the Supreme Court relative to women. Teacher's Guide. For high school and perhaps junior high students.

Bingham, Marjorie Wall and Susan Hill Gross. 1980 and ff. *Women in World History.* Upper Midwest Women's History Center, Hamline University, 1536 Hewitt Avenue, St. Paul, MN 55104. (612) 644-1727.

A series of volumes including: women in Ancient Greece and Rome, Medieval/Renaissance Europe, Russia/USSR; Israel, Islam, and Japan; and Africa, China, Islam, India, Latin America from earliest times to present. Narrative texts for grades 9-10, usable with younger and some older students. Teacher's guide for each volume and filmstrips/videos for some.

Bridenthal, Renate, Claudia Koonz and Susan Stuard, eds. 1987. *Becoming Visible: Women in European History.* 2nd ed. Boston: Houghton Mifflin, 1987.

Twenty chronologically organized chapters, with specialists in each period covering economic, political, social, and cultural history. Written for college student use, it is still the single best introduction to the field of European women's history for teachers at all levels, and can be read by able 11th and 12th graders. Recommended as an introduction, and continuingly useful reference, for teachers; and for selective student use in honors/AP European history/ Western Civilization courses.

Cirksena, J. Diane and Valija Rasmussen. *Women in United States History.* Upper Midwest Women's History Center, Hamline University, 1536 Hewitt Avenue, St. Paul, MN 55104. (612) 644-1727.

Nine chronologically-defined volumes, each with teacher's guide, designed to "facilitate the integration of women's history into U.S. history courses." Target group 9th and 10th grades, but usable for earlier and perhaps later grades.

DuBois, Ellen Carol and Vicki L. Ruiz, eds. *Unequal Sisters: A Multicultural Reader in U.S. Women's History.* 2nd ed. New York: Routledge, 1994.

Articles by scholars about female slaves, Cherokee and Seneca women, strikes, suffrage militants, sexual politics , the cosmetic industry and the cultural construction of gender, Chicana feminist discourse, and more. State of the art multicultural resource, but best for those with a knowledge base in women's/feminist history. Comprehensive current bibliographies on women of color. Teacher background.

Evans, Sara M. *Born for Liberty: A History of Women in America.* New York: The Free Press, 1989.

Narrative account of women's history, with some new perspectives on the familiar periods and topics of U.S. history courses. Deftly woven into the text are many striking quotations from women of varied backgrounds. Scholarly but readable. Lists books for further reading by topics. Recommended as introduction, and continuingly useful reference, for teachers, and for selective student use in honors/AP U.S. history classes.

Field, Janet Scarborough, Elisabeth A. Middleton and Sarah J. Walker. *A Selected High School Reading List in Women's Studies: A Resource for Educators with Guide Included.* 1994. University of Texas at Austin, WMB 206A, Austin, TX 78712. (512) 471-5765.

Annotated bibliography especially strong on biographies and autobiographies, U.S., British, and World; some on U.S. and World history, as well as economics, political science, psychology, geography, sociology, and women's studies classics. Neither authoritative nor exhaustive, with idiosyncratic selections, and reading levels not indicated, but useful given the dearth of up-to-date bibliographies of student accessible materials.

Filene, Peter Gabriel. *Him/Her/Self: Sex Roles in Modern America.* 2nd ed. Baltimore: The Johns Hopkins University Press, 1986.

Interdisciplinary historical approach to changing definitions of masculinity and femininity since the late nineteenth century within political, economic, demographic, and intellectual contexts. Readable by able high school seniors.

Fox-Genovese, Elizabeth, and Susan Mosher Stuard, eds. *Restoring Women to History: Materials from Western Civilization*, vol. I. 1983. Organization of American Historians, 112 N. Bryan St., Bloomington, IN 47401.

Fifteen curriculum units from prehistory through the end of the eighteenth century, suggesting concepts and subject matter for lectures, reading assignments for students, topics for discussion, audiovisual aids, and bibliography for instructors. Thought-provoking and dense; designed for college use. Good for high school teachers with some background in women's history.

Flexner, Eleanor. *Century of Struggle: The Women's Rights Movement in the United States*. Rev. ed. Cambridge, MA: Harvard University Press, 1975.

Parts could be assigned to able high-school students; many of the quotations from original sources would be readable by upper elementary grades. Also teacher background. Recommended as the classic work on the subject.

Fox, Mary Virginia. *The Story of Women Who Shaped the West*. 1991.

Stories of a rancher, a single homesteader, a missionary, a sharpshooter, a politico and a writer, amidst many photographs and a scene-setting narrative. Grades 3-5.

Hellerstein, Erna Olafson. Leslie Parker Hume, and Karen M. Offen, eds. *Victorian Women: A Documentary Account of Women's Lives in England, France, and the United States*. Stanford, CA: Stanford University Press, 1981.

Over a hundred documents, including diaries, letters, advice manuals, medical, legal, and government records, grouped according to life-cycle: Girl, Adult Woman, Older Woman. Contains comparatively plentiful material at students' stage of life. Documents include childhood on a rural French estate, life in an English boarding school, courtship in America, infant care among working class. Reading difficulty varies; most selections accessible to students of varying abilities and ages, including upper elementary. Recommended as background for teachers at all levels, for more than usually student-friendly documents, and for versatility.

Hoobler, Dorothy and Thomas Hoobler. *The Trail of Which They Wept: The Story of a Cherokee Girl*. National Women's History Project, 7738 Bell Road, Windsor, CA 95492.

Thoughtful, fictionalized account of the Cherokee move from Georgia to Oklahoma, and the wrenching cultural changes that result. Grades 3-4.

Katz, Esther and Anita Rapone, eds. *Women's Experience in America: A Historical Anthology*. New Brunswick, NJ: Transaction Books, 1984.

A valuable source for bringing together a number of classic, highly influential historical essays. Recommended as a reasonably accessible starting point for teacher background.

Kerber, Linda K. and Jane Sherron DeHart. *Women's America*. 4th ed. New York: Oxford University Press, 1995.

A college undergraduate text, this collection of authoritative essays with illustrative primary source documents provides useful information for teachers. Some documents could be read by students. Best for those with a background in women's history. Selections do not overlap with Katz, above.

Kimmel, Michael and Thomas Mosmiller, eds. *Against the Tide: Pro-feminist Men in the United States, 1776-1990*. 1994.

A hundred documents by historic figures from Thomas Paine to Supreme Court Justice Harry Blackmun and Woody Guthrie speaking out for gender justice in letters, speeches, essays, poems. Grades 9-adult.

Kolb, Frances. *Portraits of our Mothers*. National Women's History Project, 7738 Bell Road, Windsor, CA 95492.

Detailed handbook reporting how teachers and students have used oral history to learn about women in their families and communities. Includes classroom activities, materials, and resources for creating a unit in oral history. Grades 4-12.

Lerner, Gerda. *Teaching Women's History*. 1981. American Historical Association, 400 A St. SE, Washington, DC 20003.

Indispensable practical manual on issues, methods, topical approaches, sources; significant coverage of racial and ethnic minorities.

Luchetti, Cathy, and Olwell, Carol. *Women of the West*. New York: Crown Trade Paperbacks, 1995 (1982).

Carefully edited journals, letters, and diaries, including those of a Paiute translator for the U.S. army, a school teacher, a French Catholic nun, a middle-class black widow, the owner of a large cattle ranch, a Mormon handcart pioneer, and a divorced physician. Two introductory chapters, one on minority women, give historical background. Contemporary photos. Recommended as pictorial resource for slow readers/younger children, as well as excerptable readings for grades 9-12, and for teacher background.

McKay, John P., Bennett D. Hill, and John Buckler. *A History of Western Society*. 4th ed. Boston: Houghton Mifflin, 1991.

Probably still the best bet among European history textbooks in terms of integrating women and working classes. Useful list of suggested readings at ends of chapters includes women's history scholarship. High school, seniors and/ or able readers.

McKisack, Patricia and Fred McKissack. *Mary McLeod Bethune*. National Women's History Project, 7738 Bell Road, Windsor, CA 95492.

Story of the worker (1875-1955) for Black equality in education and political rights. Grades 3-5.

Middle East Research and Information Project, *Women in the Middle East: Image and Reality, 1992-94 and Women and Work, Women and Politics, Women's Rights, Gender and Family*. Middle East Research and Information Project, 1500 Massachusetts Ave. NW, Suite 119, Washington DC 20005. (202) 223-3677.

Pamphlet series. Each about eight pages, with photos, statistical charts and lists for further reading. Teachers and high school students.

Morrison, Dorothy Nafus. *Chief Sarah: Sarah Winnemucca's Fight for Indian Rights*. National Women's History Project, 7738 Bell Road, Windsor, CA 95492.

Late 1800s Paiute woman's part, as successful lecturer and writer for peace and Indian rights, in the history of the West. Grades 7-12.

Moynihan, Ruth Barnes, Cynthia Russett and Laurie Crumpacker, eds. *Second to None: a Documentary History of American women*. Two volumes. Lincoln, NE: University of Nebraska Press, 1994.

Volume I covers the sixteenth century through 1865; Volume II, 1686 to modern times. The books try to "show that the daily lives of ordinary women have historical significance, ranging from the ways they provide for the survival of their communities to their emergence into the public spheres of political, social, and economic life." Many illustrations. Recommended for breadth and diversity of selections, suitability as teacher background, and student accessibility.

Murray, Janet Horowitz. *Strong-minded Women and Other Lost Voices of Nineteenth Century England*. New York: Pantheon, 1982.

Over a hundred primary source readings tell the story of middle and upper-class women's "struggle to escape the confinement of the home," working class women's "struggle to ensure her own and her family's survival," and "women's collective effort to redefine the boundaries and potentialities of womanly life." Striking contemporary illustrations are a resource in themselves. Selectively assignable to almost any student readers from grade 9 and up; pictures for younger ages. Recommended for breadth of possible student use, and as teacher background.

Nakano, Mei. *Japanese American Women: Three Generations 1890-1990*. National Women's History Project, 7738 Bell Road, Windsor, CA 95492.

Excerpts from personal interviews combined with demographic information give an account of historical change through personal experience.

*Norton, Mary Beth et al.* A People and a Nation: A History of the United States. 3d ed. Boston: Houghton Mifflin, 1990.

A textbook that, while no panacea, is among the better options for inclusiveness of underrepresented groups and ideas. High school.

O'Faolain, Julia and Lauro Martines, eds. *Not in God's Image.* New York: Harper and Row, 1973.

Collection of mostly brief documents from prehistoric Greece to the nineteenth century, by and about non-exceptional women in Europe, giving wage scales, conditions of employment, laws governing behavior, excerpts from manuals and sermons, biological and medical views, diaries and letters, interspersed with brief explanatory notes. Recommended as a source for student readings, upper elementary age and up.

Organization of American Historians. *Restoring Women to History.* 1988. OAH, 112 North Bryan Street, Bloomington, IN 47408. (812) 855-7311.

Teaching packets for integrating women's history into courses on Africa, Asia, Latin America, the Caribbean, and the Middle East. Intended for college teachers, but the introductions to each section are immensely useful overviews of the basic issues and information for pre-college teachers at all levels. Recommended to all who deal with world history, as the only resource that gives a relatively easy entry into basics of women's history in various areas of the world.

Pearson, Jim. *Women of the American Revolution.* 1994. National Center for History in the Schools, University of California, Los Angeles, Moore Hall 231, 405 Hilgard Avenue, Los Angeles, CA 90024.

Fifty-two page instructional unit based on primary sources for student reading and analysis. Grades 5-8. (Note: The Center for History in Schools has other titles. Ask for catalog.)

Pleck, Elizabeth, et. al. *Restoring Women to History: Materials for U.S. History*, vol. II. 1984. Organization of American Historians, 112 N. Bryan St., Bloomington, IN 47401

Covers Reconstruction to 1790s. Format and approach same as Fox-Genovese, above.

Porter, Cathy. *Women in Revolutionary Russia.* New York: Cambridge University Press, 1987.

Narrative with lots of illustrations, some maps, short excerpts from original sources. Grades 8-10, could be supplemental later.

Rappaport, Doreen. *American Women: Their Lives in Their Words.* New York: Harper Collins, 1992.

Spokespersons from each period tell of women's roles and the evolution of feminist consciousness. Excerpts from letters, speeches, diaries and interviews are tied together in a narrative frame. Grades 7-12.

Reese, Lyn and Jean Wilkinson, eds. *Women in the World: Annotated History Resources for the Secondary Student.* Metuchen, NJ: Scarecrow, 1987.

Although somewhat dated for a bibliography, still worth a look since there is so little else.

Riemer, Eleanor S. and John C. Fout, eds. *European Women: A Documentary History 1789-1945.* New York: Schocken Books, 1980.

Accounts by unrenowned women on the topics of women's work, women's politics, women and the family, woman and her body, drawn from public sources — periodicals, magazines, pamphlets, broadsides, testimony to government commissions. Working class, and to a lesser extent upper class, women are represented in addition to middle class ones. Compared to the other two European document collections, this focuses on women's voices only. No overlaps. Alternative source for able 11th-12th grade student readings.

Seeking Educational Equity and Diversity (SEED) Project. Information from Peggy McIntosh, Wellesley College Center for Research on Women, Wellesley, MA 02181; or Emily Style, 286 Meeker Street, South Orange, NJ 07079.

Summer workshops prepare seminar leaders from both public and independent schools to subsequently hold regular year-long meetings with ten-twenty teachers of all subject areas in their own school, discussing readings in common and ways to make their curriculum more gender-fair and multicultural. The National SEED Project recommends readings, films, and videos, from which seminar leaders choose those appropriate to their school. Recommended as excellent professional development for individuals, and a peerless way to create a knowledgeable group that can spearhead curriculum revision efforts.

Stevenson, Louise L., ed. *Women's History: Selected Course Outlines and Reading Lists from American Colleges and Universities.* Vol. I: American History. 3rd rev. ed. New York: Markus Wiener, 1993.

Useful for high school and to some extent junior high, for its listing of texts and document collections, as well as scholarly works by century (alas, without publication dates), as well as minimally annotated list of feature and documentary films; and for syllabi which give information about various ways of conceptualizing "American women's history."

Stomfay-Stitz, Aline M. *Peace Education in America, 1828-1990: Sourcebook for Education and Research.* Metuchen, NJ: Scarecrow Press, 1993.

Historical narrative of the curriculum, writings, and contributions of numerous American men and women who have tried to introduce teaching about peace into American schools. Over 700 citations, photographs, extensive bibliography, and resource directory. (Note: Scarecrow Press allows teachers to order a book and keep it for thirty days to see if it's what they want; then pay for it, or return it in saleable-as-new condition. P.O. Box 4167. Metuchen, NJ 08840; (800) 537-7107 or (908) 548-8600.)

Swerdlow, Amy, Renate Bridenthal, Joan Kelly, and Phyllis Vine. *Families in Flux.* Rev. ed. New York: The Feminist Press, 1987.

Historical development of family forms, review and analysis of contemporary variations in the U.S., utopian and other alternatives to traditional family structure. High school student text; teacher's guide available.

■ ■ ■ ■

## CHAPTER SIX

## SCIENCE

*No two plants are exactly alike. They are all different, and as a consequence,*
*you have to know that difference. I start with the seedling,*
*and I don't want to leave it. I don't feel I really know the story*
*if I don't watch the plant all the way along.*
*So I know every plant in the field.*
*I know them intimately, and I find it a great pleasure to know them.*

*—Barbara McClintock, 1978*

Overall, science education does not do well by girls. However, it does not do all that well by boys either.

In spite of the fact that scientific thinking is of great value to everyone in both intellectual and everyday contexts, that people trained in scientific ways of thought are increasingly needed by society, and that scientific jobs pay almost 50 percent more than non-scientific ones requiring the same amount of schooling, there has been a marked drop in the total number of young Americans preparing for scientific careers in the last few years. In the natural sciences and engineering, bachelors' degrees awarded declined by 25 percent from 1986 to 1991.

For women, there has been a slowing, and in some cases even a reversal, of gains made in scientific fields from the 1960s to the 1980s. Women in 1992 still earned only about 15 percent of these degrees; among them only about 6 percent were Asian American, 3 percent Latina, 1.5 percent African American, and less than 1 percent Native American. There are nearly three times as many white male, but only a quarter as many white female scientists and engineers in the work force as would be expected given each group's representation in the population. Moreover, a consistently higher proportion of women than men are, after graduation, under or unemployed in technical fields (Ginorio 1995, 4; Association of American Colleges 1994, 2; Linn 1993/94, 3; Kahle 1992, 9).

Yet it is well documented that girls and boys as 7th graders have the same level of interest in careers in science, and the same positive perceptions of science; and nine as well as thirteen-year-olds' performance on national science proficiency tests does not significantly differ by gender. Something happens to turn students, and especially girls, off science from junior high through college. Of the students who, as sophomores in high school, claim they are interested in studying science and engineering, 20 percent will have lost interest by their senior year. Attrition is twice that during freshman year in college, and continues thereafter until only 0.24 percent of the originally interested sophomores will end up having completed a Ph.D. in those subjects. (1980s data by NSF. Tobias 1990).

Inability to do the work does not adequately explain students' avoidance or dropping out of science courses. Only about a third of college freshmen who switched out of science and engineering have done so because they found the course work too difficult; and among students with the same tested ability and grades, females have less self confidence in their ability to do science, and more avoid doing so, than males.

*"I came away from the course feeling that turning kids on to chemistry was not a goal... I*
*was weeded out because I didn't like the impersonality and the size of the class, because I was not*
*as motivated as others to 'ace' the exams, because the material never really captivated or*
*stimulated me..."*
*—girl in introductory chemistry course, quoted in Tobias 1990*

**Girls in school are discouraged at higher rates than boys; and some of the information we have suggests possible roots for their discouragement in:**

> ➤ lesser exposure to science-related toys and activities of girls
> ➤ lesser encouragement of girls to tinker with technology, from pre-school on
> ➤ culturally promoted willingness of boys, but not girls, to be competitive, confident risk takers
> ➤ the socialization of girls to be cooperative and relationship- and context-oriented, whereas the common style of science teaching emphasizes individual work, competition, analysis of discrete detail, and abstraction from context
> ➤ girls' perception that even if they were getting good grades, they were not really doing well, nor achieving the same depth of understanding as boys
> ➤ the general perception of science as "masculine," heavily dependent on inborn talent, and involving a life of dedication that demands an exceptionally heavy commitment of time
> ➤ girls' knowledge of the difficulties for women in combining a career in science with family and children

The roots of girls' relative lack of engagement with science are varied. Studies since the 1980s have shown that girls in elementary school had the same interest in extracurricular science activities as boys, but had had many fewer actual experiences with using science-related equipment or doing science-related field trips; and while they may have had equally frequent experiences with living plants and animals, they had substantially fewer with magnets and electricity. Between grades 7 and 11 the number of girls who have "tried to fix something mechanical" had decreased, while the number of boys increased markedly.

Self-rating of ability in science and math is the highest predictor of choosing a science major. Girls' — but not boys' — confidence in their ability and expectations for success in science courses decline as they progress through school, although their grades in these subjects do not. In college, though women science majors had higher overall grades than men during their first two years, they dropped out of science at higher rates. On achievement tests, girls at all ages (nine, thirteen, and seventeen) selected the "I don't know" response significantly more often than did boys. By eleventh grade, girls have less positive attitudes towards science; are less interested in science careers than boys; and score substantially below boys on science proficiency tests — though the gender gap in science performance shrank significantly during the late 1980s. Male peers play some part in discouraging girls from taking, or excelling in, science, as do African-American peers in labeling such behavior as "acting white."

Enrollment patterns in science courses are stereotypically gender-skewed; the "harder" the science, the more male-identified it is, and the more boys predominate in courses in it. Girls outnumber boys in the "soft" social sciences. In natural science, there is approximate parity in life sciences, but not in physical sciences: girls and boys enroll about equally in biology courses; fewer girls in chemistry; and a lot fewer in physics. These differences are connected with, but not wholly accounted for, by the amount and kind of mathematics needed in these disciplines.

Anxieties about whether, and how, it might be possible to integrate doing science with having a family plays a significant part in women's reservations about science, and have a trickle-down effect to the pre-college level. Recently, men also have begun to be concerned about the strains of balancing science and family, influenced by the increasing number of young male scientists with a working wife as well as small children, and the increasing impact of ideas about fathers' participation in parenting.

(McLaren and Gaskell 1995, 137-139; Ginorio 1995, 3, 6, 9-11; Association of American Colleges 1994, 2; Linn 1993/94, 4; Antony 1993/94, 10-11; US Dept. of Education 1992, 48; Kahle 1992, 11; Tobias 1990, section 1; Stage et al. 1985, 247)

Research on gender bias in teaching tools as a possible contributory factor in turning girls off has been focused on the humanities. But there is one significant research study of five mid-1980s textbooks for 7th grade life science in South Carolina public schools. While overt sexism does not occur (for instance career discussions include both women and men), there are ways in which they continue to disadvantage girls. In all there are more pictures of men, shown in more active roles; the discussions that do include women are perfunctory; and the texts are thin on those science-related skills that girls are typically more deficient in (for example, spatial and investigative skills), therefore shutting them out of the possibility of improvement in these areas. (Rosser 1990, Chapter 6).

Recent changes in scientists' methodologies and attitudes towards science are more in keeping with girls' acquired style of thought, but have not yet made much of an impact on science teaching in schools. In the last two decades or so, various scholars have suggested the possibility that the dominant scientific style of "knowing," characterized by emphasis on critical and even adversarial thinking skills, abstract analysis, objectivity, and a distancing of the observer from the object of study, is to some extent culture-bound. It has been influenced by the fact that most people who have done science have been men, whose masculine world view tends to value autonomy, distance, and an ability to keep a tight, sharp focus while ignoring context considered irrelevant. While this approach is that of most women scientists as well, it does not come as easily to them, conflicting as it does with the emphases of female socialization. Extra doses of training for girls in the "masculine" style are known to be successful.

> *"With physics you are dealing with situations that they have to be almost perfect for you to work with — like air has no friction — so it's harder to take things that you've learned and look at the real world with it. So it's not as exciting . . . as doing formulas and things like that. . . . In physics, amazingly enough, I've always gotten B's, which is a surprise, because I don't know what I'm doing."*
> —*senior girl, quoted in McLaren and Gaskell 1995*

However, there appears also to be a different style that comes more easily to women and to African Americans which is also scientifically valuable. It tends to be more global than analytical; is characterized by paying more attention to interactions, relationships, and events that are contextual, and were typically ignored or scanted in traditional science; accumulating more data and remaining longer in the observational stage before theorizing; targeting different kinds of problems, often more holistic, global, or cross-disciplinary, or viewing them in divergent ways; using methods drawn from various disciplines or fields of knowledge; development of theories that tend to be relational, interdependent, and multicausal; and questioning the possibility of "objectivity" in science, since the culture-based attitudes and preconceptions of scientists and funders of science influence the kinds of questions asked, the methods used, and the results obtained.

That this alternative style is a scientifically successful one has now been shown in the work of a number of scientists, and carries credibility in the scientific community. It is not one, however, that is deliberately taught in most science classrooms, though it should be; not only because it would benefit girls, but also because it would benefit boys.

Boys need extra doses of training in not rushing observations, not theorizing too far ahead of their data, taking time to think through various aspects of the problems they deal with, developing more patience, and more of what Nobel Prize winner Barbara McClintock has called "a feeling for the organism."

(McLaren and Gaskell 1995, 154; Mimms, 1994; Sperry 1993; Rosser 1990, Chapter 4; Root-Bernstein 1989; Harding 1986, passim; Keller 1985, Parts 2 &3; Keller 1983; Shade 1982; Kuhn 1970)

> *"[When he asked his classmates about what they were studying, they were not able to] articulate an answer. I wonder if this is because they lack communications skills or because they haven't yet had the time to reflect on what they have learned, or perhaps because they don't really know much about their subject — if knowledge means a deep, thoughtful understanding, rather than a superficial ability to regurgitate formulas."*
> —*male student in physics course, quoted in Tobias 1990*

In science teaching, it is important not only to target compensatory work for those students whose skills and confidence need strengthening, but also to target those features of the discipline itself, and the way it is taught, that would benefit from flexibility and diversity.

Many interventions that seek to integrate women and minorities in science still aim at working with under-represented groups in order to help them to fit into, adjust to, negotiate, or survive the existing system of science (and mathematics) education. Such empowerment continues to be important. However, some institutions have begun to make changes in the system; and it is clear that many white male students also benefit from changes that were introduced because they were expected to serve women and minorities (Ginorio 1995, 21).

For instance, changes made in 1987 in Harvard's introductory course in chemistry that are in line with some of the above research were credited three years later with a near-doubling of enrollment, a better performance on the average by all the students, and higher subsequent rates of continuation in advanced chemistry courses.

Changes included the teacher's:

> - deciding to "cover less and uncover more"
> - using parables/narratives to reinforce science information
> - requiring students to "guess" at answers before doing the work, and to think about the problems qualitatively before plugging in numbers
> - abandoning grading on a curve, instead measuring all work relative to the standard defined by the teacher
> - instituting "resurrection points" in grading, which allows students to compensate for poor performance on earlier tests if they can demonstrate competence by course-end (Tobias 1990, 59-60)

Because of the great importance of parental influence both in self-confidence and course selection (discussed in detail in the mathematics section), schools need to collaborate with parents in efforts to attract students to science and help them be, and feel, successful in it.

Schools need to take the initiative in acquainting parents, individually through college counselors and advisors, and collectively through articles/editorials/comments in school publications, workshops, and forums, with the importance of science for both their daughters and sons; the kinds of experiences and attitudes that contribute to success in scientific disciplines; and the wide variety of careers in which scientific training is useful or necessary.

A more active role still may be taken by schools in:

> - recommending science-related books to parents to help them participate in, or promote, science activities and science-related thinking with their children (For some suggestions see **Resources**, page 81)
> - suggesting low-cost activities that families can do at home which promote and support children's interest in science
> - providing programs for parents that help them promote their children's interest in natural phenomena and foster scientific ways of thought

(The suggestions above draw on information in Greenbaum 1993/94, 17-18.)
For working with parents, check also the suggestions in the section on mathematics.

*E*ducators can promote more in-depth understanding, reduce anxiety that inhibits performance, and build student confidence in their ability to do science by using some of the following activities and resources.

- From pre-K on, give students lots of hands-on experience.
- From pre-K on, support students in cross-gender play activities.
- Encourage the use of building toys, woodworking, tinkering, blocks, and active play for girls; and experiences with figure-ground images and puzzles that flip the importance in interpretation between context and detail for boys.
- Consider taking the time, especially early in the year and in introductory courses, to do more work in depth, even if it may mean sacrificing some breadth.
- Give a general overview of new material about to be covered and how it connects with previous material; refer to the overview occasionally, asking students how details fit.
- Include in content taught opportunities for letting students see that scientists' making mistakes; exploring what prove to be blind alleys, and being proven wrong are integral parts of the scientific enterprise.
- Include information about the importance of creativity, divergent thinking, and intuition in scientific work.
- Model the possibility of alternative ways of solving problems.
- Encourage students to seek multiple solutions.
- Give students a role in planning activities, designing investigative techniques themselves, and identifying resources, as well as doing experiments already set up for them by the teacher.
- Use hands-on activities that are readily accessible (an elementary school group investigated whether water fountains on different floors tasted different, which was most tasty, and why; a high school group monitored pollution levels in a local body of water; others could look into the effects of meditation and exercise on blood pressure and heart rates, etc.)
- Help students understand the scientific texts they read by explaining ways in which such texts differ from narrative.
- Judge what students say by content, not style; do not assume that those who speak hesitantly and with circumlocutions ("I'm not sure . . . but maybe . . . perhaps . . . wouldn't it?") do not have valuable contributions to make.
- Keep working with the student called upon until he or she has achieved a reasonably successful answer, instead of answering the question yourself if the student does not do so satisfactorily (or at all . . . ), or turning to another student for the answer.
- Explore the level of students' understanding by asking them to: explain their reasons for giving the answers they give; apply what they seem to have learned to a different context or set of circumstances; translate from words or numbers to pictures or diagrams and vice versa; make connections between different parts of the work covered; and/or teach what they know to someone else.
- Be alert to the fact that silence about their ability may be detrimental to those students who have already internalized a negative self-image, and anticipate failure. Such students need frequent positive feedback and accurate, unsparing, but kind criticism that focuses on the actions that need to be taken for improvement.

- Suggest to students that they should view criticism positively, as helpful in telling them where and how to invest their effort, rather than negatively, as a put-down or a questioning of their ability.
- Encourage students to form study-groups and support each other in the work they are doing, instead of looking down on the giving and receiving of help, and needing to beat each other out of some "top spot."
- Encourage students, in talking to themselves and to others, to keep to the here-and-now instead of generalizing: "I did poorly on today's test," not "I can't do physics."
- Encourage students to avoid trying to make themselves feel bigger by belittling someone else; to register their objection to someone else's attempt to belittle them or put them down.
- Encourage students to stand up for someone else they see being ridiculed or hassled, and to recognize that it shows more courage, strength, and "manliness" to protect, rather than to attack, others, and even more to stand up against peers' ridicule.
- Give opportunities to students to work at their own rate. Wait for five to ten seconds at least after asking a question, as well as after she or he answers, to allow for elaboration.
- Don't allow anyone to answer for a minute or more after asking a question, insisting that everyone think about it for awhile (this benefits both girls, who tend to take longer to organize their thoughts, and boys, who tend to blurt out the first thing that comes into their heads).
- Give some untimed tests.
- Give some take-home tests.
- Monitor assessment, making sure it measures that which is valued in the course. (A teacher serious about developing cooperation would do well to consider evaluating how successfully students are able to work cooperatively.)
- Diversify evaluation techniques, using some that allow students to demonstrate the full spectrum of skills involved in science by designing and carrying out an experiment demonstrating a principle being taught; writing a grant proposal for a scientific project; listing real-life situations in which a particular scientific proposition would be salient; or researching and assessing the kinds of scientific investigations that would be needed to solve a real-life problem.
- Consider abandoning grading on a curve.

Teachers can emphasize the relatedness of science to other disciplines, to relationships within subject matter, and to collaborative approaches, by some of the following:

- Create opportunities, and time, for those teaching science at the elementary, middle, and high school levels to get together and exchange information about the use of manipulatives, cooperative groupings, and hands-on learning in which the former have more expertise, as well as recent advances in subject matter that are more likely to be familiar to the high school people.
- Promote the integration of the science curriculum with other core disciplines.
- Collaborate with English teachers. Students can write essays on scientific topics for English, and do lab reports and science research papers in accordance with the writing skills emphasized in English.
- Collaborate with history teachers in acquainting students with the history of science and with the women and men of various origins who contributed to its development.
- Collaborate with the arts department in teaching students precise observations and their translation into visual terms, as well as the translation of verbal or numerical into visual information and vice versa.

- Give a general overview of new material about to be covered, and how it connects with previous material; refer to the overview occasionally, asking students how details fit.
- Link older with younger students in working together on a long-range scientific project, such as investigating and monitoring water quality, erosion, recycling technologies, or animal and plant populations in the community.
- To reduce possible domination of lab partnerships or project groups by the more self-confident and experienced students, pair students with approximately the same level of assertiveness and experience with each other. Have students within each group take turns about who does what, such as setting up, doing the experiment, taking notes, writing up lab reports, and cleaning up.
- Hook up students with quality summer and/or special enrichment programs in science to give an additional boost both to those who are already science buffs, and the hesitant ones, perhaps from groups traditionally underrepresented in science.

*T*eachers can reduce the perception of scientists as solitary white male geniuses who bury themselves in laboratories, by some of the following:

- Counteract the perception that "scientists are born, not made."
- Expand students' definition of who uses, and needs, science, perhaps bringing in people such as electricians, county extension agents, photographers, dietitians, veterinarians of both genders and different racial/ethnic backgrounds to talk with students about how they use science in their work.
- Bring students into contact with scientists willing to talk about how they overcame obstacles in their paths, and how they are able to combine their careers with fulfilling personal lives — including families.
- Check teaching resources (textbook, AV materials, displays) for gender and ethnic/race inclusiveness wherever this is salient.

Both schools and teachers can work with parents to keep them abreast of the critical need for continued study in science for both their daughters and their sons, and of college/career requirements and opportunities in scientific fields.

(The above suggestions are based on information in Ginorio 1995; Equity Coalition 1993/94; Woodrow 1993; Chapman 1992; National Coalition 1991; Rosser 1990)

Please check the sections on **COMMUNICATION** and **What Schools and Teachers Can Do** in the chapter about mathematics for additional information that might prove helpful.

## RESOURCES

Note: Items marked *(P)* are recommended to parents.

Clewell, Beatriz Chu, Bernice Taylor Anderson and Margaret E. Thorpe. *Breaking the Barriers: Helping Female and Minority Students Succeed in Mathematics and Science*. San Francisco: Jossey-Bass, 1992.
Intervention strategies and guidelines.

Cornwell, Catherine R. *Science EQUALS Success*. Charlotte, NC: Charlotte EQUALS/Charlotte-Mecklenburg School System, 1990. From Education Development Center, 55 Chapel Street, Newton, MA 02160.
Field-tested, hands-on, cooperative, spatial, multi-step problem-solving discovery science activities for grades 4-9, designed to meet needs of females and minorities while empowering all students. *(P)*

Kass-Simon, G., and P. Farnes. *Women of Science: Righting the Record*. Bloomington, IN: Indiana University Press, 1990.

Kreinberg, Nancy. *I'm Madly in Love with Electricity; and Other Comments About Their Work by Women in Science and Engineering*. 1983. From Lawrence Hall of Science, University of California, Berkeley, CA 94720, Attention: Careers.
Useful as source for teachers, mostly late elementary through mid-high school. *(P)*

McGrayne, S.B. *Nobel Prize Women in Science: Their Lives, Struggles, and Momentous Discoveries*. New York: Birch Lane Press, 1993. *(P)*

McNeal, Ann. "My Favorite Books on the Relation of Women and Minorities to Science." *Feminists in Science and Technology* 6 (1) Fall 1992. From School of Natural Science, Hampshire College, Amherst, MA 01002; or e-mail mmurrain@hamp.hamshire.edu

Rosser, Sue V. *Female-Friendly Science: Applying Women's Studies Methods and Theories to Attract Students*. New York: Pergamon Press, 1990.
Synthesizes a lot of information on pedagogy, curriculum change, women's ways of knowing, applicable in contexts other than science as well; also presents several theoretical approaches critiquing science as a discipline, and practical ways of attracting women and non-elite groups to science. Extensive scholarly bibliography. Written for college, but useful for high school.

Schiebinger, Londa. *The Mind Has No Sex?: Women in the Origins of Modern Science*. Cambridge, Mass.: Harvard University Press, 1989.
A scholarly but readable (even by able seniors) account of the rise of modern science in 17th and 18th century Europe, examining scientific institutions and the gender boundaries they set; women's participation in science; and how biological sciences' understanding of gender became embedded in debates over women's ability to do science.

Sprung, Barbara, Linda Colon, and Sandra Jenoure. *Playtime is Science: Implementing a Parent-Child Activity Program*. 1990. From Educational Equity Concepts, 114 E. 32nd Street, New York, NY 10016. (212) 725-1803.
Intended to help parents and teachers of children aged 4-7 to work on scientific concepts together, using materials easily found at home and in classroom, targeting higher-order thinking skills, estimation, problem-solving. *(P)*

Verheyden-Hilliard, Mary Ellen, ed. *American Women in Science: Biographies for the Elementary Grades*. Bethesda, MD: The Equity Institute. (If hard to find, contact Programs for Educational Opportunity, 1005 School of Education, University of Michigan, Ann Arbor, MI 48109, or National Women's History Project, 7738 Bell Road, Windsor, CA 95492.)

Books for elementary students to read or have read to them, with titles such as Engineer from the Comanche Nation, Mancy Wallace, and Scientist and Governor, Dixie Lee Ray. For grades 1-4. *(P)*

■ ■ ■ ■

## CHAPTER SEVEN

## ENGLISH LITERATURE AND LANGUAGE

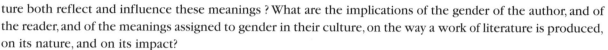

*Read not to contradict and confute,*
*nor to believe and take for granted,*
*nor to find talk and discourse, but to weigh and consider.*

*—Francis Bacon, 1625*

*L*iterature has always posed the question: What does it mean to be, and act, as human? To this central question, women's studies criticism adds others. It asks: What does it mean to be, and act, as a gendered human, and how does literature both reflect and influence these meanings ? What are the implications of the gender of the author, and of the reader, and of the meanings assigned to gender in their culture, on the way a work of literature is produced, on its nature, and on its impact?

The verbal areas in which gender — the socially assigned meanings of being male and female — may come into play include approaches to literature; the influence of content on students' values as well as self-image; reading and writing skills; and oral communication. Teaching and learning of every kind of literature is enriched by drawing on information arising from the women's studies critical tradition.

The first phase of the new scholarship on women focused on a critique of the predominantly male literary tradition, examining the images of women presented, and identifying omissions, misconceptions and stereotypes as well as cases of outright misogyny. While this critique on occasion tipped over into the militantly adversarial, much of it continues to offer valid insights.

Teachers acquainted with this approach can broaden students' critical stance towards the works they read. They can help students analyze the images of womanhood and manhood presented; the implications of the stereotyping of both, and of the exclusion, marginalization, and trivialization of women in some works and genres; and structure, imagery, content and language as potential reflections and promoters of limitations on choices for both genders, and of sexual inequality.

Teachers can also help students to consider texts in several different ways. In dealing with analysis of the aesthetic qualities and formal literary properties of a text, and in "close reading" that insists on the separation of the literary work from all non-literary context, viewing through the lens of gender can generate additional insights about the nature of genres, the choices and formal working out of themes, archetypal images, metaphors, and word-choices.

Additionally, students can be encouraged to:

> ➤ Explore the cultural and personal background of the author that contributed to the way he (or she) has handled content, concepts, language, and style.
> ➤ Consider the questions of whether the text can, or should, be divorced from the author; and what the advantages, and disadvantages, of doing so are for understanding and appreciating the text.
> ➤ Examine the claim that literature is important because it treats themes, from the local and parochial to the universal, of which the latter is to be more highly valued. (In discussing the potential of cultural influence on universal themes, if students are familiar with the plot of *Hamlet* an excellent resource is "Shakespeare in the Bush," a hilarious, and true, account of the reinterpretation of that story into their own cultural idioms by the Tiv in West Africa (Bohannan 1966 (1980)).

Re-examination of the traditional canon by women's studies criticism was accompanied by an investigation of how a "literary tradition of classics," composed of canonical works, comes to be accepted and perpetuated by the decisions, governed not solely by considerations of literary merit, of a series of gatekeepers such as publishers, established journals, compilers of anthologies and writers of textbooks. What is commonly called literary history is actually a record of choices. Which writers have survived their time and which have not depends upon who noticed them and chose to record that notice (Bernikow 1974, 3).

Most importantly perhaps for the encouragement of those contemplating curriculum revision, it is documented that major changes in the canon had, in fact, already taken place at various times. Authors of previously high repute such as Irving, Cooper, Lowell, and Longfellow dropped out of the canon; those of currently high repute such as Melville and Twain were not so considered sixty years ago; and relatively numerous women authors had been part of the canon (included in textbooks and anthologies, for instance) in the period after World War I. By the 1950s, however, women authors were rarely anthologized or taught. Significant change in this respect has come in the last decade, but it has been slow to arrive at the high-school level (Lauter 1994; Templin 1994; Lauter 1991; Rabinowitz 1988; Lauter 1984).

A national survey in 1989 of high school English courses found that the list of most frequently required books had changed little compared to twenty-five and even eighty years ago. Shakespeare, Dickens, Melville, Twain, and Steinbeck have remained central; in some schools there has been no broadening of the traditional canon at all, in others changes have begun on the fringes, mostly in elective courses (Applebee 1989, 16).

A comparison of books most widely assigned in schools in grades 7-12 in 1988 and 1963 showed both that changes in the canon have occurred, and the relatively conservative nature of the change.

| 1988 | | 1963 | |
|---|---|---|---|
| **Book** | **% of Schools** | **Book** | **% of Schools** |
| *Romeo & Juliet* | 90 | *Macbeth* | 90 |
| *Macbeth* | 81 | *Julius Caesar* | 77 |
| *Huckleberry Finn* | 78 | *Silas Marner* | 76 |
| *To Kill a Mockingbird* | 74 | *Our Town* | 46 |
| *Julius Caesar* | 71 | *Great Expectations* | 39 |
| *The Pearl* | 64 | *Hamlet* | 33 |
| *The Scarlet Letter* | 62 | *Red Badge of Courage* | 33 |
| *Of Mice and Men* | 60 | *Tale of Two Cities* | 33 |
| *Diary of Anne Frank* | 56 | *The Scarlet Letter* | 32 |
| *Hamlet* | 56 | | |
| *Lord of the Flies* | 56 | | |

(Source: *Teacher Magazine*, 1989, 31)

Accelerated change is suggested by the fact that, in 1989, the College Board added to the recommended authors list for AP language six women writers (including Joan Didion, Antonia Fraser, Lillian Hellman. and Margaret Fuller); and eleven to the AP literature list (including Anne Bradstreet, Willa Cather, Kate Chopin, Louise Erdrich, Toni Morrison, and Alice Walker) (The College Board News, 1990). It is this kind of decision that contributes to the validation of inclusion in the canon.

The next phase of women's studies criticism focused on writings by women authors, and examined the history, themes, genres, styles, and archetypes in the literature by women. This process included restoring the reputation of women authors of merit who, valued in the past, had dropped out of the canon, and establishment of scholarly recognition and a body of criticism for contemporary women writers. As a result, a canonical list of women authors has evolved, encouragingly for those looking to diversify the outstanding authors they introduce students to with the assurance that they are not thereby diluting excellence.

More recently, critical attention has been focused on the issue of difference. Some critics argue for the indistinguishability of writing on the basis of gender. Others claim that women bring different points of view and insights, different ways of handling content, as well as distinctive modes of expression to writing, and also different expectations and backgrounds to reading. Currently, many critics are exploring the issue of differences — especially those of race and class — among women authors themselves.

Clearly, there are both similarities and differences in the writings by women and men; and nationality, class, race, and other factors may add to, interact with, or override gender differences. In some cases, the effects of author characteristics do not appear to create distinguishably different works. Other works are significantly influenced by gender. In teaching, students can be sensitized to noting the differences gender makes in those circumstances where it is salient; and to recognizing the impact of the differences on literary aspects as well as on content of their reading (Kelly 1995; Templin 1994; Pope 1989, Chapter 2; Moi 1985, Chap. 2-4).

There are at least two powerful arguments in favor of including women authors, and authors of a wide range of different backgrounds, among books students read in school.

One is that, if literature has to do with ways of being human, readers, especially children and adolescents, need exposure to the great variety of ways to be human, and the great variety of ways that humans have found to speak about themselves and the world. They need to be able to construct a more than one-dimensional concept of the "other" and to acquire enough familiarity with "otherness" to find it neither threatening nor contemptible. They also need to examine the "other" in order to appreciate ways it is similar to, as well as different from, themselves.

Secondly, when the young are finding out who they are and what they can become, what they read plays a major role in answering questions about their identity and their place in the world. Whether they can experience finding both those like, and those unlike, themselves in their reading, will affect their answers and will affect also the kind of world they build as adults. There is considerable research showing that books do influence children's attitudes. Reading about girls and boys in non-stereotypic roles, for instance, reduces readers' gender-stereotyped attitudes, and multicultural readings produce more favorable attitudes towards nondominant groups. (AAUW 1992, 62; Campbell and Wirtenberg 1980).

> *"From preschool to grad school, literature is the main subject that presents gender images and provides concrete models of manhood and womanhood."*
> — *Nell Noddings, 1992*

Given that children are influenced by what they read, what they read needs to be assessed for its potential influence. The message about gender-appropriate behavior sent in books is one such influence. Children's literature has been much studied for the messages it sends about gender images and inequities in terms of stereotypic depiction of both males and females, and exclusion/marginalization/trivialization of the latter. Analyses of both Caldecott Award winning and nonaward books in the last two decades show some welcome changes, including increases coming close to parity in representation of female characters in titles, central roles, and pictures. However, gender stereotyping continues. Male characters continue to be represented as active and independent, females as passive and dependent. Boys are shown solving problems five to eight times more often than girls; whereas the latter are shown in nurturing roles about eight times more often than boys (Kortenhaus and Demarest 1993; McDonald 1989).

Characterizations in what they read play a part in suggesting to children that the "appropriate" way to behave is boys doing no nurturing, girls doing no problem-solving. Such limiting of the self, however, is dysfunctional for both boys and girls in the contemporary world. There is no need, of course, to stop children from reading good literature because its message is not what one might wish; but they may need to have the message identified and explained, in order to be able to disregard or discount it.

Literature is a form of socialization. It tells how — in what languages and images — we should understand our experience. From liberal and conservative forces alike, its justification is typically couched in terms of its usefulness in cultivating larger sympathies, instilling national and cultural identity, and serving as a conduit of moral concerns. As such, literature is monitory, exemplary, cautionary, both mythic and local to our culture and dominant ideology (Pope 1989, 28-29).

That the kinds of heroes students are exposed to in stories affect what they will value, and what they are likely to imitate, has also been widely documented. Therefore, we need to pay some attention to the messages sent by the heroes, male and female, of the works students read. Male heroism expressed in conflict and violence is still very prevalent in the literary works students study, and the books they read, though female heroism as passive self-sacrifice may have become rarer.

There are at least two ways to counter any negative effects. Efforts can be made to explore the costs, to themselves and to others, of the choices made by heroes, female and male, in student readings, as well as alternatives that might have been available to them. Students can also explore the social and cultural reasons why these characters might not have had alternatives, or might have found that those available came at too high a cost. Teachers can also make efforts to find readings of literary merit that present to students a wider range of male and female heroes.

Schools and teachers inevitably send powerful messages concerning values by their choice of student readings, whether they intend to or not. Meter, rhyme scheme, and alliteration may be value-free, but the texts they are used in are not, nor are the illustrations chosen to demonstrate their use. The teaching of reading and of literature cannot be divorced from the teaching of values. With the best intentions to be value-free, all choices (and even deliberate refraining from choice) send messages that have a value component. Since such messages are inevitable, it is preferable that they be by deliberate choice, rather than inadvertent.

In the choice of books for young children especially, and in much of juvenile literature, the canon of fairy and folktales that makes up a significant proportion exists mostly in versions that have been described as "relentlessly chauvinistic" (Myers 1990, 278). It is not, for instance, the variant of the Red Riding Hood tale in which she is a sturdy peasant girl who cleverly outwits the wolf on her own, does not get eaten and does not need a woodsman to rescue her, that is widely known.

There is a case to be made for careful review of the didactic nature of the literature chosen for, and recommended to, young readers. What does it teach? How does it inculcate and alter values? Yet a wholesale replacement of old, culturally significant, favorites with the compensatory, corrective, and the more contemporarily therapeutic or inspirational, however well-written and of whatever literary merit, is not a good answer either. Ideology must be disentangled from evaluation; positive role models don't always make for great literature; and effective works of art don't always say what readers (or teachers, or critics) think they should.

It is possible and sometimes desirable to teach works the values of which one deeply disagrees with. In such cases, it is helpful to make one's own positions, and the reasons for it, known to students; to raise problematic aspects of, or issues in, the work for discussion; and to capitalize on the opportunity to point out why some particular set of ideas embedded in a literary work may be hurtful, undesirable, or objectionable, without insisting that students choose between author's and teacher's point of view.

Some balance, alertness to the meanings of the choices made, and trust in the good sense and strong stomachs of the young who can digest the most awful junk food (in all senses) and thrive on it, are needed.

*"Perhaps you are what you read as much as you are what you eat, but as every parent knows, healthful carrot sticks do not inevitably oust candy bars. Teacher models encourage us to make available the widest range of reformist literature; reader models remind us that the reading process is idiosyncratic, that literary charm sometimes counts more than sturdy good sense, and that positive lessons for living can be culled from seemingly refractory materials."*
—Mitzi Myers, 1990

*S*ystematic differences in life experiences influence the reactions of females and males as readers. Because gender affects children's experience, in the kinds of toys they are given, the experiences they are exposed to, and the kinds of behavior encouraged and discouraged, gender exerts influence not only on the author, but on the reader as well.

The knowledge boys and girls have available to them to draw on in trying to construct understanding from a text differs. Studies have found that high school students' memories of events and of characters' goals and motives were distorted in accordance with the gender stereotypic schemas that they had built up in their heads (Chapman 1993, 26). Recent analysis of possible test bias has shown that students of both sexes were more likely to leave problems with unfamiliar content unanswered, and less likely to solve such problems correctly. Moreover, in this study familiarity was correlated with stereotypical content for girls but not boys.

At least part of the reason that male students often complain about "girls' books" being "boring" is their lack of systematic acquaintance with the socially, emotionally, and often also conceptually different female world. This lack of acquaintance is far less on the part of girls with boys' worlds. Girls' acquaintance with the male world is less culturally penalized and girls are less committed to preserving gender stereotypes for themselves or others than are boys.

Resistance on the part of boys to reading "girls' books," and the fact that their resistance is likely to be disruptive acting out, undoubtedly has played a considerable part in the subject matter of books chosen to be read in schools. (Whatever resistance girls may have to reading boys' books is more likely to manifest itself less disruptively, through passive tuning out.) Allowing boys to continue depriving themselves of reading experiences that would widen their horizons and contribute to their education is not in their best interest. Boys' resistance can be overcome, as many teachers know. The availability of books for younger readers with female protagonists who are considerably less gender stereotyped than has been the case in the past has undoubtedly helped (Segel 1986).

Another gender-related issue in reading is the propensity of girls to focus on narratives and literature, while boys focus on nonfiction in their leisure reading. Both need help and encouragement to broaden their literary diet.

*T*he quirks of gendered language necessitate some attention to the effects of usage, such as pronouns and metaphors.

Twenty years of consciousness raising about the exclusionary effects of some common English usages has made an impact, and led to changes in the language used in newspapers and textbooks. However, the changes are far from universal. It continues to be necessary to reiterate that use of the supposedly generic "he" and "man" *does* exclude women.

There is strong research evidence that, preschool through college, students (especially males) interpret these terms as referring specifically to males, rather than to both men and women. Alternatives such as "they" and "people" result in higher rates of including women and reduce the differences between male and female responses. However, for the highest rates of inclusiveness explicit reference to both seems to be needed: "his and hers," "she or he," "women and men" (Johnson 1980, 18-19; Thorne, Kramarae and Henley 1983, 10; Scott and Schau 1985, 220).

There is evidence that language intended as generic but actually exclusionary can have undesirable effects on students' learning. Among college students given identical essays to read that differed only in that one used "they" or "he and she," the other consistently "he," male students remembered the content of that essay using the latter form better, whereas females were better at remembering the former (Crawford and Chaffin 1986, 16).

The usage of always putting the male first (he and she, men and women) also sends subliminal message with cumulative effects.

In addition to consistent exposure to generic man and the male pronoun (and based on an analysis of 100 college texts, an educated American's exposure to "he" will exceed one million times before she graduates from college (Deats and Lenker eds.1994, 267)), there are two additional characteristics of English that are likely to impact differently on females and males, though neither seems to have been specifically researched. One is the metaphorical conceptualization of intellectual discourse as combat; the other, the metaphorical conceptualization of story-plots as conflict (LeGuin 1989, 165-70; 190-91).

Both combat and conflict fit better with the male stereotype than with the female as seen in the following excerpt from a speech: "Occasionally we are fortunate enough to have students of piercing intelligence. Such students are important, because we require an able opponent with whom to fence in the classroom, so as to exhibit to the others what the thrust of an argument is about. However, we must take care to always have the upper hand, to win thumbs down, to avoid being hoist with our own petard. If we find ourselves pressed at the end of a class, with our back to the wall, we may have to resort to barbed comments, strong-arm tactics, to go for the jugular, to cut their argument to pieces, to bring out our big guns or the heavy artillery. We can justify this because in so doing they get a view of the cutting edge of scholarship; and we can explain this to them in a post mortem of the previous day's exchange during the next class" (Ayim 1984, 1-2).

The combative, adversarial aspects of intellectual argument, deep-rooted legacies from demonstrable historical roots in classical, renaissance, and nineteenth century civilization that are built into some of our most basic notions about how to inquire, how to argue, and how to learn and teach, have been documented by other scholars (Ong 1981, Chapter 4; Lakoff and Johnson 1980, Chapters 1 and 15). Females have been socialized to be uncomfortable with aggression; the ritualized verbal combat (Your claims are indefensible. You disagree? Okay, shoot! If you use that strategy he'll wipe you out. I demolished him.) does not come as easily to them as it comes to males.

*"Try to imagine a culture where arguments are not viewed in terms of war, where no one wins or loses, where there is no sense of attacking or defending, gaining or losing ground. Imagine a culture where an argument is viewed as a dance, the participants are seen as performers, and the goal is to perform in a balanced and aesthetically pleasing way. In such a culture, people would view arguments differently, experience them differently, carry them out differently, and talk about them differently..."*
*—George Lakoff and Mark Johnston, 1980*

Similarly, customary analysis of narrative in terms of conflict is a way of conceptualization that plays into male stereotypes and feeds an adversarial way of thinking. It is to the advantage of both genders to expose them to alternative conceptualizations.

*"From looking at manuals used in college writing courses, and from listening to participants in writing workshops, I gather that it is a generally received idea that a story is the relation of a conflict, that without conflict there is no plot, that narrative and conflict are inseparable... Existence as struggle, life as a battle, everything in terms of defeat and victory: Man versus Nature, Man versus Woman, Black versus White, Good versus Evil, God versus the Devil — a sort of apartheid view of existence, and of literature."*
*—Ursula K. LeGuin, 1987*

Though there are many gender-related differences in the verbal realm, differences in reading performance between girls and boys are very slight, perhaps even smaller than had been thought. The perception that boys have more difficulty learning to read tends, however, to persist; and boys continue to perform significantly below girls in writing.

Girls have been traditionally thought to be innately superior to boys in verbal ability. Some support for this can be found in the fact that girls continue to outscore boys on the College Board's English Composition, Literature, and Standard Written English Achievement Tests, and that almost twice as many girls as boys took the English Language and Literature Advanced Placement Tests. Girls also outscore boys at all ages on the nationwide reading and writing proficiency tests; on the latter, at all ages, by the largest margin of difference between genders on any scores in the four subject areas (reading, writing, mathematics, science) measured. On both the comprehension and vocabulary measures of the SAT, however, males marginally outperformed females in 1994. The gender gap in favor of males shrank, compared to the 1980s, but was the same in 1994 as in 1972, the scores of both groups having declined substantially (World Almanac 1995, 223; College Board 1994, SAT, iii; College Board, 1994, AP, 13; US Department of Education 1992, pp. 42,44,46,48).

Teachers in the early grades nationwide identify two to four times as many boys as girls as having reading disabilities. Recent studies however show that reading disabilities are actually no more frequent in boys than in girls (Education Week 1990, 14). Stereotypical expectations probably play a part in their perceived problems, as does young boys' sometimes disruptive overall behavior in class. It is noteworthy that boys in other countries are not seen as "problem readers," and research has now discounted the theory that girls' being developmentally more advanced gives them an edge in reading (Stage 1985, 272-273).

## What Schools and Teachers Can Do

To enrich teaching of the traditional canon, add ideas drawn from women's studies critical literature by doing some of the following:

- Add women's studies perspectives to shed new light on the study of the classics. In teaching epics such as the *Iliad* and the *Odyssey*, analyze such aspects of these texts as the influence of Greek ideas about nurturing/dangerous aspects of femaleness on the depiction of Greek and of nonhuman females in Homer; Homer's concept of heroism and honor as suggested by his different male, and at least one female characters (Penelope); what alternatives to modern concepts of manhood and womanhood are validated in epics; and Andromache's and Hector's different approaches to problem-solving (Cohen 1995, passim.) In teaching *King Lear,* examine Cordelia's and Lear's attitudes in the light of Gilligan's work on differences of emphasis in the morality of justice and of caring among men and women (Kazemek 1995, 77-80). In teaching *Romeo and Juliet*, examine the role played by the family feud in terms of its being an activity whereby the sons of the family prove themselves to be men through violence on behalf of their fathers; and the private/female public/male contrast between the domestic, cozy, informal, supportive household indoors, and the strife-ridden streets, where claims to manhood are asserted at the cost of civil peace (Kahn 1980, passim).
- Help students explore differing interpretations of canonical texts. Women's studies/feminist critical perspectives (with relevant bibliographies) are included among the five contempo-

rary critical approaches featured as essays appended to the text in the critical editions series *Case Studies in Contemporary Criticism*, Ross C. Murfin, series editor, by Bedford Books of St. Martin's Press. *Heart of Darkness, The Scarlet Letter, Portrait of the Artist as a Young Man, Hamlet*, as well as *Wuthering Heights, Frankenstein*, and others are available as teacher resources or for able senior students.

- In considering genre, note its gendered character (epic poetry vs. romances, or the sentimental vs. the realist novel, for instance), and ask why some genres are associated more with men or with women, and held to be more, or less, important, valuable or excellent than others.
- Teach students to recognize implicit assumptions in the texts they read, including those made about the characteristics of, and relationships between, women and men, and the ideological persuasiveness concerning issues of gender, intended or otherwise, that may be found in literary and other texts that are not overtly about this topic at all (Kelly 1995, 104).

*E*xplore the literary impact of gender with students by pairing two stylistically very similar, but in approach to subject matter and point of view very different, works of literature, or works on the same topic by male and female authors:

- Pair George Orwell's *1984* with Margaret Atwood's *The Handmaid's Tale* as examples of dystopias by canonical authors. Have students compare the significant part played by language in both books, as well as the characters, plot, values, and literary devices. Discuss what characteristics and concerns of each writer's society they drew on for these works.
- Pair Ernest Hemingway's *The Sun Also Rises* with Zora Neale Hurston's *Their Eyes Were Watching God* for a comparison of images by two canonical authors of individuals alienated from mainstream culture.
- When teaching *Jane Eyre*, have students also read Jean Rhys' critically well-received *The Wide Sargasso Sea*. In this case, you have two women authors giving a very different view of the same character; the latter is an account of Mr. Rochester from point of view of his first wife, the crazy one he keeps in the attic, whose story it is. Or contrast Bronte's image of middle class nineteenth century women in *Jane Eyre* with Kate Chopin's, in *The Awakening*; or *Jane Eyre* with *Oliver Twist*.
- When teaching Hemingway, have students also read the short story "The Women Men Don't See" by James Tiptree (in Sargent 1977), and discuss the marked similarities of style and male character, and the equally marked conceptual differences. Examine also similarities in the "tough-guy" biographies of the authors — perhaps before revealing that Tiptree is the pseudonym of senior citizen Alice B. Sheldon. (Already a Hugo and Nebula winner, Sheldon was nominated for another Nebula award for the above. She withdrew it because so much of the praise for the story concerned the evidence it gave that a man could write with full sympathy about women that she felt the prize if awarded would involve false pretenses.) (LeGuin 1989a, 185)
- Give students Margaret Atwood's poem on the subject of desire (Atwood 1972, 22) and pair it with Sydney's "Thou Blind Man's Mark" (Norton Anthology Vol I, 1962, 423) on the same topic, without identification. Ask students to try to come to a consensus, by discussion in groups, whether both are by men, both by women, or one by a man the other by a woman, in which case which is which; and to report to the class the result (with minority positions, if no consensus was possible); and to explain on what basis they arrived at their decision.
- Subsequent discussion can range over stereotyped expectations about authors' gender; the differences in the literary devices used in the two poems, and their effects on the reader;

whether the differences in approach to desire are genuinely reflective of gender differences in this respect, and how far such differences might themselves be stereotyped; the relative importance of time period and gender; and the relative difficulty of getting published, if female, in the past compared to today. (Some students have tagged the Sydney poem "male" on the basis that it must be an early poem because of the language, and argued that at "that time" women poets would not have published. If they do so, they might be introduced to some. Several women poets contemporary with Sydney are included in Cosman, Keefe, and Weaver, 1978.)

- The approaches suggested here can, of course, be adapted for use with other works. For example, explore the impact of gender on human society and character through literature by teaching a work initially labeled "science fiction," but by now accepted into the canon (Bloom 1994, 564): *The Left Hand of Darkness* by Ursula LeGuin (for grades 11-12, and perhaps 10). Its theme is betrayal and fidelity, and the nature of the "other," in this case the narrator, male Earth ambassador to an alien world the inhabitants of which are not gendered at all. Sexual only for brief periods months apart, and with no control over whether they become male or female, all experience *both* biological reproductive roles repeatedly in a lifetime. When not in the sexual mode, they are neuter, and socially androgynous. The book explores the meanings of sameness, otherness, and its effects on perceptions, character, relationships, and society, using myth, language, and metaphor; as well as telling an exciting and moving story.

*T*o present students with a greater diversity of literary approaches, points of view, and human experiences, consider adding more works by women authors from different periods and backgrounds to the curriculum:

- Develop your own, and your students', acquaintance with the gradually expanding "canon" of women writers by now routinely taught in colleges, and increasingly making their way into secondary school literature courses. Introduce students to selected writings from these authors by choosing from works featured in *The Norton Anthology of Literature by Women* (Gilbert and Gubar 1985) and anthologies such as Bridges (Muller and Williams 1994), or the *Winchester Reader* (McQuade and Atwan 1991), for reliably high-quality selections that also include works by women and men from a variety of backgrounds. For additional canonically "validated" authors, among other possible sources Bloom's list in *The Western Canon* (Bloom 1994) may also be consulted.

- Consider the possible role of literature as an affirmation not only of the greatest excellence achieved in a limited set of exemplars, but also of the widest possible range of human potential in verbal expressiveness. Doing so would sanction greater inclusiveness not only of different women authors, but of a greater variety of genres, some of which have strong female representation (reading diaries, letters, and transcriptions of creative oral expression as well as poetry, novels and so on), and of exemplars within a genre (folktales as well as novels; guerrilla theater as well as Shakespeare).

- Assign parallel excerpts from men's and women's diaries or autobiographies. (See **Resources**). Do diaries show any gender-associated features? Are diaries more, or less, influenced by gender stereotypes than other kinds of writing? What differences are there between "formal" literature and the informal writing shown in diaries?

- Discuss the claim that, to learn what women have felt and experienced, texts written by women are likely to be more revealing. Set this issue in the wider context of other groupings of literature. Are works by Russian authors more revealing of Russian ways of thinking than those written about Russian ways of thinking by writers of other nationalities? What special features do Holocaust survivors bring to writing about the Holocaust? What differences are there for the reader in reading Wiesel's works as opposed to oral accounts by survivors, Anne Frank's diary, or fiction about the Holocaust by non-Jews?

- Introduce students to women as authors and protagonists in the leisure reading fields. Some examples are: in detective/science fiction, Lois McMaster Bujold's series (*Brothers in Arms, The Warrior's Apprentice, The Vor Game,* and others) with a young, compassionate military genius space-hero who compensates with wit for his physical disabilities; C.J.Cherryh's "Chanur" series whose hero overcomes her culture's conviction that biology unfits males for rationality, and that different species are condemned to insoluble enmity, and where a human is the alien; Dorothy Gilman's "Mrs. Pollifax" stories about a retired housewife-turned-CIA operative; Ursula LeGuin's many works for different ages (for junior high, try *The Wizard of Earthsea* series, among numerous others).

*T*ry to examine literature for the values it embodies, help students to analyze literary characters in terms of the values they exemplify, and how those values are, or are not, congruent with students' own values on the one hand, and the values prevalent in the society the authors wrote for on the other, by doing some of the following:

- Introduce the sociohistorical dimension of literary works to students as an alternative approach to the exclusive focus on text promoted by the formalism associated with New Criticism. Use texts as primary sources, analyzing the author's frame of reference, and ways she or he reflects some particular group's cultural assumptions at the time and place of writing.

- Have students come up with their own definitions of what it is to be heroic from lists of individuals whom they consider to be heroes. Ask them to compare their ideas with the characters of both female and male heroes in the books they have read. A discussion on different gender standards of heroism, cultural differences in what is considered heroic, and which aspect of heroism is emphasized, as well as differences between "protagonist" and "hero" in literature, and the concept of "anti-hero" can be explored.

- Use parody to expose underlying assumptions in stories and language. Ask students to construct a story that is a reworking of familiar fairy tales, following the revised plot lines suggested below. Discuss what assumptions were upset or negated by the new plot lines. Ask how much of the original tale their new version could have, and how much it did, preserve. An extension is asking students to suggest new twists to familiar tales or myths. With early to mid-elementary grades, this exercise may be done by starting with reading them the wolf's view of what happened, and his startlement at being told by Red Riding Hood that he looks "foolish and ugly in granny's nightgown" (Vozar 1993); or the story of the paper bag princess, who outwits the dragon and rescues the prince (Munsch 1980). (I am indebted for this idea to Carol Feiser Laque's presentation of it at the North Central Region National Women's Studies Association Annual Conference, October 1978, Indiana University; to Garner 1994, and Tatar 1992, Epilogue.)

Try these plot lines:

*Sleeping Beauty*: A powerful witch demands that the Handsome Prince marry her, but the Prince refuses. She casts an evil spell upon the Prince; he falls into a deep sleep. A Princess, hearing of his great body, sense of humor, and integrity, goes to negotiate his release with the witch. They meet for coffee. What happens?

*Red Riding Hood*: The story ends with Red scolding the woodsman for trying to settle a conflict by applying more violence; talks the wolf into regurgitating grandma, and Red, grandma. and wolf set up an alternative household together, based on division of labor. Write the whole story with this end in view.

*Snow White and the Seven Dwarves*: Instead of saying "Mirror, mirror, on the wall, who is the fairest one of all," the Queen joins the Gray Panthers, and drafts the seven dwarves to organize and operate a meals-on-wheels program for senior citizens. Given this scenario, what would Snow White be doing?

- If you teach *Hamlet* ask students to read Atwood's three-page "Gertrude Talks Back," in which the queen tells her son she is not wringing her hands, she is drying her nails; and that, since Claudius did have a slight weight problem, she'd be obliged if Hamlet stopped hurting his stepdad's feelings by calling him "the bloat king" (Atwood 1994). What different messages does it send about the characters and the relationships in the play than does Shakespeare's version? What are the differences in the underlying assumptions of the two authors?

- Teach critical reading/listening/viewing skills as they apply to popular writing and mass media in general, not only to literature, and how to analyze the messages, including those about gender, and values, being sent. Students need tools to distinguish reality from myth, recognize commercial as well as political rhetoric, and to be able to approach critically not only the texts of the "classics," but editorials, magazines, song lyrics, and TV as well, and to recognize different kinds of manipulation and uses of literary devices (See the **ARTS** chapter for additional ideas and resources).

*T*o counteract exclusionary messages unintentionally sent by some features of English usage, help students recognize and defuse gender-related quirks of language by doing some of the following:

- Model the use of gender-fair language, such as "she and he," "men and women," consistently. Teach students to be sensitive to gender-fair writing, ask them to use it in their own work, and reward them for doing so — if only by praise.

- When teaching about metaphors, challenge students to create alternative metaphors both competitive/violent/male-interest stereotypical, and cooperative/caring/female-interest stereotypical. (Try organic, growth and creation-oriented metaphors instead of conflict-oriented ones for intellectual discourse, for instance.)

*T*o improve students' ability to communicate effectively, help them towards understanding gender differences in communication styles, and towards versatility in using the beneficial features of both styles, by doing some of the following:

- Discuss with students gender-associated differences in speech and behavior styles, their advantages and disadvantages, and the merits and negatives of possible changes.

- Explain that the message sent may not be the message received; and that taking for granted that intention will be understood can lead to problems. Use the computer convention smiley-face :) used to signal in e-mail that the message is intended to be funny to help make the point. For a case study of a failed male joke resented by female students, its disruption of previously friendly relations, and the discussion between the two parties to help straighten out the situation, that can be adapted for older students, see Lyman 1987.

- Ask students to summarize points made by earlier speakers before making their own statement.
- Announce occasionally that, having asked the next question, you will not allow anyone to answer for a minute (or other amount of waiting time you decide on).
- Wait for five to ten seconds after a student has apparently finished speaking, in case she or he has more to say. Encourage fuller answers by follow-up questions: "Tell me more about that . . . " "What in the reading makes you think . . . ?"
- Bring balance to student contributions by giving each the same number of pebbles or beans at the start of class; having each "pay" one unit for every time they speak until their units are spent, and mildly penalize all with unspent units at the end of class.
- Assign half the students, randomly chosen, the job of asking challenging questions during one or two classes, the others to ask supportive, speaker-sustaining questions. Switch assignments for the next class or two. Or give "secret assignments" in sealed envelopes to individuals about what part to play in class discussions (having explained roles in small-group discussions): devil's advocate, conversation promoter, mediator, summarizer, challenging questioner, and so on. After a week or so, challenge students to write down who they think played what parts, and what they base their guesses on. Rotate assignments.
- Restrain students who dominate discussion by not allowing interruptions, limiting the time any student can hold the floor, or limiting the number of times anyone may speak.
- Coach those who speak in a hesitant way, with too many qualifiers and hedgings, by taping their comments and having them rework their wording, then practicing a more assertive delivery on tape.
- When a student answers hesitantly, or with a rising inflection that turns the answer into a question, confront the uncertainty directly and turn it into an asset. You might say: "It sounds as though there might be some doubt here. Let's look at all the reasons why it might be correct, and reasons for doubt," and lead the student, perhaps with help from other students, toward building a reasoned stand for their position, given all the pros and cons. Or ask directly: "What makes you doubt? What makes you give this answer in spite of the doubts?"
- Help students to recognize that challenges from others, even hostile challenges, can be turned to good account in helping to clarify one's own position. Instead of fearing or resenting such challenges, they can be used productively, instead.
- Set a discussion of the gender aspects of language in the wider context of the social functions of language, one of which is inclusion into groups and exclusion from them. Consider with students professional jargon, computer hackers' language, social control of access to elite positions through language (Shaw's *Pygmalion* might be used here, or Black English), and reasons why in-group/out-group dynamics might, or might not, be applicable in the case of gender.

*T*o improve all students' verbal abilities, help young readers to enjoy reading a variety of books, and to become competent writers in a variety of modes, by doing some of the following:

- Convince students, and their parents, that the best way to make competent readers is to have them read a lot.
- Enlist the help, and hold up the example, of admired/respected adult male role models to help young boys identify reading as an appropriately male occupation. You might, for instance, solicit a brief review of their favorite book from (whomever you can appropriately target in your community), and prominently display the review, a photo of the reviewer, and a copy of the book somewhere in the school.

- To help restless younger students with the demands placed on them by reading, intersperse it with physical activity based on it such as acting out the story, miming it, or "translating" it into two or even three dimensional visual terms.
- Since girls' knowledge base derives more heavily from the reading of fiction, and boys' from nonfiction, give special encouragement to remedy the imbalance.
- Lead students to writing by doing more frequent, brief writing in class from the early grades on. Class discussions may be stopped occasionally, and students asked to summarize the points made so far; or ask them to write a brief reaction (perhaps alternating analytical/ critical and personal, or asking for both) to a reading, an experience, or a discussion.
- Give students practice in a wide variety of both reading and writing from early grades on. Expose them to creative, critical/analytical, descriptive, technical (directions and scientific reports) and rhetorical/persuasive, and personal reaction readings; and ask them to write in all of these ways and more.
- Help reluctant journal-writers by giving it an image other than the female-identified "Dear Diary" approach. It may be helpful to call it a "log" rather than a "journal"; describing its rationale as "talking back to the author, telling her or him about what bugged you as you read them; and questioning them on all the points you've found unclear," and/or keeping the journal on computer backed up with a hard copy.

Rereading their journal can help convince students, especially those with low self-confidence, that they have indeed grown as readers, writers and thinkers.

(Many of the suggestions in the last two sections are based on information in Chapman 1993, which contains other suggestions on reading, classroom interchanges, and writing.)

## RESOURCES

Note: Items marked *(P)* are especially recommended for parents with younger children.

Altan, Susan, *Many Women's Voices: A Bibliography of Authentic Women's Voices,* I and II. Washington, D.C.: National Association of Independent Schools/Committee for Women and Girls in Independent Schools, 1991 (I), 1993 (II).
Author/title list of reading selections for high school, both for teacher background and student reading. Arranged by ethnicity or category such as Asia/Philippines, Asia/Japan, International/Urban, Jewish American, Native American /Lakota Sioux, and United States/Working class. Books cited include fiction, autobiography, poetry, essays, interviews, and other genres by women writing about their own cultures and lives.

Bankier, Joanna, and Deirdre Lashgari, eds. *Women Poets of the World*. New York: Macmillan, 1983.
Almost 250 poets represented, mostly by only one or two poems. Ten introductions to the language groupings discuss historical and sociological contexts as well as prosody and imagery. Broad coverage of minority women in America. Most of the content readable by high school students, some by those younger.

Barnstone, Aliki and Willis Barnstone, eds. *A Book of Women Poets from Antiquity to Now.* New York: Schocken Books, 1992.
International selections, smoothly translated. Interesting for leisure reading as well as the classroom; selections vary in difficulty, some suitable for elementary level. *(P)*

Bauermeister, Erica, Jesse Larsen and Holly Smith. *500 Great Books by Women: A Reader's Guide*. New York: Penguin, 1994.

Annotated list organized by topics such as Art, Choices, Growing Up, Power, Work. Classic and contemporary works from Lady Nijo's thirteenth century Japanese court diaries to Toni Morison, Alice Hoffman, Isabel Allende, Barbara Tuchman, Maya Angelou. Some nonfiction. Brief annotations capture flavor.

Boyd, Herb and Robert L. Allen, eds. Brotherman: *The Odyssey of Black Men in America: An Anthology*. New York: Ballantine, 1995.

One hundred fifty selections from slave narratives, memoirs, social histories , biographies, novels, short stories, autobiographies, position papers and essays. "The world that Black men experience as adolescents, lovers, husbands, fathers, workers, warriors, elders." Includes works by W.E.B.DuBois, Louis Farrkhan, Jesse Jackson, Booker T. Washington, Malcolm X., Magic Jonson, Miles Davis, Mohammed Ali, Countee Cullen, Sidney Bechet, Langston Hughes. Teacher resource.

Busby, Margaret, ed. *Daughters of Africa: An International Anthology of Words and Writings by Women of African Descent from the Ancient Egyptian to the Present*. New York: Ballantine Books, 1994.

Two hundred women writers of African descent from all over the world, arranged chronologically. Includes literary novels, short stories, poetry, essays, journalism, memoirs, diaries, letters, plays, folklore, historical fiction, science fiction. Black female experience "of love, loss, hope, despair, dreams, nightmares, birth and death." Includes works by Ama Ata Aidoo, Octavia Butler, Nikki Giovanni, Billie Holiday, Jamaica Kincaid, Ntozake Shange, Sojourner Truth, Harriet Tubman, Phyllis Wheatley, Gwendolyn Brooks. Teacher resource.

Davidson, Cathy E. and Linda Wagner-Martin. *The Oxford Companion to Women's Writing in the United States*. New York: Oxford University Press, 1994.

Some 800 entries, some brief biographies not restricted to literary figures (Mead, Carson, Anthony) and longer essays with basic, authoritative, and clear information. Separate, detailed essays on wide variety of topics: each of a wide range of ethnic literatures; brief survey style road maps to specific periods, colonial to contemporary; chronological and thematic survey of women's poetry; entries on canon formation, mentoring, ecofeminism, women's movement, Civil War, men and feminism.

Field, Janet Scarborough, Elisabeth A. Middleton and Sarah J. Walker. *A Selected High School Reading List in Women's Studies: A Resource for Educators with Guide,, rev. ed.* 1994. Women's Studies, WMB 206A, University of Texas at Austin, Austin, TX 78712.

Annotated pamphlet listing books written by and about a culturally diverse cross-section of women, Includes novels, autobiographies, biographies, folktales, short stories, essays, journals, diaries, and historical narratives as well as some psychological, economic, and sociological works, arranged by academic department, with some suggestions for thematic uses (titles to use for teaching "coming of age," "the Victorian Era," or "the experience of Latina women.") Teacher resources, and works for upper elementary and up, though more in the "and up" category. Appropriate age levels not always made clear, but are usually inferable. A useful resource.

Gilbert, Sandra M., and Susan Gubar. *The Norton Anthology of Literature by Women: The Tradition in English*. New York: W.W. Norton, 1985.

Over 150 authors from every English-speaking country, ranging from Bradstreet and Wheatley to Dickinson and Wharton, Woolf, and Walker, spanning the period from the Middle Ages to today and the gamut of genres: poetry, drama, journals, letters, short fiction, essays, and three complete novels. Each period is introduced by a historical essay, each author by a biographical and critical headnote.

Hull, Gloria T., Patricia Bell Scott, and Barbara Smith, eds. *All the Women Are White, All the Blacks Are Men, But Some of Us Are Brave: Black Women's Studies*. New York: The Feminist Press, 1982.

Intended for college, but useful for high school. Provides literary essays on major writers, and carefully annotated bibliography for further access to black women poets, novelists, playwrights, and composers, as well as political theory, guidelines for consciousness-raising about racism and much else. Teacher resource.

**McKissack, Patricia.** *Flossie and the Fox*. New York: Dial Books for Young Readers, 1986.

Tennessee folk tale about young black girl whose mother warns her to look out for a fox. When she meets one, she outwits it. Useful as a variant on the Red Riding Hood theme. *(P)*

**McQuade, Donald and Robert Atwan, eds.** *The Winchester Reader*. Boston: St. Martin's Press, 1991.

A thematically arranged anthology of prose — essays , stories, and quotations — intended for use in first year college composition classes, but fine for high school seniors and probably juniors as well. About half of those included are not literary figures but journalists, historians, scientists, scholars, and activists. Includes Thomas Edison, Thomas Jefferson, Ho Chi Minh, Gloria Steinem, Walter Lippman, Loren Eiseley as well as Joan Didion, Mark Twain, Virginia Woolf, James Baldwin, Lin Yutang. Includes useful biographical notes on the writers. Unusually extensive instructors' manual includes writing-before-reading exercises, and very detailed, often imaginative teaching strategies. Could work as student text.

**Meyers, Ruth, Beryle Banfield, and Jamila Gaston Colon, eds.** *Embers: Stories for a Changing World*. New York: Feminist Press and Interracial Books for Children, 1983.

Includes autobiographical and historical narratives and poems grouped into thematic units such as friendship, families, freedom fighters, breaking barriers. Selections are short, easy to read, upbeat, and each has moral aspects. Teachers' edition has text in tiny type, surrounded by wealth of innovative ideas for classroom use, resources, background information, and projects. Specifically designed for grades 4-6. Student text. *(P)*

**Miller, Casey, and Kate Swift.** *The Handbook of Nonsexist Writing*. 2nd ed. New York: Harper & Row, 1988.

Useful, sensible, and sensitive. The standard book on nonsexist writing recommended by *The Chicago Manual of Style*.

**Moffat, Mary Jane and Charlotte Painter.** *Revelations: Diaries of Women.* New York: Random House, 1974.

Samples of the diary form by thirty-two women from the early nineteenth century to the recent past, from many countries. Selections include some well-known writers, some relatives of well-known writers, some artists, and some unknowns. Included are Anna Dostoevsky, Sophie Tolstoy, Dorothy Wordsworth, as well as Katherine Mansfield, Selma Lagerlof, George Sand, Anais Nin, Kathe Kollwitz, Marie Baskirtseff. Teacher resource. (Alternative collections listed in Field, above.)

**Muller, Gilbert H. and John A. Williams, eds.** *Bridges: Literature Across Cultures.* New York: McGraw-Hill, 1994.

Excellent, well-balanced selections of fiction, poetry, and drama grouped thematically: women and men, caste and class, faith and doubt, children and families, war and peace. Among authors included are Anton Chekhov, Louise Erdrich, Walt Whitman, Chinua Achebe, Amy Tan, Langston Hughes, Gerard Manley Hopkins, Leslie Marmon Silko, Lorraine Hansberry, Yukio Mishima, and their ilk. Useful brief biographical profiles of authors and glossary of literary terms. Slim teachers' guide is rather simpleminded, but may spark some ideas. Could work as student text. Recommended for quality and variety of literary selections.

**Ostriker, Alicia Suskin.** *Stealing the Language: The Emergence of Women's Poetry in America*. Boston: Beacon Press, 1986.

A lucid, scholarly, and passionate examination of the works of a wide range of contemporary American women poets that sets their work into a literary, historical, and political context and contributes to the reader's personal appreciation of the poetry discussed. Teacher resource.

**Part, Annis.** *Archetypal Patterns in Women's Fiction*. Bloomington, Indiana: Indiana University Press, 1983.

An analysis of the works of over 300 British and American novelists, major and minor, including working class and minority women, offering insights that could be applied to whatever fiction is being taught.

**Phelps, Ethel Johnston, ed.** *Tatterhood and Other Tales*. New York: The Feminist Press, 1978.

Authentic folk tales from many countries featuring spirited, enterprising and funny heroines in appealing and entertaining tales. Book of the Month and Young Parents Book Club selection. For ages 6 and up. *(P)* NOTE: The Feminist Press has a number of other high quality children's books. For a catalog write to them at 311 E. 94th Street, New York, NY 10128.

Riley, Patricia, ed. *Growing up Native American: An Anthology*. New York: William Morrow 1993.

The works about childhood of twenty-two Native American writers, women and men from fifteen nations across the United States and Canada, including short stories, excerpts from novels, and autobiographical sketches from well-known writers as well as the less known, among them Black Elk, Louise Erdrich, N.Scott Momaday, Leslie Marmon Silko, Sara Winnemuca Hopkins, Luther Standing Bear, Lame Deer, Simon Ortiz, Ella Cara Deloria, Anna Lee Walters. Mostly chronological arrangement, nineteenth century to now, with section on schooldays. *(P)*

Rubin, Michael, ed. *Men without Masks: Writings from the Journals of Modern Men*. Reading, Massachusetts: Addison-Wesley, 1980.

Selections from the diaries of thirty twentieth-century men from various countries and backgrounds: "soldiers and explorers, school boys and mama's boys, gurus and football players." A minority are by writers (Franz Kafka, Thomas Merton) and those famous for other reasons (photographer Edward Weston, explorer Richard Byrd). Teacher resource.

Sadker, Myra, David Sadker, and Joyce Kaset. *The Communication Gender Gap*. The Mid-Atlantic Center for Sex Equity. The American University School of Education, Washington, D.C.

Booklet for high school students and adults with twenty-item quiz, whose answers give substantial information about how women and men communicate with each other; exercises in assessing communication patterns among adults and in classrooms; suggestions on how to end the gender gap.

Sadker, Myra and David Sadker. Failing at Fairness. New York: Charles Scribner's Sons, 1994.

Appendix of recommended reading: "Wonderful Women and Resourceful Girls: Books for Children to Grow On," ranges from picture books to myths and fairy tales, biographies, historical and realistic fiction, fantasy and adventure, with age-level suggestions. *(P)*

Savanna Books, 858 Massachusetts Avenue, Cambridge, MA 02139.

Mail-order catalog of a wide range of nonstereotyped, culturally diverse books. *(P)*

Whalley, Liz and Liz Dodge. *Weaving in the Women: Transforming the High School English Curriculum*. Portsmouth, N.H.: Heinemann, 1993.

Suggests books and poems by women authors to use with ninth and tenth graders, with brief reviews of the works, comments on student reactions to them, ways to use women's works in tandem with traditional male authors, and classroom activities. Also describes women authors to include in survey or period courses of American and English literature, from seventeenth and eighteenth centuries respectively until the present, giving a good enough "feel" for works and their teaching possibilities to allow decisions to be made about using them. Includes extended discussions of pedagogy and testing, and copious annotated bibliographies of student and teacher resource readings. Recommended for depth, breadth, hands-on usefulness, and variety of reading suggestions; good for those just getting their feet wet, as well as for veterans of inclusiveness.

■ ■ ■ ■

## CHAPTER EIGHT

## MATHEMATICS

*since mathematics can speak to the infinite*
*imagine me as 1 to the first power*

—*Nikki Giovanni, 1975*

Gender-related differences in attitudes and behavior with respect to mathematics continue to be of concern. Lower female participation in mathematics contributes to the loss by society of potential contributions by women, to continued occupational segregation of the sexes, to women's lower incomes, and to individuals' not living up to their full capabilities. To the extent that females as a group develop less confidence than they justifiably might have in their math ability, are unconvinced as to the usefulness of mathematics for their future, and become reluctant to be intellectually independent risk-takers, they will be screened out of the elective, higher level mathematics courses. Without these courses, they will be unable to study many subject areas, handicapped in the study of many others, and shut out of many of the highly paid, traditionally "male" jobs.

But math avoidance is not an exclusively female problem. There are also many boys who believe they can't do math, who avoid taking math courses, whose discomfort about math failures is deepened by the feeling that, as males, they ought to be good at math, whose intellectual growth and career choices are narrowed; and whose potential contributions are a loss to society.

**Since the 1970s, there has been a flood of scholarship on the topic of gender and mathematics. Over twenty years of research has established that:**

➤ the relationship between gender and mathematics is very complex

➤ large variations between groups of females exist both in comparison to other groups of females and relative to males

➤ race, ethnicity, socioeconomic status, parental attitudes and expectations, the particular school, and even the specific teacher all affect math-related thinking and behavior

➤ the largest gender differences tend to show up in the middle class, and among whites and Hispanics; the smallest, among African Americans

➤ race, ethnicity, and socioeconomic status correlate with larger differences between groups than does gender

➤ within-gender differences consistently dwarf between-gender differences

➤ the magnitude of between-gender differences in performance also varies depending on the kind of operation measured, as well as the format and the content of the test given; it tends to be largest on tasks that require explanation, interpretation, and application

➤ girls generally do better on mathematics tests that emphasize computation, arithmetic-and-algebra skills, logic, essay or open-ended items, and those that mirrored curriculum content; boys on word problems, arithmetic-and-geometry skills, and multiple choice items

➤ many of the interventions developed to benefit girls also benefit boys' attitudes to and performance in mathematics

➤ no overall differences have been noted in the ways boys and girls solve arithmetic problems; and even at the level of the most difficult questions on the SAT, there is a very large gender overlap in the methods used

- there are some stereotype-congruent statistical differences in some of the ways males and females approach some specific kinds of mathematics problems, and these may appear as early as the mid-elementary grades
- a perception of math as "male-appropriate" continues to exist, and for girls is associated with lower math achievement at every grade level
- intervention can make a difference, and can lead to the achievement of parity in mathematics for earlier under-performing groups

**Some of the areas in which intervention is needed have been identified as:**

- overcoming unwarranted lack of confidence in the ability to do mathematics
- reducing anxiety that inhibits performance
- increasing understanding of the future importance of mathematics for everyone
- reducing perception of mathematics as a "masculine" field
- alerting teachers to both the commonalities and the differences in girls' and boys' relationship to mathematics, as well as to what might be done to empower both to live up to their potential
- using a variety of approaches, including collaborative, problem-solving oriented, hands-on, self-monitoring, and student-responsible ones under high challenge/low threat conditions
- equalizing expectations that parents and teachers have for boys and girls in mathematics

(Willis 1995, 264-266; Fennema 1993, 17, 21; College Board 1992/93, 22; AAUW 1992, 30; 54-55; National Coalition 1992; Caine and Caine 1991; Leder 1990, 13; Eccles 1989, 47-50; Peterson and Fennema 1985, 309-310; Stage 1985, 240-245)

*A*t the high school level, there has recently been a significant reduction in the disparities between girls and boys. Girls' mathematics scores on national tests have risen. An increasing proportion of girls have taken advanced level math courses prior to taking the tests, and they have been placed in high ability mathematics classes at higher rates.

Perhaps as a result of the twenty years or so of concern and intervention, the gender differences in math performance that had traditionally shown up in high school have declined consistently during the last decade or two.

On the national mathematics proficiency test taken at age 17, the male-female gap shrank from 8 points in 1973 to 3 points in 1990. On the ACT, the gap shrank from 2.7 points in 1980 to 1.2 points in 1994, and on the SAT from 46 points in 1975 to 41 in 1994. (Note that the three tests use different scales, so the size of the differences they indicate is not directly comparable.) (World Almanac 1995, 223; U.S. Dept. of Education 1992, 46).

The changes are undoubtedly linked with the fact that an increasing number of girls are taking advanced mathematics courses, from Algebra II to pre-calculus through calculus, though the increase is by far the smallest at the most advanced level.

The ACT reported that in 1994 for the first time an equal proportion of males and females taking the test had studied Algebra II. On the 1994 SAT, 34 percent of the girls taking the test had taken pre-calculus compared to 25 percent in 1987; and 19 percent calculus compared to the 15 percent in 1987.

Considerable racial and ethnic differences continue to exist in the male advantage relative to females in mathematics performance. The gender gap is by far the least significant among African Americans.

SAT figures continue to show that performance disparity varies in different groups. Girls trailed boys by the largest margin among Hispanic students other than Puerto Ricans (48 points); by slightly less in white and Asian American groups (44 and 43 points), and slightly less still among all other groups. Among black students, however, the gap was less than half that of the white and Asian-American groups (18 points) (Miller 1994, 10-11). Other research confirms that among African-American groups, gender is a less salient factor in mathematics behavior. Studies, albeit not on national samples, have found either no gender differences in mathematics achievement and course participation, or ones favoring girls (Catsambis 1994, 201).

Two features may explain this. Given what is known about the importance of parental expectations, past research that shows black fathers expecting both their sons and daughters to be independent and assertive, and black mothers having higher expectations for their daughters, though not math specific, is at least suggestive (Washington and Newman 1991, 24). Moreover, the drop in overall self-esteem experienced by all students between junior high and high school, and among whites more markedly by girls, is experienced more markedly by boys rather than girls among the black groups studied; and black boys' self-esteem dropped especially sharply in the academic area (Madhere 1991).

A different change, but one clearly connected to the decrease in the disparity between female and male performance, has taken place in girls' math course placement. A 1988 national study of eighth and tenth grade math placement in public schools showed a higher percentage of girls than boys in the high-ability classes (and 80 percent of the schools had eighth grade classes "tracked" this way.) Before the late 1980s, either there was no difference in this respect between the genders, or the difference favored boys (Catsambis 1994, 205).

*I*n spite of the demonstrable accrual of pluses, all is not yet equal for girls in mathematics.

Overall, boys (though not African-American boys) consistently continue to have more confidence in their own mathematics ability than girls. Girls continue to tend to underestimate, boys to overestimate their own current and likely future achievement in mathematics, relative to their past grades and normed test performance.

Girls continue tending to blame their own lack of ability for their failures, and attribute their successes to luck, or to the test having been easy. Boys tend to blame their failures on their own lack of effort, or an unfair test or teacher, and attribute their success to ability.

Girls generally continue to be more dependent than boys on learned algorithms, and more unwilling to risk failure, to speculate, to question.

From about tenth grade on, boys tend to outstrip girls in mathematics test performance, as well as in favorable attitudes towards mathematics and in course-taking. This is not, however, consistent across all groups: in Hawaii, for instance, non-white girls outperform boys in mathematics (Ginorio 1995, 6).

The most marked gender differences in performance continue to show up among the highest-performing students, even when the number of math courses taken is held constant, and on the cognitively most complex problems.

Middle class white boys continue to be the ones who rate the future importance to them of mathematics most highly, compared both to boys from other racial/ethnic groups and to girls from all groups.

By high school, more boys than girls have decided to pursue math/science careers, with white boys being most likely to do so and Hispanic girls least. In college, only women with a very high aptitude for math choose a science major, though men of a wide range of math abilities do so (Ginorio 1995, 6).

Math/science self-rating of ability is the highest predictor of choosing a science major (Ginorio 1995, 6); low confidence in and underrating of their own math ability, continuing to occur starting in elementary school, results in a significant narrowing of choices, in a disproportionately high number of cases for girls.

Finding, and shrinking, the difference takes adding and subtracting small increments.

Thousands of studies have investigated reasons for the differences. The consensus is that there is no one reason. Rather, a number of variables can be identified that play a part in the existence of the gender gap. There are small but consistent cultural pushes and pulls on girls that continue to influence girls' under-performance in mathematics.

Their parents', teachers', and peers' expectations, as well as the impact of the mass media, mold girls' expectations of themselves in mathematics as in other fields.

The influences that shape girls' and boys' mathematics-related attitudes and behaviors begin to operate before the differences in performance itself begin to show up; and they cast a long shadow. Knowing about them is important for all who deal with math-related issues and students at any age, especially since research studies confirm the very important part played by teachers in mathematics-related outcomes for students.

> *"My interest as a teacher has been in igniting that spark, in supplying both the knowledge of algebra and that desire to see what it can do. To this end I was a very tough and demanding teacher. I had high standards. I pushed and prodded. I laughed. I supported. I tutored. I used what worked for me. I did not try to bend myself to fit a method. I did not demand uniformity from my students. I demanded rigor. I insisted on thought. I applauded. I hugged. I cried. I had a variety of approaches to each idea, each problem, and if my ways did not work, I turned to the class for help."*
> —algebra teacher quoted in Independent School, fall 1994

**Studies that focused on a comparison between those classrooms in which boys and girls had similar confidence in their math ability, and those where the gender gap in confidence was large, found that generally in the former:**

- ➤ all students were required to participate actively
- ➤ equality of participation was promoted by everyone being called on, not only those who raised their hands
- ➤ there was relatively less social comparison and less competition
- ➤ students spent more time working on problems on their own, and interacting one on one with the teacher, as and when they needed help
- ➤ there was relatively less time spent on all-class drills, and more on individualized learning strategies, hands-on learning, problems with practical applications
- ➤ there were more open-ended learning situations and more opportunities for creative solutions (Eccles 1989)

*I*n elementary school, there has traditionally been little if any difference in boys' and girls' mathematics performance — and this continues to be true. National Assessment of Educational Progress mathematics proficiency tests between 1973 and 1990 at both ages 9 and 13 typically show only a point or two difference, in some years in favor of girls, in others of boys (U.S. Dept. of Education 1992, 42).

Boys by and large from preschool on have more informal, outside of school experiences that have some relevance for mathematics. Estimating trajectories in ball games, rotating objects (including their own bodies) in space, keeping scores in their own games as well as athletics, and discussing them in spectator sports (e.g. batting averages), making measurements in model-making and woodworking, and using building blocks and toys such as Lego, Tinker Toys, and Meccano — all these behaviors, known to hone spatial ability, and to an extent involving prediction, validation, and numbers, are more characteristic for boys than girls. On the average, boys come to school having had more exposure to mathematics-related concepts and experiences than girls have had, and some of this disparity continues in elementary school.

While the relationship between spatial skills and mathematics achievement is unclear, there does appear to be one. There is considerable evidence for consistent under-performance for girls compared to boys on (in descending order of magnitude): measures of mental rotations, judgments involving horizontality/verticality, and the ability to isolate a figure from a confusing background or "field." Training is known to help close the gap (Hyde 1990; Stage et al. 1985, 241; Linn and Petersen 1985a, 62, 63, 67; 1985b; Liss 1983, 149-150).

There is also evidence that while both males and females performed better when the same spatial task was described as measuring aptitude for occupations stereotypical of their own gender, the boost in performance for males on male-stereotyped tasks was considerably greater. Such results provide a strong argument for some degree of cultural influence on differences in spatial cognition performance, as well as support for the already well-documented greater investment of males in gender stereotypes (Sharps, Price and Williams,1994).

Gender differences in the approach to academics that have long-term impact on learning and especially mathematics learning, begin to develop in elementary school.

In terms of academic style, the early grades, which typically demand neat, careful work, following directions accurately, learning the rules, and getting the answer "right" fit well the feminine gender role stereotype. Girls adopt it readily, thereby earning teacher approval.

Boys are more likely to resist, from around third or fourth grade on. They seek their peers' rather than teachers' approval, and a major way to gain it is by "toughness," a defiance of authority. In middle and upper elementary grades, boys tend to put a ceiling on the amount of academic effort they are willing to expend, in order to avoid being labeled a goody-goody or a teacher's pet (Adler et al. 1992, 173, 177). They tend to act messy, lazy, and unwilling to follow directions.

Risk-taking in improvising, "fudging," guesstimating, extrapolating from minimal data, consequently fits in well with boys' peer-group culture. Having had experience with failure, and not been penalized for it by those whose opinion is important to them (their peers), they do not fear it; and knowing that error is often due to their not having done the work, and having their teachers also tell them that they would succeed if only they worked harder, it is not surprising that they do not question their own mathematical ability. Failure is obviously accounted for by lack of work; if, in spite of it all, they succeed, what else could it be due to than ability?

It is symptomatic that third and sixth grade boys' (but not girls') most consistent arithmetic error is due to not learning the rules, the algorithms, correctly. Girls' errors, on the other hand, are typically verbal ones. In word problems, they make errors by looking for "key words" as clues and misinterpreting them: taking "altogether" to mean addition was required, for instance, regardless of the actual parameters of the problem. Other research documents continuing errors of this type for women, such as in fractions confusing the meaning of "of" as multiplication or division (Marshall and Smith 1987, 378-9; Tobias 1988, 3).

Girls tend to persist in rule-conforming and teacher-pleasing behaviors in later elementary school and beyond; they are neat, their work is clean, their homework done, their academic effort high. What other reason can there be for their failure than that they just don't have the ability? Especially when they are praised for doing everything "right," and for having worked so hard, when they succeed? Because they are anxious to do the right thing, and are more oriented to female adult approval than are boys, they experience failure far less, and fear it more.

> "... [O]ne woman, looking directly at the math specialist, said:'How do you feel when you make a mistake in math?' He thought quite a long while, and then replied:'Do you want the truth? I find my mistakes interesting. And my misunderstandings even more so. They are like windows into my thinking.' There was an audible gasp from the group. You can understand why, I'm sure. These were people for whom, all their lives, making a mistake had seemed the deepest pitfall, the thing to avoid at all costs, and here, right in front of them, an expert was saying that those errors are not just okay but a source of learning and deeper understanding."
> —quoted by Tobias in Academic Connections, 1988

It is congruent with the differing academic styles developed by boys and girls that the largest gender differences have shown up, as early as fourth grade, in mathematical tasks requiring explanation, interpretation, and application of mathematical knowledge; and that girls generally do better on mathematics tests that emphasize computation, arithmetic-and-algebra skills, and those items that mirror the curriculum.

A large number of studies specifically investigated to what students at various ages attributed successes and failures, and to what teachers attributed them. There is great consistency in the findings.

The teachers studied tended to attribute boys' mathematics successes to ability, girls' to effort. Girls typically attribute their failures to an unchangeable factor — lack of ability — and their successes to factors they have no control over: luck, or an "easy test." Boys typically attribute their failures to variables such as their not having done the work, or factors outside themselves: unfair test, incompetent teacher; and their successes to ability. This, however, is not the case among Asian Americans, a consistently mathematically high-performing group, who emphasize the importance of effort for success more strongly, compared to those from other groups who emphasize ability more (Catsambis 1994, 200; Whang and Hancock 1994; Tapasak 1993, 356; Fennema 1993, 21; Eccles et al. 1993, 844; AAUW 1992, 54-55).

The effects of well-learned computation rules by girls and not by boys in elementary school may be compounded by boys' highly visible mistakes being likely to attract teacher attention and additional instruction, which the girls do not get because they are already doing well on the kinds of problems being tested. The fact that the girls' early success may mask rote learning without genuine understanding does not surface until later, when having to make a change in previously successful and rewarded techniques has become difficult (Marshall and Smith 1987, 382-383).

*S*ocietal factors play a part in the differential confidence levels developed by girls and boys during the elementary years. While as early as the first three grades boys have been found to expect to do better than was warranted by their test scores and grades in arithmetic and girls worse. One study that controlled for race and class found the difference to be statistically significant in the white middle class, but not in the mixed black and white working class school studied. This research showed the strong influence of parents, discussed below. The middle class parents expected boys to be better at mathematics than girls; and the parents' expectations had a net influence on the boys' unwarranted optimism, and the girls' equally unwarranted pessimism, regarding their future arithmetic achievement (Entwhistle and Baker 1983, 208-209).

The influence of gender-role expectations, starting in the first four grades, is shown by a number of studies. In the ones focusing on early elementary grades, each sex consistently reports greater perceived competence in gender-role congruent activities; not surprisingly, boys in mathematics and sports, girls in reading and music (Eccles et al. 1993, 830). There is evidence that girls may have low confidence in math, but high confidence in verbal subjects; six- to eight-year-old girls perform at a higher level when a game is labeled "for girls," and boys when the same game is labeled "for boys"; and that labeling a traditionally masculine task as "feminine" or "neutral" causes sixth-grade girls to raise their expectations of, and to place a higher value on, success at the task (Skolnick 1982, 31). There is also evidence that females both expect to and actually do better at tasks defined as feminine, and males vice versa, even when the content of the task is neutral and unchanged (Mark 1983, 4). Boys in the early elementary grades are also under greater pressure to conform to their stereotypic gender role, and therefore have a strong incentive to perceive themselves as able in areas stereotyped as "masculine," such as mathematics (Eccles et al. 1993, 844). This helps to explain the discrepancy between their actual performance and their assessment and prediction of it.

At the high school level, where the significant differences in performance become more visible, the higher the level of mathematics the more being a good student changes in the direction of active exploration, risk-taking, rule-challenging, and away from one right answer towards multiple possible solutions. To be "good at math" at these higher levels requires attitudes and behaviors that fit boys' acquired style much better than girls' (Erickson and Schultz 1992, 477). To succeed, the latter would need not only to change their style, but change it to one that is not congruent with the "feminine" stereotype and hence causes discomfort.

> *"The difference between understanding and knowing is an enormous one ... So I am struggling with how much I can put into something in order to truly know it, i.e. be able to replicate, explain, know why, not just how. It's really hard, but there is so much in the math that can be so much more than just numbers."*
>
> —*journal of a high school girl quoted in Countryman, 1992*

It is noteworthy in this context that both girls and boys have been found to be more likely to omit problems with unfamiliar content on mathematics tests, and less likely to solve such problems correctly; and that in at least one study familiarity was correlated with stereotypical content for girls, though not for boys (AAUW 1992, 55).

That both girls and boys continue to use the style they acquired in elementary school is suggested by a small-scale study of the problem-solving strategies used by students who were in the top scoring group of SAT mathematics test-takers. Among these able math students, although there was substantial overlap in strategies used to solve the problems on the test, there was an important difference. Girls were more likely than boys to use algorithmic strategies, following rules or procedures; boys more likely to use insight and estimation (College Board 1992/93, 22). Among the able group of math students where the greatest gender differences in performance show up, girls clearly continue to lean more heavily than do boys on a style that has some draw-backs in higher level problem-solving.

It is unclear whether girls' slower, more deliberate working style might also be a factor in the performance gap at the higher levels, in leading them to leave the last, and most difficult, problems on a timed test unanswered through lack of time rather than lack of knowledge or ability.

Loss of confidence hits different racial and ethnic groups differently in high school. By the tenth grade, white and Hispanic girls, but not African-Americans, have been found to judge their own mathematics performance to be lower than did the boys in each group, even though their actual level of achievement was not different (Catsambis 1994, 210). African-American boys have been found, in some studies, to lose confidence in their own academic abilities more markedly than African American girls, starting in junior high; and the latter's high academic achievement-orientation to be braked in circumstances where they were competing with African-American boys (Madhere 1991, 58; Washington and Newman 1991, 24). Research in the independent school context, however, has found higher general self-esteem among African-American boys and girls both than among white students (Cookson 1991).

Lack of confidence is also demonstrated by the fact that more girls than boys report they are afraid to ask questions in math class, a gender difference that does not show up in other subjects, and does not hold true for African-American girls.

Given these attitudes, it is not surprising that by high school age, more boys than girls have decided to pursue math/science careers, with white boys being most likely to do so and Hispanic girls least. (The white boys were also the most likely to have engaged in extracurricular activities relevant to math/science.) The career-choice gender differential was consistent within each achievement level, each level of liking for mathematics, and in each socioeconomic group (Catsambis 1994, 205-207).

In evaluating these career-decisions, it needs to be taken into account that career potentials and earning incentives are greater for men than for women. The National Longitudinal Study of the High School Class of 1972 shows that the women averaged higher grades in college than men, including in statistics and in calculus. However, they found their opportunity for promotion in their firm, and for career advancement, less satisfactory than men (Adelman 1991). And, of course, their earnings continued to be lower as well.

It is important also to note that all the gender differences discussed throughout are statistical, and that there is a great deal of overlap between the genders, as well as both girls and boys whose beliefs, attitudes, interests, values, styles, and performance are counter-stereotypic. The same, of course, is true with regards to race and ethnicity.

*P*arents' beliefs about their children's mathematical competence, and the importance of the subject for them, play a significant part in the development of gender differences in students' attitudes toward mathematics, and their enrollment in mathematics courses.

A number of studies have shown that:

> - parents', and especially mothers', confidence in their children's math abilities has a greater impact on those children's confidence in their own math ability than do grades
> - parents widely believe that males have more math talent than females, and that math is harder for their daughters than their sons
> - those who have this belief tend to underestimate their daughters' and overestimate their sons' math talent, compared to the children's grades and performance on normed tests
> - parents' underestimation of their daughters' math ability does not coincide with any lack of confidence in their daughters' general academic ability
> - parents are more likely to attribute their sons' math successes to talent, and their daughters' to hard work
> - both parents commonly believe that math, especially advanced high school math, is more important for sons than daughters, and are in agreement that they would be more likely to encourage their sons to take advanced math courses
> - parental advice is noted by students as one of the most important influences on high school course decision making (Eccles 1987, 47-49)
> - parental expectations influence children's expectations of their own probable success (Entwhisle and Baker 1983)
> - white girls' parents, unlike Asian-American parents, support their daughters' decisions to avoid entering math and science competitions (National Coalition 1991)

One's own, and significant others', confidence in one's ability to do well in mathematics is clearly related to mathematics performance. Research evidence has shown a drop in confidence preceding a decline in achievement in girls in the middle-school years (AAUW 1992, 28). That the level of confidence is not, by itself, sufficient to explain gender differences in mathematics achievement is, however, suggested by the case of Asian-American students. As a group, Asian Americans consistently outperform those from other ethnic backgrounds on mathematics tests. Yet they have lower self-perception and lower confidence in their own math ability than do students from other racial/ethnic backgrounds, in spite of their higher levels of achievement (Whang and Hancock 1994). Other factors, then, can outweigh relatively low confidence levels.

*P*romote in-depth understanding, reduce anxiety that inhibits performance, and build students' confidence in their own mathematical ability, by doing some of the following:

- Add more activities to the curriculum at the lower grades to boost spatial skills for those who need it. Try informal activities such as making and experimenting with paper airplanes; identifying pairs of objects that could make similar shadows; making mobiles; and making pentominoes and predicting, then validating, which of them can be folded to make open boxes; as well as more formal activities, such as Cuisinaire rods (Skolnick 1982).
- Use hands-on activities, visual representations, and physical materials to build abstract concepts.
- Make it easier for students to build connections by giving a "bird's eye" overview of the subject matter to be covered (Tobias in Wood, 50).
- Help students towards independence as problem-solvers by having students read the book and do the problems before class discussion of the topic, as an alternative to the more traditional sequence of lecture followed by reading the book and doing the problems (an extensive research study found such a change improved girls' performance on coordinates, proof-taking and applications — perhaps because they had to put more intensive effort into working out themselves how to approach the problems) (AAUW 1992, 71).
- Ask students to keep a mathematics journal, keeping track both of how they have figured out ways of solving the mathematics problems they had to work with, and their feelings as they faced such work (Countryman in Wood 1993, 31).
- Make opportunities for, encourage, and reward "creative floundering."
- Have students, when appropriate, not only "show their work" on paper, but explain in words the reasons why they did what they did.
- Reward interesting approaches to solutions even when they do not lead to correct answers.
- Ask questions that do not have only one right answer.
- Have students check, and comment on, each others' homework. Occasionally, have the teacher check and comment on both homework and on the peer comments.
- Give open-ended questions and problems as homework and on tests.
- Give some open-book tests, rewarding understanding rather than memorization.
- Allow ample time to interact with material without formal evaluation, but ensure frequent feedback by self-checking or communication with peers or teachers.
- Encourage students to see errors as a natural and indeed indispensable part of the learning process, as feedback that shows what needs attention.
- Hold open-ended oral conferences to evaluate progress some of the time, instead of timed written tests.
- Ask students to reflect on the work being done in class by having them write periodically their answer to questions such as: What do you think were the main issues or points being made in this series of lessons? What was the muddiest issue in this week's work?
- Be alert to unintended messages in statements made. "There, there, don't feel bad, you've done your best," to console a child for having done poorly on a test is entirely well-intentioned — but sends a micro-message about ability. So does, more overtly though still with the best of intentions, "I'll be glad to give you extra help; I know girls often have trouble with numbers."
- Help both girls and boys to arrive at more realistic self-assessments.

- Speak to students out of class, or write them a note, praising them for doing especially well or having improved on tests, or in class participation.
- Counter students' self-denigrating statements such as "I'm dumb!" with "No, you have made several mistakes, which have helped you to know what you need to do next," or "I'm no good at this!" with "Look at your earlier tests and see how much better you are doing."
- Do all you can to discourage students from dropping out of, or choosing not to take, elective math courses "because I'm only getting a B (or a C...)."

*H*elp students become more aware of their own mental processes and more in control of their own learning; model a "think-aloud," letting them hear how you yourself work through a problem, as introduction to the following:

- Work one-on-one with a student as training for written test taking, having the student read each question aloud then tell you, step by step, what action he or she will take in response to the question. This allows the teacher to see exactly what the student's problems are, and to give appropriate help.
- Encourage students to verbalize, to each other or to themselves, saying what they are doing as they are doing it, when they are working problems.
- Encourage students to join together in out-of-class study groups. Have students write out, in complete sentences and without using any numbers or mathematical symbols, how they arrived at their answer.
- Use several diagnostic written tests, graded but without the grade "counting" towards the eventual recorded grade, before giving a final evaluative test with a grade that counts.
- Have students correct, and grade, their own or a peer's diagnostic test, asking them to explain in writing their reasons for the evaluation they gave.
- Help students feel more in control of their own learning by giving them choices on tests ("Do any five of the following eight problems?") and some say in whether they are ready to take the test.
- Have students, individually or collaboratively, in class or for homework, construct quiz and test questions; use the good ones for review and in diagnostic testing.
- Reconsider the frequency of "extra credit" questions that benefit only the elite few.
- Give some evaluative tests that are untimed.
- Consider alternatives to grading on a curve, which evaluates students' performance relative to that of another, rather than relative to a standard set as the one to be reached, or improvement relative to student's own previous work.
- Have students keep all their quizzes, tests, and journals, and assign them the task periodically of reviewing their past work and writing down what consistencies and changes they see.
- Ask students periodically for anonymous written feedback on what they like, do not like, and wish were different about the course and the class.

*B*uild on the known connection between discussion and deepening understanding, and girls' favorable response to cooperative, boys' to competitive classroom activities, by some of the following:

- Monitor the balance between competitive and collaborative activities. (For information on collaborative learning, see Slavin 1983; Slavin 1987; Fiske 1991, 81-86.)
- Be alert to the fact that group-work does not necessarily improve math achievement, and that some research suggests not only that competitive activities have some detrimental influence on girls' math achievement, but that cooperative activities have some detrimental influence on boys', at least at the elementary level (Fennema 1993, 22; Fennema and Leder 1990, 136).
- Combine cooperative and competitive styles by having teams rather than individuals compete.
- Consider alerting students to potential collaborative problems due to gender differences in communication styles, by discussing with them the differences and likely misunderstandings noted in the section on **CROSSCURRENTS IN COMMUNICATION**, page 16.
- Consider using pairs, perhaps occasionally single-sex or same ethnicity, to solve problems in collaboration; have pairs share both solutions and explanations of their methods.
- Before starting group work, give students some training in small group process, to enhance chances of success.
- Observe group interaction for balance in help asked and help given, and for help asked in non-specific ways indicating merely general confusion. (Some junior high studies found boys, among high-ability white middle class students, consistently unresponsive to requests for math help couched in non-specific terms in group work, while girls were very likely to ask.) Give help in pinning down the problem: "I can't tell where to put the brackets," rather than "I don't know what to do" (Webb and Kendersky 1985).
- Balance diversity in working groups (gender, ability, race, ethnicity, class) with occasional homogeneity (all-friends, all-girl, all-black, all-high-performing); and student choice with carefully teacher-chosen group membership.
- Be alert to the advantages and the disadvantages of both homogeneous and deliberately diverse groupings.
- Balance the benefits of leaving the same people in a working group for a considerable time, to allow them to become familiar with each other and build trust, with the benefits of exposing students to different personalities, styles of working, and group dynamics by shifting group membership.
- Have students working in a small group take turns explaining, helping the one explaining, keeping notes, and questioning the ones explaining; and ask them to debrief each round, identifying what behaviors they will try to improve on the next round.
- Have teams take turns — group A designing problems for group B to solve and group C evaluating both A's problems and B's solutions.
- Look for opportunities for "jigsaw" assignments, in which each member of the group is given part of the information needed to solve the problem assigned.
- Encourage the formation of study groups to work together on out-of-class homework assignments.
- Work one-on-one with students specially resistant to collaborative styles, often because it does not fit their "cool," "tough," or "macho" image of how they think they ought to be.

*R*educe perception of mathematics as a "white male" field, and provide role models, by some of the following:

- Do not schedule single-section elective advanced math courses in the same slot as single section elective courses typically popular with girls.
- Inform students about career-opportunities in math-related fields.
- Give information about fields of college study, and employment opportunities, where students might not realize mathematics is important.
- Invite alumni/ae of diverse racial/ethnic backgrounds now majoring in mathematics, or working in a mathematical or technical field, to address the school community and talk with interested students.
- Include the work of women mathematicians in the curriculum (many ways of doing so are presented in Perl 1978), and inform students about other outstanding women/minority mathematicians whose work does not fit the curriculum.
- Use word problems, and real-life data for graphing and statistics, the vocabulary and subject matter of which includes/is of interest to both genders and to students of different backgrounds.
- Arrange a lunch for girls in Algebra I to meet with girls taking Calculus to talk about their experiences with and feelings about mathematics.
- Ask older girls in honors or advanced placement courses to talk to boys and girls at lower levels about strategies useful in the subject, or to tutor younger students with difficulties.
- Invite women and minority mathematicians to visit classes and as speakers at assemblies.
- Collaborate with the English department in assigning students essays on mathematical topics.
- Communicate to parents, collectively, individually, orally and in writing, the importance to their daughters as well as their sons of mathematics.

*H*elp parents to support and encourage both their daughters and sons in mathematics by some of the following:

- Hold a Path to Math night periodically, to explain to parents what their children are doing in their math class, and what parents can do at home to help.
- Have math resources in your library that you encourage parents to take out.
- Offer a math workshop to parents occasionally on something like Venn diagrams or Fibonacci numbers or statistics, to spark their interest and defuse their discomfort with math.
- Offer mother-daughter workshops in math.

(The above suggestions draw on information from Ginorio 1995; Sanders 1994; *Independent School* Fall 1994; Chapman 1993; Countryman 1992; Garibaldi 1992; National Coalition 1991; Tobias 1988; Shanker 1988; Webb and Kenderski 1985; Skolnick 1982.)

## RESOURCES

Note: Items marked **(P)** are especially recommended for parents.

Burns, Marilyn. *Math for Smarty Pants*. Boston: Little, Brown, 1982.
Stories, activities, problem solving. Grades 4-8. **(P)**

Campbell, Patricia. *Math, Science, and Your Daughter: What Can Parents Do?* Undated brochure, available from Campbell-Kibler Associates, Groton Ridge Heights, Groton, MA 01450, or call WEEA Publishing Center at (800) 225-3088. **(P)**
Highly readable and strategy oriented, recent research-based information on what works in math and science programming for girls.

Edeen, J. and S. and V. Slachman, *Portraits for Classroom Bulletin Boards: Women Mathematicians*. Palo Alto, CA: Dale Seymour Publications, 1990.

Clewell, Beatriz Chu, et al. *Breaking the Barriers*. San Francisco: Jossey-Bass, 1992.

Clewell, Beatriz Chu et al. *Intervention Programs in Math, Science, and Computer Science for Minority and Female Students in Grades Four through Eight*. Princeton, NJ: Educational Testing Service, 1987.

Countryman, Joan. 1992. *Writing to Learn Mathematics*. New Hampshire: Heinemann, 1992.

Kaseberg, A., N. Kreinberg and D. Downie. *Use EQUALS to Promote the Participation of Women in Mathematics*. Berkeley, CA : University of California Math/science network, 1980. **(P)**
A classic. Teacher training, and sampling of strategy games, spatial activities, and logic problems targeted to raising confidence and interest in mathematics.

National Coalition of Girls' Schools. *Math and Science for Girls*. Concord, MA: NCGS, 1992. For information call (508) 369-1484.
Easy-to-absorb summary of research and suggestions on how to use it in curriculum and classroom; activities; extensive lists of resources.

Ohanian, Susan. *Garbage Pizza, Patchwork Quilts and Math Magic: Stories about Teachers Who Love to Teach And Children Who Love to Learn*. New York: W.H. Freeman, 1992. **(P)**
First-hand account of innovative, problem-solving oriented, highly effective mathematics teaching in many K-3 classes. Some are very detailed, running to several pages and quoting what teacher and students said; others are summaries encapsulating approaches, ideas, or replicable suggestions. Reproductions of chidren's work. Heartening and useful, with short sections for administrators and parents. Recommended for high interest and versatility.

*Outstanding Women in Mathematics and Science* (picture series). From National Women's History Projects, 7738 Bell Road, Windsor, CA 95492; (707) 836-6000.

Parker, Marla, ed. *She Does Math! Real-Life Problems from Women on the Job*. Washington, D.C. : Mathematical Association of America, 1995. For information call (800) 331-1MAA. **(P)**
Presents brief career histories of thirty-eight professional women, including how much math they took in high school and college, how they chose their field and ended up in their current job; and several math problems typical of those they meet on the job. Subjects of the problems are Algebra, Geometry, Trigonometry, Calculus, Statistics, Physics, Chemistry, Computer Science, Health Sciences, and Business, among others. High School; worth checking for middle school/junior high. Recommended for its "real-life" flavor and innovative approach.

Perl, Teri. *Women and Numbers*. San Carlos, CA: World Wide Publishing, 1993.

Perl, Teri. *Math Equals: Biographies of Women Mathematicians and Related Activities*. Menlo Park, CA: Addison-Wesley, 1978. *(P)*

Readable account of lives and work of nine women mathematicians, and mathematical activities related to the work of each, accessible to those with elementary school mathematics and geometry. Junior/senior high. Recommended for mathematical as well as historical interest.

Sanders, Jo. *Lifting the Barriers: 600 Tested Strategies that Really Work to Increase Girls' Participation in Science, Mathematics and Computers* 1994. Available from Jo Sanders, P.O. Box 483, Port Washington, N.Y. 11050; (212) 642-2672. *(P)*

List of resources, including conferences, in-service training programs, and publications. Recommended for wealth of very specific, snappy, simple suggestions.

Secada, W.S., Elizabeth Fennema, and L. Byrd. *New Directions for Equity in Mathematics Education*. Cambridge: Cambridge University Press, 1993.

Women's Educational Equity Act Publishing Center. *Add- ventures for Girls: Building Math Confidence*. Available from Education Development Center Inc., 55 Chapel Street, Newton, MA 02160; (800) 225-3088. *(P)*

Elementary and middle-school activities in separate volumes. Other math-related items available; ask for catalog.

Women's Educational Equity Act Publishing Center. *Spatial encounters. (P)* (See address above.)

Exercises in spatial awareness that combine fun and learning, with emphasis on real-world applications. K-12 to adults. Recommended for joint parent-child projects.

Woodrow Wilson National Fellowship Foundation. *Woodrow Wilson Gender Equity in Mathematics and Science Congress*, 1993. Princeton, NJ: Princeton University. For information call (609) 452-7007.

Comprehensive information on current research, many suggestions for classroom ctivities, extensive bibliography and resource lists, including organizations,programs, and institutes for both students and teachers. Recommended as teacher resource.

■ ■ ■ ■

## CHAPTER NINE

## ARTS

> *Beauty is in the eye of the beholder.*
>
> —*Margaret Wolfe Hungerford, 1878*

The new scholarship on women and gender has been gradually incorporated in arts courses in a variety of ways. In general, doing so has made arts instruction both more inclusive and more critical. Greater inclusiveness has resulted in more frequent and more in-depth consideration of not only the elite arts of high culture, but also of decorative arts, crafts, folk, and popular art, and of non-Western artistic expressions as well. Within each of these, greater efforts have been made to include and analyze both women artists' creations and the depiction of women in the arts.

This more critical stance has resulted in the examination of changes in the criteria of artistic excellence, and a questioning of how the criteria themselves are developed and applied. Another area of interest has been the examination of the image and the place of the arts in both the broader society and in the school community itself.

**The following avenues have been followed to various extents in different courses by teachers of diverse interests and instructional aims:**

- ➤ Study of women artists' work, and that of people of color and non-Western peoples, in various genres and styles, and their inclusion in chronological and stylistic surveys on the basis of their artistic merit

- ➤ Investigation of women (and others) as the subject matter of art. This approach can lead to consideration of the kinds of images presented in the arts of women, men, and "out groups" (racial, ethnic, occupational, religious, cultural, and other) during various periods; the role of the arts as reflecting, maintaining, promoting, or creating stereotypes; the relation between the arts and ideology; and the results of art's functioning as a reflection and expression, or critique and transformer, of the wider culture.

- ➤ Exploration of what the standards of artistic excellence are, how they are known, how and by whom they are set, how they have changed, and in what ways they may be culture-bound

- ➤ Discussion of the bases on which some art forms and genres are considered more significant than others; and reasons for, as well as results of, such rank-ordering (Needlework and textiles, for instance, consistently important avenues of artistic expression for women, have traditionally hardly even been considered "art," although they anticipated subsequently recognized artistic approaches such as collage, geometric abstraction, and optical illusion.)

- ➤ Broadening the concept of "art" to include decorative arts, design, and crafts, areas in which women and non-elite groups have been more active (quilts and Native-American pottery), leading to multicultural and cross-cultural appreciation as well as additional criteria of critical analysis

- ➤ Broadening the scope of visual literacy to include how formal elements such as color, line, placement, space are used to create a common visual system, the claim of which to represent reality accurately needs investigation (This includes developing students' interpretive skills and competence in understanding pictorial conventions, and how images make meanings. both in the traditional arts and in mass media such as advertising or videos.)

➤ Consideration of the process of becoming an artist, and how differences in women's and men's experiences and opportunities have influenced their themes, styles, and the media and genres they have worked in

➤ Investigation of the historical and socio-cultural contexts in which art has been, and is, created and viewed, leading to: exploration of the different meanings brought to the creation and appreciation of arts by those of different backgrounds—chronologically, geographically, socio-economically, culturally, and psychologically; investigation of the effects on the arts of the institutions that teach, fund, exhibit, promote the arts and of the ways in which they have worked to include or exclude various kinds of art and various groups of artists; and examination of the potential social and political agendas at work in particular images and the settings in which they are presented

➤ Alertness to the choice of period and genre (While not decisive in making the choice of what to teach, it should be remembered that some choices permit more varied critical approaches, and greater inclusiveness, than others.)

➤ Realization that very traditional periods and themes can be reconceptualized in interesting ways (A study of the Renaissance, for instance, can include the impact of the new, theoretical status granted to painting, sculpture, and architecture not only on the kinds of arts created, but on who could create art.)

*I*t is important to recognize that art education in many schools suffers from its feminine identification. It is often not included among the academic disciplines, is considered a "soft" and easy option, a permissive and undemanding refuge from work in other courses. Art is often a loser in the battle for students' time when the need for drama rehearsals or music practice is pitted against the need for athletic practices. It may be taught by a part-time teacher, who is, without special efforts to avoid it, likely to remain peripheral to the school community with low visibility and little or no participation in decision making. In lower and middle school, art is often taught by grade-school teachers, whose expertise, since they are not "specialists," may not be taken seriously.

Schools should recognize that the art department is often taken for granted as a provider of domestic services to the institution, expected to decorate the school for holidays, do lettering, programs, and posters — whether or not such services are congruent with the demands of the discipline.

Art may be considered to have emotional rather than intellectual worth, as a way to help young students build self-confidence since there are no "errors" possible, and thus discontinuous with skills-and-concepts-oriented university level instruction. On the other hand, art education in some schools suffers from being too successful in avoiding any "feminine" characteristics, resulting in an overly academic orientation that teaches about art at the expense of involving students in *creating* art, and engages in tough and competitive grading.

Art education often parallels the conceptual passing of a child from the female-identified, nurturing lower and middle school (where teachers are in fact overwhelmingly women) to the "tougher," male-identified high school, with its higher proportion of male teachers. What message does this send to students?

All the above insights and alternatives have implications for the arts program, and suggest possible ways of rethinking arts courses.

(Sources for this section were Collins 1995; Wolfe and McNally 1994; Lauter 1993; Blaikie 1992; Haskell 1989; Neuls-Bates 1982; Hedges and Wendt 1980; Harris and Nochlin 1977)

# What Schools and Teachers Can Do

*S*chools can maintain appropriately the intellectual integrity of creative arts, and counteract both overly "feminine" and overly "masculine" perceptions and characteristics of the arts program by considering some of the following:

- Offer (some) arts courses that build on each other, for which lower levels are prerequisites to the higher, on the pattern of language or mathematics courses.
- Institute Advanced Placement arts courses.
- Make sure there are at least some full-time faculty in the arts department.
- Investigate the feasibility and possible benefits of introducing arts requirements, if there are currently none.
- When writing comments, advisor letters, or talking with parents about students in the arts, be specific about the skills and competencies they are acquiring.
- Encourage collaboration between arts and the other disciplines/departments: mathematics and music, visual arts and computer science, drama and English, dance and athletics, all the arts and history. Bring in guests from those departments to talk to students, and offer to guest-lecture or run a one-class (or longer) workshop in your specialty in appropriate other courses; refer to those other subjects in your own work with students, and inform colleagues about information from arts disciplines that they could use in their own work.
- Encourage collaborative artwork by students. Have them work on murals, quilts, and collaborative sculpture.
- Create more opportunities for interdisciplinary arts endeavors such as musicals; involve students from visual arts in designing, building, and painting the sets, as well as those from music, drama, and dance in the performance.

*T*o support both boys' and girls' participation in all aspects of the arts program consider doing the following:

- Encourage full student attendance at visual arts exhibits (consider holding a proper opening, with a reception), as well as at dance, music, and dramatic performances, as vigorously as attendance is encouraged for athletic events.
- Give as high visibility in school publicity efforts to the arts as to athletics and academics.
- Invite both male and female artists as guest speakers at assemblies and other public events.
- Support and encourage the participation of boys in drama and dance; point out to football players the benefits of the bodily skills developed in dance, and to those aspiring to careers in politics and business, of training in dramatic skills.
- Teach about women's as well as men's art, not only to provide role models for girls but to expose both boys and girls to a fuller spectrum of artistic possibilities and achievements.

*U*se the following curriculum units as springboards to develop your own ways that some of the ideas above may be used in schools:

### 1. HELP STUDENTS LEARN ABOUT WOMEN ARTISTS AND THEIR WORK.

➤ **A. Study women artists** (or African American, Asian American, Native American, or others artists) at a local museum. Have students select some about whom enough information can be generated, and produce an informative booklet about them and their work that other students could use as a resource when visiting the museum. This activity combines art, language arts, and social studies, and has resulted in students' increased awareness and appreciation of women and/or non-elite artists and some of the challenges they faced in becoming accomplished and recognized as professional artists. It has been shown to be successful with fourth graders, and could be adapted for higher grades.

➤ **B. Investigate the degree to which women's art is influenced by gender.** Start with a class or small group discussion on the topic, resulting in students' prediction about whether, how much, and what kind(s) of differences there might be between the work produced by female and male artists. (With older students, consider introducing the variables of time, place, and class into the discussion.)

Present students with an exhibition of reproductions, without identification, of artwork by both male and female artists, trying to find "matches" in style and period, such as Mary Cassatt and Edgar Degas or the constructions of Lee Bontecou and mobiles of Alexander Calder. After students have viewed the exhibits, ask them to determine for each whether the artist was a woman or a man, and record their guesses anonymously on slips of paper.

As variations you could:

- Ask students to discuss the reasons for their choices before tallying and revealing the results, and the actual gender of the artists. Afterwards, discuss the influence of culture-bound expectations on both artists and audiences. Students may also create a gallery of their own artwork, unsigned, and try to identify which were done by girls or boys, or have another class make the guesses, again followed by discussion. (I am indebted to Ann Foreman and Mary Howe, lower school art teachers in 1988 at Hathaway Brown School in Cleveland, Ohio, for the above suggestions.)

- Have students study forms of artistic expression by women (and/or various racial/ethnic/cultural groups) in the United States through reproductions; look for similarities/differences of themes, subject matter, and of artistic style such as the use of color, texture, form, line, and symbols.

- Share with students, or let them research, what countries and cultures have influenced American music. Discuss artistic differences in the various kinds of music, teach students about women and men who have been great performers in the various traditions, and teach them to sing songs from them (McCormick 1994, 95).

### 2. ALERT STUDENTS TO GENDER MESSAGES IMPLICIT IN MEDIA, AND OTHER, IMAGES.

**Ask students to collect advertisements** showing women and men from a variety of print media, making sure that both those pitched to women and men are included (Field and Stream as well as Ladies Home Journal), noting on each the source. Pool the students' finds and separate them into male and female images. Group, within each category, those images that seem to be sending the same message about the women/men depicted. Ask students to determine what the predominant messages about each gender are, according to the pictorial representations collected, and compare the messages about each gender.

The exercise can be taken further. If men/women are portrayed differently to a male and a female audience, ask which representations, if any, are in conflict with, or exaggerations of, reality; collect "museum art" representations, perhaps divided into periods, to see if gender differences in depiction exist, if, so, what they are, and whether there have been changes over time; or do a similar exercise with TV commercials, or TV shows such as soap operas or sitcoms. This exercise can be adapted to any age-group.

### 3. HELP STUDENTS UNDERSTAND ALTERNATIVE VIEWS OF AESTHETICS AND THE ARTS THAT ARE GENDER-ASSOCIATED, BUT NOT MUTUALLY EXCLUSIVE.

Give students the two sets of descriptions provided below, presented in a way that allows viewing them side by side. Make sure, through class discussion, that everyone understands both views clearly. Then ask students to come up with what they consider to be positive, and what negative, features of each view, and to explain their reasons for their assessment.

Follow by asking students to consider themselves, and their own views about art. Do they approximate one or the other? Which? What features of the less-favored view do they nevertheless find attractive? Which features of their more-favored one are problematic? Why?

If they had to, for their own lives, pick one or the other in its entirely, which would they pick? Why? Would their opinion change if they were to decide on a career as a professional artist? Which view comes closer to approximating their current creative output?

If they wanted to create the most favorable climate for producing the art that would be most desirable for humanity, which view do they think would better promote it? What composite view, combining features from both views, would they consider to be optimum? Why? How did they decide on what art would be "most desirable for humanity"? This exercise is most suitable for eleventh and twelfth graders, but it could be adapted for younger ages.

## View One

1. Art is defined in terms of formal properties, qualities and principles.
2. "Art" is clearly separate from "non-art."
3. Forms and objects of art are ranked in a hierarchical order. Those least useful to daily life are most highly valued.
4. Aesthetic values are completely divorced from moral values.
5. Good art meets standards of excellence established by trained taste setters (critics, scholars).
6. The artist is a maker of forms equal to or more important than nature, and independent of culture.
7. The artist learns the specific techniques of one, or a few closely related, media through formal education, and apprenticeship with a master.
8. The artist seeks to develop an individual stamp on works created, so it is immediately distinguishable from works by others; but wishes to nullify any relationship between personal life and the art produced, in order to make the latter "universal."
9. The audience's task is to appreciate the work of art as a thing in itself, having used the correct standards to ensure that it is indeed "art," and having established the category it belongs to (epic poem or lyric; post-impressionist, or surrealist, etc.) Time should be set aside from daily life to take in art, once the ability correctly to respond to it has been cultivated.
10. The professional has additional responsibilities in encounters with art: works are to be compared, evaluated according to their relative success or failure according to the established standards for their category, and likes and dislikes set aside in favor of an objective, impersonal assessment.

## View Two

1. Art is identified through exemplars and models instead of trying to define it.
2. Boundaries between "art" and "not-art" are identifiable but can change, and may depend on context.
3. Art's value depends on the degree that it is able to increase the sense of life in its creator(s) and audience(s).
4. Aesthetic values have a moral component.
5. Good art reaches beyond its society of origin to suggest alternative ways of being.
6. The artist creates within an interactive system that includes both nature and culture.
7. The artist learns techniques in any one or more of several possible ways — including formal education, craft tradition, apprenticeship, and self-teaching.
8. The artist may work in collaboration with others, and the artwork is assumed to reflect and interact with the values of a particular culture; the aim is production not of a highly individual, but rather of an authentic work.
9. The audience tries to understand the work of art in relation to its cultural setting, rather than defining it or setting it into categories; fullest response to it involves not only aesthetic, but religious, political, and social sensitivity, which may come from education or experience.
10. The professional has the additional responsibility of interpreting works of art to those who do not belong to the artist's community of origin, so they can more fully appreciate it; and to evaluate art according to its potential to empower people to live more effective, moral, and satisfying lives. Since objectivity is impossible, likes and dislikes should be declared up front, so those being informed about the work of art can take them into account.

(The two views were distilled from information in Lauter 1993, 31-32).

## RESOURCES

Baker, G. *Teaching Strategies for Music. Planning and Organizing for Multicultural Instruction*. Reading, MA: Addison-Wesley, 1985.

Blood-Patterson, P. ed. *Rise up Singing.* Bethlehem, PA: Sing Out Corporation, 1988.

Collins, Georgia and Sandell, Renee. *Women, Art, and Education*. Reston, VA: National Art Education Association, 1984.

Epstein, Vivian Sheldon. *History of Women Artists for Children*. Denver: VSE Publisher, 1987.
Thirty women artists from the 16th century to the present, discussed with historical context. For elementary level.

Goffman, Erving. *Gender Advertisements*. New York: Harper and Row, 1976.
A classic and subtle analysis of what signals are sent about gender, and how, by the visual images represented by advertisements. The categories of analysis could be applied to other visual media. Great abundance of pictures useable with younger children; text is teacher background and able high school level.

Hedges, Elaine and Ingrid Wendt, eds. *In Her Own Image: Women Working in the Arts*. New York: The Feminist Press, 1980.
Presents the work of Western women artists in sculpture, painting, graphics, photography, ceramics, needlework, music, and dance as well as in various literary genres. Explores relationships between women's social condition and their art, as well as the experience of women artists from diverse national, ethnic, racial and economic backgrounds from their own viewpoints. Usable with high school and selectively earlier.

Jezic, Diane Peacock. *Women Composers: The Lost Tradition Found*, 2nd ed. New York: The Feminist Press, 1989.
Musical and biographical material about twenty-five composers from the eleventh to the twentieth centuries, discussed in the context of traditional music history and analyzed for information on what conditions it takes for a woman to be a composer and for her works to survive. Set in broader context of teaching about women and music. Listing of available scores and recordings.

Kilbourne, Jean. "Killing Us Softly: Advertising's Image of Women," and its updated sequel " Still Killing Us Softly." Cambridge Documentary Films, Box 385, Cambridge, MA 02139; (617) 354-3677.
This twenty-nine minute color film/video is a sure-fire discussion starter. Best to preview it before presenting to students.

Lauter, Estella. "Re-enfranchising Art: Feminist Interventions in the Theory of Art." In Hein and Korsmeyer, eds., *Aesthetics in Feminist Perspective*. Bloomington: Indiana University Press, 1993.
A reasonably clear, brief, concise, accessible, and well-balanced explanation of basic concepts in feminist art criticism, not easily found elsewhere.

*National Museum of Women in the Arts Catalog*. New York: Harry N. Abrams, Inc., 1987.
Brief biographical information about the artists with works in the collection, and both color and black and white reproductions of their work.

Neuls-Bates, Carol, ed. *Women in Music: An Anthology of Source Readings from the Middle Ages to the Present*. New York: Harper & Row, 1982.
Letters, diaries, autobiographies, interviews, reviews of both notable and lesser-known composers, performers, patrons, and educators. Most selections accessible to competent high school readers.

Organized Against Sexism and Institutionalized Stereotypes (OASIS). "Stale Roles and Tight Buns: Images of Men in Advertising." From OASIS, 15 Willoughby Street, Brighton, MA 02135; (617) 782-7774.

Videotape and slide show, paralleling the Kilbourne one on women listed above.

Pendle, Karin, ed. *Women and Music: A History*. Bloomington: Indiana University Press, 1991.

Women's contributions to performance, composition, patronage from antiquity to present; discussion of feminist aesthetics, lots of musical examples readily available in scores and recordings. Sections on women in popular music and jazz, and in non-Western music. Grades 9-adult.

Rubenstein, Charlotte Streifer. *American Women Artists from Early Indian Times to the Present*. New York: Avon, 1982.

Relation of women's art to their social and cultural circumstances in discussions of period, style, and genre. Biographical information; description and evaluation of works, including excerpts by the artists and their critics; significant representation of women of color. Two hundred and thirty-five crisp black-and-white and forty-nine color illustrations. High school seniors could tackle the reading.

Sills, Leslie. *Inspirations: Stories about Women Artists*. Morton Grove IL: A. Whitman, 1989.

Views lives of O'Keeffe, Kahlo, Neel, and Ringgold through the works of art they produced. Lots of high-quality color reproductions. Grades 4-10.

Stolz, Mary. *The Noonday Friends*. New York: Harper and Row, 1965.

A juvenile novel that illustrates the difficulty one man has in providing for his family and also become established as an artist. A good basis for comparing with the problems faced by women in similar circumstances. Can be read aloud with 4th graders.

Waller, Susan. *Women Artists in the Modern Era: A Documentary History*. Metuchen, NJ: Scarecrow Press. 1991.

Selections from sixty-one primary source documents: artists' letters, journals, and memoirs; critics' reviews; and reports of artists' societies and schools, from mid-eighteenth to mid-twentiethth centuries in the U.S. and Europe. Includes the famous such as Vigee-Lebrun, Kaufmann, Bonheur, Bashkirtseff, Hepworth, as well as amateur artists and women in ceramics and textiles. This press will allow teachers to order the book and keep it for thirty days to see if it's what they need; then either pay, or return the book in salable-as-new condition, with no charge. For a catalog call (800) 537-7107 or (908) 548-8600.

■ ■ ■ ■

## CHAPTER TEN

## COMPUTERS

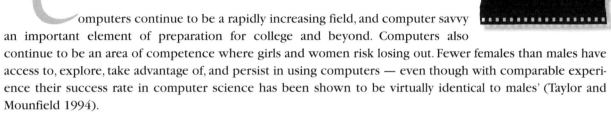

*This is the Space Child with Brow Serene*
*Who pushed the Button to Start the Machine*
*That made with the Cybernetics and Stuff*
*Without Confusion ...*

*—Anonymous, c. 1980*

Computers continue to be a rapidly increasing field, and computer savvy an important element of preparation for college and beyond. Computers also continue to be an area of competence where girls and women risk losing out. Fewer females than males have access to, explore, take advantage of, and persist in using computers — even though with comparable experience their success rate in computer science has been shown to be virtually identical to males' (Taylor and Mounfield 1994).

In 1994, more than twice as many boys than girls nationwide planned on taking advanced placement in college in computer science, and almost three times as many boys than girls gave computer/information sciences as their intended college major. This, although about the same proportion had taken computer math course work in school, and the kinds of course work taken — programming, data and word processing, and math, science, English course use — was also very similar (The College Board SAT, 1994, 2,5,8). That computer specialization was already associated with males in high school is suggested by the fact that four times as many boys than girls took the 1994 lower level computer science advanced placement test, and seven times as many the higher level one (The College Board AP 1994, 13). These were the biggest imbalances among all AP subjects.

The incidence of computer use by girls in school settings varies, but still lags behind use by boys. In K-6 schools, a 1991 survey found the percentage of computer users who were girls varied as much as 30 percent to 50 percent. More importantly, girls' attitudes towards technology, including computers, continue to differ from boys' in ways that are to the females' disadvantage.

The identification of computers as mathematics-related "masculine" number-crunching machines has decreased substantially, but overtones of earlier perceptions linger. The image of those really good with computers continues to be that of the virtuoso male "hackers" or "computer jocks," brainy, eccentric, single-minded, solitary, even antisocial, who spend their days and nights on the computer. This is not an image with which girls, and some boys, find it easy to identify.

Girls' approach to computer use is typically the same as that discussed in the section on mathematics: girls tend to do it by the rules, to get a particular job done, rely on others for help when stuck, and are anxious about the possibility of doing something wrong and even of harming the machine by misusing it. They use computers for homework about one third more often than do boys (Lazarus and Lipper 1994, 12).

Boys tend much more to "mess around" with a computer to see what they can make it do. They waste a lot of time, and run into many dead ends, but they acquire a lot of know-how and confidence in the process. Boys also have the advantage of bringing early extracurricular experiences of tinkering with mechanical and electrical devices to their work with computers that girls typically lack.

> *"[In a roomful of machines] she played with everything and it got broke. They came in and rescued her and she paid for everything by earning the money and mother helped out."*
> *—a 12-year old girl's invented story about technology, related in Bank Street, 1991*

$M$uch competence in computer operation comes from the use of computer games. In the early 1990s, 85 percent of computer game users were boys, and video games for home computer use are overwhelmingly marketed to boys. Although there have been some positive changes, most of these games are heavily male-stereotypic. Moreover, they feed into a very narrow band of the male stereotype: aggression. Because of the heavy doses of violence the games use to engage interest, they are detrimental to boys in the male behavior they model. They are also detrimental to girls, for whom violence runs counter to their gender-role socialization and therefore has less appeal. Girls' lack of interest in computer games can serve as a brake on their participation in the computer culture.

Males are more involved in other than game aspects of computers as well. They are more likely to use computers in idiosyncratic, self-initiated ways: doing unguided exploration, fooling around with programs to see what they can be made to do, joining computer clubs (Taylor and Mounfield 1994, 293). They are 85 percent of people using the Internet and other on-line services, and 69 percent of those who are home-users of on-line services (Lazarus and Lipper 1994, 12).

In elementary schools where computer use is mandated, there is no significant difference in girls' and boys' abilities with computers. It is during high school, when computer courses are largely elective, that girls' interest in, and use of, computers declines. Fewer girls than boys participate in computer courses and activities. Moreover, among those who choose to do so, a higher proportion of girls than boys drop out, so much so that gender by itself has been found to be a significant predictor of persistence in computing. In college and graduate school, the gender gap continues to widen. Men report higher use of computers in word processing, statistical analysis, and electronic mail. In the workplace, the kind of work done with computers has become gendered. Work in factories microwiring computers and in offices entering data is done largely by women; designing new hardware/ software, and programming, are done largely by men (Lazarus and Lipper 1994, 12; Taylor and Mounfield 1994, 293; Lorber 1994, 50, 208; Mundorf et al. 1992, 172).

In addition to attitudinal, performance, and usage differences, girls also just plain have less access to computers than boys. Studies in the mid-to-late 1980's found boys more than girls had the use of a computer at home or at a friend's house. Among students who had not yet received computer instruction at school, 64 percent of boys and 28 percent of girls reported knowing how to work with computers. Boys were also three times more likely to be enrolled in computer camps and summer programs (Levin and Gordon 1989; Chen 1986; Miura and Hess 1984). In the 1990s, males have continued more likely to have access to, and use, computers at home, and to have more computers with modems (Quoted in Taylor and Mounfield 1994; also Lazarus and Lipper 1994, 12).

The lower precollege participation of girls in computer courses and activities is greatly to their disadvantage, both in terms of their performance in college computer courses and as career possibilities. Recent research shows that, for girls, any prior experience with computers improved their chances of success in a college computer course, and that prior ownership of a computer was a significant predictor of success for both girls and boys. Whatever promotes comfort, feelings of competence and of self-confidence for girls in computer environments (all of which experience can do), improves their performance (Taylor and Mounfield 1994, 303).

One analysis of the variables that influenced access and use of computers in schools suggested that among a number of other factors, the commitment to equity of administrators and coordinators was significant(Bohlin 1993, 157).

To make computers accessible to both girls and boys, consider doing some of the following:

- House the computers outside the math department, or decentralize them altogether.
- Make clear to students the importance of computer know-how in diverse fields of knowledge and in various careers.
- Consider the language used when talking about computers. For instance, "giving commands to the computer" sends a different message, creates different mental pictures, and sets up different expectations, than does "choosing from a menu," whose implications are more female-user friendly.
- Have students use desktop publishing software to produce stories written on computer in English class.
- Have students post their reactions to class analyses of readings in English, foreign language, and other classes on a computer forum, and respond to each others' comments the same way.
- Encourage out-of-class use by everyone by requiring that (some) homework be done on computer.
- In teaching programming, be alert to the kinds of subject matter that the programs are written for.
- Teach LOGO or PILOT instead of the more mathematically oriented BASIC.
- Widen applications by encouraging desktop publishing, computer art and music, and record keeping involving the construction of databases and spreadsheets for extracurricular activities.
- Before buying, evaluate software for female as well as male student appeal and for gender stereotyping.
- Address game playing, which heavily attracts boys and tends to exclude girls.
- Pair teams of an older girl and boy with a younger girl and boy to teach the latter computer use or new applications.
- If access is an issue, pair boys and girls, and have them take turns at the keyboard; and/or use a sign-up system.
- Involve parents, especially mothers, whose own computer avoidance is a detrimental model for girls.
- Promote advanced computer training for girls as well as boys with parents.

(Information in this section is based on Sanders 1994; Brunner and Honey 1992; Bitter 1992; Bank Street 1991; Clayborne 1991; Sutton 1991; Kramer and Lehman 1990.)

**RESOURCES**

*Debugging the Program: Computer Equity Strategies for the Classroom Teacher* Project on Equal Education Rights, 99 Hudson Street, 12th floor, New York, NY 10013. (212) 925-6635.

*IDEAS for Equitable Computer Learning.* Center for Educational Equity, American Institutes for Research, PO Box 1113, Palo Alto, CA 94302. (415) 493-3550.

*The Neuter Computer: Computers for Girls and Boys.* Women's Action Alliance, 370 Lexington Avenue, Room 603, New York, NY 10017. (212) 532-8330.

Sanders, Jo. *Lifting the Barriers: 600 Tested Strategies that Really Work to Increase Girls' Participation in Science, Mathematics and Computers.* 1994. From Jo Sanders, P.O. Box 483, Port Washington, NY 11050. (212) 642-2672.

List of resources, including conferences, in-service training programs, publications, and computer equity expert trainers.

■ ■ ■ ■

## CHAPTER ELEVEN

## THE INFORMAL CURRICULUM: ATHLETICS

*Glory lies in the attempt to reach one's goal and not in reaching it.*

—*Mohandas K. Gandhi, d.1948*

The playing field has been seen historically as a training ground for sound moral character. This accounts in part for the great emphasis it has consistently merited in schools. Athletics are intended to affect not only bodies, but also minds and personalities — to teach dedication to shared goals, loyalty to teammates, grace under pressure, stoicism in defeat, modesty in victory, the game outweighing the glory, and honor due worthy opponents.

Playing fields have also functioned as proving grounds for masculinity. For the last century or so, sports in the United States have served as a gateway, perhaps *the* gateway, to being a man. Over a quarter of elementary school boys regards athletics as "the best thing about being male," and almost three quarters dream about being sports stars when they grow up (Sadker and Sadker 1994, 85).

Fathers, and father-figure coaches, initiate young boys into male language and traditions by shared sports-talk, and by watching and critiquing athletic events together (Whitson 1990). Parents (especially fathers), as well as schools, as a rule have a very great investment in having boys perform well in athletics; and very great pressure is put on boys from a tender age to engage and excel in sports. In doing so, they are expected to exhibit the stereotypic male traits of toughness, which may demand playing with injuries; of high competitiveness, which may demand winning at any price; and of aggression, which may demand an outlet through violence.

It is not only fathers and schools who put a premium on boys' sports performance. Perhaps most importantly, their peer group does also. Among elementary school children, boys' popularity is closely linked to their athletic ability, as is their ability to come out on top in the informal pushing, shoving, and roughhousing, and the formal fights that not infrequently lead from contact sports.

While the aggressive, belligerent, and athletically able boys have their peers' admiration, the least athletically able and weakest are not only the least popular but also the most often hurt and least frequently helped (Adler, Kless and Adler, 1992, 172-173). Adults may need to pay more attention to the value systems being developed in boys' informal, as well as formal, sports.

The danger of an over-emphasis on athletic performance swamping the desirable traits and tipping over into their undesirable exaggeration is increased by the early introduction to athletics as a spectator via TV, and continued exposure to professional sports, where violence is almost taken for granted.

> *"Imagine a young boy watching football. Normally, running into someone with all your weight and force and knocking that person down with a good chance of injuring him, is viewed as bodily assault and could subject a person to arrest. But in football this behavior is called tackling or blocking and is widely admired and respected. If a player can get away with late hitting or spearing — both of which are illegal — he will be considered particularly clever and adept."*
> —*Myriam Miedzian, 1991*

The violence in professional sports may be due more to owners' commercial interests — "It attracts spectators who come to see 'red ice' " — than players' inclinations, but children watching do not realize this. What they do realize is spectators' approval for the violence, and the continued showing of it, without censure, on screen. The link between watching violence on TV and the development of violent behavior in those watching it is very extensively documented (Mortimer 1994; Barry 1994; Eron 1980; Berkowitz 1964). Parents themselves may model violence for their children in sports contexts: in recent years, it has been reported that one hundred referees of children's sports are attacked by parents each year (Cited in Horgan 1995, 37).

Violent language toward both opponents and players also creates a climate favorable to violent behavior. In rallies, in conversation, and in yells during the game, calls are for opponents to be destroyed, mangled, massacred, slain; and the contest is not infrequently conceptualized not as winning, but dominating; not showing oneself better trained and more skilled than the opposition, but literally able to physically beat them, even when this is not actually carried out. (In individual cases, it may be.) Teammates often, and some coaches sometimes, put down players who are not considered tough or competitive enough by what many regard as the ultimate insult: labeling them effeminate by derisively calling them "girlies," "fairies" or other, more explicit, epithets. Players may describe themselves and each other, with admiration, as "kamikaze," or "assassin" (Miedzian 1991, Chapter 11).

Sports play a significant role, moreover, in reinforcing fierce competition, and a will to win that may not count the cost either to oneself or to others. This is especially likely in the absence of consistent affirmation that winning is not only not the *only* thing, it is not even always, necessarily, or perhaps at all, the most important thing.

In contrast, parental attitudes towards girls' sports participation tend to the neutral; few by now discourage it entirely, but strong emotional pressure in favor of it is not common. A 1988 report on parent attitudes documents most parents then saying that sports were equally important for girls and boys, providing important benefits for both (Thorngren and Eisenbarth 1994, 2). Schools perhaps more than parents encourage girls' athletics, but in few instances as heatedly as boys'. While playing is considered acceptable, and perhaps even desirable for girls, dedication often is not. Parents may be uncomfortable with a daughter who continues to be a "tomboy" beyond early adolescence; being a serious competitor may raise questions about a girl's femininity or sexual orientation; and female athletes may encounter indifference, disapproval, or ridicule. Some who experience this bias, or fear it, may over-compensate by becoming apologetically over-feminine off the field. High-achieving female athletes' accomplishments are often less highly valued than comparable performance by males.

Not surprisingly, girls' perception of their own competence in sports is lower than boys' from as early as first grade on, a perception contradicted by objective tests of their physical abilities, as well as their teachers' ratings. Moreover, although elementary-age girls think they are less able than boys in sports overall, they rate themselves higher than do boys in some specific (non-male-stereotypic) activities, such as tumbling (Eccles et al. 1993).

That participation in sports may have positive effects on girls' self-esteem is suggested by recent research, the most dramatic effects showing up among Hispanic, African-American, and white rural and urban girls (Schultz 1991, 7).

In junior and senior high school, the physical ability gap between girls and boys widens, certainly in those characteristics that are demanded in the most highly valued, and high-profile, sports: height, weight, muscle mass, and cardiovascular capacity all statistically favor males. Women have the physiological advantage in a more effective aerobic ventilation system, better temperature control mechanism, and better insulation against long exposure to cold. They are the ones holding world records in ultra-long-distance swimming, running, and walking; and are consistently the winners of the Alaskan Iditarod dogsled race (Hargreaves 1994, 284-285).

However, the sports demanding endurance and flexibility, the characteristics where females are statistically superior, do not get much publicity; and either cannot practically be part of school programs, or are less highly valued (compare gymnastics with football). Moreover, the physiological gender gap that increases with maturation is emphasized by schools that highlight the contact and team sports (such as football, wrestling, basketball) where the disparity is greatest, at the expense of individual or "lifetime" sports which males and females could play together with considerable overlap in performance, such as golf, tennis, running, and some martial arts (*New York Times* 1989, 28).

The characterization of athletics as male is very obvious from the public images presented. In 1989 men's sports in America got 92 percent of the TV coverage, women's 5 percent (the rest being mixed or gender neutral). In 1990, in four of the top-selling newspapers in the U.S., stories of men's sports outnumbered those on women's twenty-three to one. While media images of male athletes glorify their strength, power, and even violence, those of women athletes focus on grace, fluidity of movement, beauty. It is symptomatic that women body-builders claim that "flex appeal is sex appeal" (Lorber 1994, 42-44).

Gender stereotyping in athletics works to the disadvantage of both sexes. The heavy emphasis on athletic prowess for acceptance and status in preadolescent and adolescent male peer groups, especially when reinforced by parents and/or school, creates problems for the small, awkward, scholarly, artistic, or plain uninterested. Athletic expectations weigh particularly heavily on African-American boys. And the strong potential link between athletics and violence, both on and off the field, is a problem that needs constant watching.

For the good male athlete, who is strongly reinforced for physical performance in competitive games by parents, school, and peers, as well as by girls who give football stars preference in dating, problems arise in college and later. It is after high school graduation that negative images of athletes (dumb jock, bully, insensitive, winner-at-all-costs) become more salient. Increased time demands by the greater variety of sources for self-validation in college, as well as by women in more adult dating relationships, conflict with demands of practice, and with self-definition as "athlete" (Sabo and Runfola, 1980). Those who nevertheless persist in such self-definition find competition much stiffer, and are more at risk for failures of confidence. For most men, the great investment of time, effort, and ego they have made in the high-profile team sports since Little League, has little payoff after graduation. Few men play football, wrestle, or even play basketball either professionally or for recreation after college.

Girls have made great strides in athletic participation in the last two decades. In 1972, about 4 percent of girls in high school took part in athletics; in 1987, 26 percent; in 1994, 37 percent, but parity is clearly still some way off. As of about five years ago, Asian-American and African-American girls nationally participated in athletics at lower rates than whites; and Hispanic girls at the lowest rates of all. Moreover, almost all sports continue to be perceived as male-appropriate by students, who identified only figure skating, gymnastics, jumping rope, and cheerleading as female (Thorngren and Eisenbarth 1994, 1; AAUW 1992, 45-46). The last point is particularly ironic, since cheerleading, when it emerged in the late 1880s, was an exclusively masculine activity. When women first entered it during World War I, their doing so was resisted as female encroachment on a male prerogative. Men began dropping out of cheerleading only in the 1940s; however, by 1970, cheerleading was considered a "naturally feminine" occupation (Davis L.,1990, 153).

From elementary school on, girls' sports are less likely to be team activities than boys; and from adolescence, girls' physical activities tend to focus increasingly on individual exercise and "fitness." In college, significantly more of their sports play becomes individual than it had been in grade and high school. This contrasts markedly with men, half of whose preferred physical activity in college is still team sports, although in this group also there is a decline from childhood. Six- to eight-year-old boys spend as much as 75 percent of their playtime in ball games with a group of six or more playmates (Vaughter, Sadh, and Vozzola 1994, 99-100). The much, and increasingly, higher proportion of time spent by boys in team sports has implications for the differential development of interpersonal competitiveness and aggressive physical contact, both promoted more by team than by individual sports.

There is a dearth of female athletic coaches as role models for girls, and as models of adult female athletic know-how for boys. In independent schools, male faculty is typically much more likely to act as coach than female; and there is an even greater dearth of non-white female faculty coaches. In high school and collegiate sports, as men's and women's sports departments were merged in response to Civil Rights legislation, the number of women coaches coaching female sports has actually declined, though the number of female participants increased dramatically; and women coach fewer than 1 percent of boys' teams (Hargreaves 1994, 179; Thorngren and Eisenbarth 1994, 5).

A mid-1980s study showed that about half of both girls and boys in high school believed that their physical education teachers expected more from boys than girls. Teachers were in fact found to apply higher performance standards to boys. In grades 1-12, teachers were observed to interact more with boys than girls, and overwhelmingly to call on boys as leaders or for a demonstration. Coeducational classes worked better for girls than single sex, and made no difference to boys, in terms of skill development. Girls felt they made more improvement in the coed classes, even though half of them spoke of less confidence, and displeasure with jeering and belittling comments from boys, in mixed classes. Direct intervention by teachers when hostile or demeaning behavior took place reduced its incidence (Geadelmann et al. 1985, 326-329).

Informal baseball, soccer, and basketball games on school playgrounds are typically boys-only. Fear of teasing by peers is a formidable deterrent to volunteering for what is shaping up as an opposite-gender team, or choosing an opposite-gender player for one's own team. Observation of fourth through sixth graders and anecdotal information suggests that the most "integrated" games are those like kickball and handball, to which access is open-ended, needs no one's permission, and can be done just by deciding to join. Among schools studied, the one with the most "integrated" playground (two thirds of playgroups single-sex, compared to the usual of about 80 percent) had rules, developed jointly by students and teachers, for admitting new players to ongoing games. Informal mixed teams are also quite common in neighborhood situations (Thorne 1993, 50-55).

Is it in female athletes' best interests to have their own teams and coaches to avoid being "swamped" by male teammates and given less attention by coaches, and to have their own space, in which their talents can unfold unhampered? Or is it better for them to learn on mixed teams that they can win over some boys, although they lose to others; that there is no question of their being held to any lesser standards; and that when they have the opportunity to try out for leadership in a mixed team, even one in which boys predominate, they will occasionally get elected captain? The question remains open.

**The optimum approach is probably to:**

> ➤ recognize that there is no one "right" answer for all circumstances
> ➤ consider the possibility of mixed teams in at least some sports, especially at the younger age-groups; and for the older, at least for intramural competition
> ➤ treat boys' teams, girls' teams, and mixed teams equitably in terms of space, scheduling, publicity, spectator support, provision of coaches, uniforms, transportation, equipment, prizes, and praise
> ➤ ensure that on both single-sex and mixed teams, coaches' attention is equitably spread to all team members
> ➤ create team spirit that helps *all* team members develop strong loyalties to each other, regardless of gender, and to validate each other rather than cut each other down — requirements as necessary to emphasize for single-sex, as for mixed, teams
> ➤ use sensitivity to the schools' ethos in considering what changes, if any, to make — but recognize that changes in the ethos itself may be desirable, and that such change can be brought about by small increments

The provision of gender-open noncompetitive options such as climbing, hiking, yoga, dance (as a sport, in addition to an academic subject), in addition and as alternatives to highly competitive individual and team sports for both boys and girls, without devaluing participation in any of the options by any student, can help dilute the "do you have to be separate to be equal?" issue.

*T*o promote optimal benefit from and equity for boys and girls in athletics, schools might consider doing the following:

* In general, put a bit less pressure on boys, and encourage girls a bit more. (Of course some girls are likely to need no encouragement, and some boys might benefit from more pressure . . . )
* Recognize that boys need flexibility enhancing and expressive training as much as girls need strength and explosive power training.
* Encourage both boys and girls to take gymnastics and dance in the primary grades, and continue to do so in high school.
* Encourage mixed-gender play by adult modeling. (A female teacher played soccer with her first graders, and found her active presence encouraged girls to join in; a male first-grade teacher taught all his class to jump rope, and drew boys as well as girls into the game). (Thorne 1993, 166)
* Introduce new, not-yet-stereotyped, activities and teach the skills involved to all.
* Try to defuse girls' tendencies to choose a sport not out of interest in the activity, but because friends of theirs have done so.
* Ask students a short time into the season what they are particularly enjoying about participation, and what they wish were different about their athletic experience.
* Consider basing some teams not on gender, but on reasonably closely matched players whether male or female. Instead of boys' track and girls' track, perhaps an A team for all who can run a certain distance in a certain time, and a B team for those below the cut-off.
* Consider having both girls and boys participate in outdoor skills activities that require cooperation. Some research suggests that when they are exposed to some risk together (as on a ropes course), an unusually cooperative atmosphere develops that transcends gender boundaries (Hargreaves 1994, citing 1986 research, 154).
* Encourage, entice, and prod female faculty into coaching on the same basis as male faculty, while remaining sensitive to problems such as childcare and helping to make whatever arrangements are needed.
* Encourage polite, friendly behavior between members of opposing teams. Start and end games with handshakes; suggest that team members single out opposing players and praise them for good performance during the game; provide refreshments to be enjoyed together by the opposing teams after the game.
* Discuss with students the negative dynamics of stereotyping and of undesirable powerplays; actively challenge their manifestations by showing disapproval of hassling, slanging, and putting down others, and encourage students to do so as well.
* Talk with coaches about the influence of language on perception, and encourage them to find ways to high morale for their teams other than the common "KILL" or "DESTROY" the opposing team — slogans that consistently appear painted on scoreboards, rocks, and water towers, as well as printed on T-shirts and caps, the latter often with the school's blessing.
* Have coaches work with their teams to eliminate shaming players as "girlies," "sissies," or "fags," and putting girls down as "dykes" as weak and incompetent, or in other ways.
* Alert both coaches and players to gender differences in communication and learning styles (see **ENGLISH**, **MATH**, and **SCIENCE** sections) that may have an impact on their work together.

- Consider making clear that winning is *not* the only thing by institutional action, including: praising teams publicly that played well even when they lose; having a major award for "outstanding promoter of fair play"; adding team awards for "most improved player" and "player who did most for team morale" as well as "most valuable player," with perhaps another award for "top scorer," since value may be measured by yardsticks other than winning scores.
- Take into account the great influence and importance of coaches as parent figures and role models. Administrators could promote professional development for them the way its is done for their classroom teaching, and, to the extent possible, arrange lighter workloads for faculty in the seasons when they coach.

## RESOURCES

Note: Books marked with *(P)* are recommended for parents.

Arnett, Chappelle. *A.C.T.I.V.E.: All Children Totally Involved via Equity*. 1980. Education Development Center, 55 Chapel Street, Newton, MA 02158; (800) 225-3088.
For elementary teachers and administrators, suggestions for promoting gender equality in physical education.

Guttman, Allen. *Women's Sports: A History*. Boulder: Colorado University Press, 1992.
Survey of European and U.S. women's participation in athletics from antiquity to the present, with brief references to African and Native American cultures. Status of women athletes, and the social context of their participation, is assessed through time. Grades 9 - adult. *(P)*

McInally, Pat. *Moms and Dads and Kids and Sports*. New York: Ivy Books, 1989. *(P)*

Uhlir, Ann. *Physical Educators for Equity*. 1981. Education Development Center, 55 Chapel Street, Newton, MA 02158. (800) 225-3088.
For secondary teachers and administrators, resources for designing gender-fair physical education programs.

*Women's Sport and Fitness*. 1919 14th St., Suite 421, Boulder, CO 80302; (303) 440-5111.
A newsletter published eight times a year, with articles on women's sports activities, nutrition, and athletic training.

■ ■ ■ ■

## CHAPTER TWELVE

## THE INFORMAL CURRICULUM: LEADERSHIP

*The Master has no mind of her own.*
*She works with the mind of her people.*

*—Lao Tzu, ca. 500 BCE*

*...although the prince may be lord and master of his subjects,*
*the subjects nevertheless make the lord and not the lord the subjects.*

*—Christine de Pisan, 1405*

The mountain of research on leadership shows that there are two basic dimensions of leadership. One has to do with getting the job done — directing; the other with motivating people to get the job done — supporting. This is as true of parents and children as it is of teachers and students, administrators and faculty, and of students leading students.

The first dimension of leadership involves strong structure, with the leader carefully defining the job to be done and planning exactly how it is be accomplished; assigning to followers the various tasks needed to achieve the goal; telling them what to do and how to do it; and diligently pushing everyone to do their tasks efficiently. This dimension of leadership puts a premium on being "authoritarian," is characteristically directive, task-oriented, instrumental, and high on rules, and is stereotypically associated with males.

The second involves strong concern for group members' needs, even beyond those obviously relevant to achieving the goal, with the leader carefully building mutual trust, respect, and rapport with followers; inviting broad participation in decision making about the definition of the goal and ways to achieve it, and in assigning tasks; and diligently promoting two-way communication about the process of approaching the goal as well as about any adjustments that may be needed. This dimension of leadership puts a premium on being "democratic," is characteristically supportive, relationship-oriented, concerned with morale, and flexible, and is stereotypically associated with females.

In spite of the stereotypes, which often influence people's behavior, research as well as historical experience has shown that both men and women can be effective leaders and supportive followers.

Traditionally, the "masculine" style was thought to be more important for a leader, with the "feminine" style a distant second in importance — a "frill," as it were. In the twentieth century, the importance of the dimension of concern has become increasingly recognized. In most groups, while the leader was the task specialist, and almost invariably male, responsibility for morale was delegated to someone with official, though lesser, status, a "socio-emotional specialist" who was almost invariably female. This division of labor was quite usual in families also.

From the late 1970s on the ideal of the "traditional manager" who is aloof, rational, critical, and cool (male stereotypical) gave pride of place to the ideal of the "transforming leader," who is receptive, expressive, supportive, and warm (female stereotypical) — with the continued recommendation, however, that the two sets of tasks both need to be performed, "though not necessarily by the same person" (Anderson 1992, 50-51, citing other research).

The last thirty years of research about leadership, however, has suggested an alternative model that is now generally accepted: the model of situational leadership. According to this, the two aspects of leadership outlined above are not mutually exclusive, but form a continuum of modes from 1) high directive/low supportive, through 2) high directive/high supportive, 3) low directive/high supportive, to 4) low directive/low supportive. Any one leader or manager needs the versatility to function in each of the various modes, and the know-how to recognize when each is appropriate.

While it was first thought that position two on the continuum, high both on task and morale, must be the best style for a leader to cultivate, it is now recognized that there is no one, best leadership style. None of the four combinations noted always best ensures efficient task achievement, high productivity, high morale, and significant growth in skills, abilities, and the meeting of personal challenges for all. The "best" leadership style depends on the characteristics of those led, and on circumstances. Successful leaders are those who have the flexibility to adapt their style to the demands of the situation, and the know-how to identify what style best fits the situation they are in.

In order to become good leaders, then, both males and females need to become comfortable with behaving in ways that may not come easily to them; that run counter to gender stereotypes. They may well be uncomfortable with behavior which they have been socialized into considering appropriate to the opposite sex, and perhaps even inappropriate for their own. They may also be anxious that such behavior will earn them condemnation from those who continue to be strongly committed to gender stereotypes. (Actually, the research we have suggests that while condemnation of non-gender-stereotypic leadership does exist, it is much weaker when the leader is known personally to those judging his or her leadership style; and decreases significantly in time as followers become accustomed to the leader as an individual rather than a representative of her or his gender.)

**In order to help students and children to become effective leaders, schools, teachers, and parents need to:**

> ➤ give them opportunities to act as leaders
> ➤ allay their fears of non-gender-stereotypical behavior
> ➤ provide opportunities and support for engaging in such behavior
> ➤ when rotating leadership in groups, avoid doing so too rapidly, giving the group and leader time to get used to each other

**The job of the leader, on any task, is to move followers towards becoming peak performers with no more need for the leader. To do so, it is helpful for adults in leadership positions to ask themselves, and help their children and students, to figure out:**

> ➤ what their own dominant style (or favored combination of styles) is or what they feel they would be most comfortable with
> ➤ what convictions or behaviors it might be helpful for them to add in order to increase the flexibility needed to fit varied situations
> ➤ how best to diagnose any particular situation in which their leadership is needed, in order to determine the particular mix of behaviors most desirable under the circumstances

*F*ortunately, research gives some general guidance about appropriateness.

The task-oriented, authoritarian style of leadership or "directing" can be good and may be necessary, not only for effectiveness but often, though not always, for morale, in the following circumstances:

> ➤ when followers are immature, inexperienced, or unmotivated
> ➤ when the task has to be performed in a hurry, under stress, or under unfamiliar or difficult conditions
> ➤ in some groups with authoritarian traditions (such as the military)

In such circumstance, the high directive/low supportive end of the continuum is likely to be a good choice. Note however that directing goes beyond saying,: "Do it because I tell you to." Rather, it involves information about what needs to be accomplished, how, when, and why; giving ongoing feedback about performance, timely advice, and constructive suggestions.

Using this style with followers who are competent, motivated, and mature, however, may send the unintended message that the leader perceives them as untrustworthy and inferior, creating offense. (Parents get strong signals that less directiveness is needed, for instance, when children protest against being "treated like a baby.")

As followers respond to the directive behaviors of the leader, begin to act more maturely, to acquire skills, and even perhaps exhibit some motivation, praise, rewards, and reinforcement are essential. Part of the reward is increasing delegation of responsibility; the leader acting more like a coach, providing both authoritative direction and moral support. Respect can begin to go both ways. and trust-building is part of the picture. The leader now is listening to people rather than just telling; paying nonjudgmental attention, encouraging openness, and empathizing with others' feelings.

Gradually, as followers increasingly gain competence, maturity, and motivation, task-directive leader behavior can diminish, while relationship is maintained and strengthened. Since the leader can now trust and respect followers, she or he can be comfortable with delegating to them and involving them in decision making; knowing them well, concern about them beyond the narrow task demands comes naturally. Here we have the circumstances in which low directive/high support is appropriate.

Traditional men may inappropriately stick to this one style when leading women, ignoring the developmental stages. Such men are reluctant to be directive and give women critical feedback even when it is needed. They are also unwilling to trust women with responsibility, even when women are ready for it. A leader's use of this style with women or girls who either need direction and criticism, or are beyond needing support, may create confusion, anxiety, and resentment.

Finally, a mature, competent group of peak performing followers get their major rewards from their success at the task itself, and from each others' companionship and collaboration. They are both competent and motivated to take responsibility, and the leader can turn running the show over to them. The function of the leader now becomes acting as a kind of consultant for unusual problems or tricky decisions; and running interference for the group with the outside world, making sure they have what they need to get on with the task. This is the low directive/low support style. (It is the style often characteristic of parents with adult children.) The presence of the leader is vital to a group at all stages of its development; but it changes from a high- to a low-profile presence. Use of the latter by a leader needs to be handled sensitively, since it may, unintentionally, create the perception of abdication, absenteeism, lack of caring, or even sabotage.

An extensive review of actual leadership behavior by women and men has shown that, in real-world situations, the only difference by gender was in women being more democratic, and using a more participatory style; whereas men were identified as being more autocratic and directive. Organizational, "real-world" studies showed no gender differences in either task orientation or relationship orientation, although some laboratory studies did so.

Some gender differences in details of leader-follower relationships that have been found are the greater accessibility of women, their greater difficulty in saying no, and their less intense work at influencing followers (they typically make fewer attempts to do so, and use a more limited range of influence strategies).

Studies also show that women leaders in organizations:

> ➤ continue to be evaluated slightly more negatively by their followers than are men
> ➤ earn more pronouncedly negative evaluations when they chose to use autocratic, non-participatory, male-stereotypic styles; when they occupied typically male positions; and when their evaluators were primarily men

The implications here are that women are likely to find it difficult to use leadership behaviors that are effective and even necessary under some circumstances for all leaders, although stereotyped as "male," and that they will have the added difficulty of potential disapproval when they do so. Part of the hostility to women in authority derives from the perception that, when a woman has authority over men of the same age and social class, she is considered by the latter to be reducing their status, rather than enhancing her own.

It has also been shown, however, that male managers who have worked with women as peers were less likely to stereotype women as unfit for management than those who have only worked with woman as sub-ordinates. The same was found true of leaders and followers at the West Point Military Academy (Powell 1988, 164). The effect of gender stereotyping of women as leaders waned after long term (several weeks), face-to-face interaction with a female leader.

A series of studies reported in 1985 suggests that women are handicapped by having had fewer opportunities to act as leaders from the very start of their education. In preschool classes' free play periods, children participating predominantly in activities in which adults strongly structured the situation, showed them what and how to do, and emphasized rules, resulted in both girls and boys being attentive, persisting in tasks, asking for help, complying with, and depending on the adults. Activities low in structure resulted in both girls and boys being more likely to initiate and make attempts at leadership, and in more aggressiveness, and more compliance with peers rather than adults. The kinds of toys, play styles, and behaviors girls have already been socialized into (see **THE "CURRICULUM" OF THE REAL WORLD**) favor their preference for the high structure activities. Sure enough, given a choice girls tended to opt for high structure activities, and spent more time with them. Both sexes, though, did participate in both.

Without adult encouragement to maintain an interest in both kinds of activities, however, what begins as a slight preference, promoted by gender-stereotypic toy choice and reinforcement for gender-stereotypic play styles by adults and media, results in choices of activities that influence choice of playmates. The interaction of these small and apparently independent choices results in children gradually becoming part of a single-sex network, within which increasingly gender-stereotyped communication and behavior styles are developed and maintained by the modeling and influence of peers (Unger and Crawford 1992, 244; Carpenter, Huston and Holt 1986).

## ➤ *What Schools, Teachers, and Parents Can Do*

*T*he educational implications of the research on leadership suggest that girls and boys need to experience both leading and following opposite-gender individuals. The easiest way to do this is to look for ongoing situations in which mixed-gender groups can have rotating, not alternating, leadership.

Such situations are easiest to come by in schools in:

- group discussions in the classroom, in lab groups, and in some extra-curricular activities
- in bringing male and female prefects together to plan mixed-gender activities

**In families these situations are found in:**

- encouraging and creating opportunities for mixed gender, mixed age informal group participation
- facilitating children's participation in planning and leading mixed gender group activities and outings with their friends, from the earliest age on

**Both girls and boys need experiences that promote the development of leadership characteristics. Such experiences offer:**

- the opportunity to take risks
- the development of self-confidence
- no fear of others' expectations
- learning from both successes and failures
- the challenge of demanding and varied assignments
  (Conger 1992, Chapter 2)

**Both girls and boys would benefit from training that alerts them to:**

- the body language and speech patterns used by, associated with, and expected of high-status and dominant individuals (high-status people of either gender claim more space with their body-postures, talk more, and attempt more interruptions than low-status individuals) (Unger and Saundra 1993, 157)
- the role in being judged unsuitable for leadership by others of both verbal and nonverbal behavior that appears to reflect low status or low power
- the fact that both actual and presumed (by others) expertise in the job that the group being led is undertaking contributes to successful leadership
- the part played by gender stereotyping in the presumed (and sometimes actual) areas of male and female expertise
- the need for would-be leaders, especially girls, to make their real competence and expertise known, since evidence of real competence can override gender-stereotyped expectations about leadership competence (Ellyson, Dovidio and Brown 1992; Wood and Rhodes 1992, 108)
- the need for adult feedback, the more immediate the better, on how they functioned in a leadership position, whether the group they led was single-sex or mixed
- the need for encouragement to seek feedback from their followers on how they were perceived as leaders, with adult support for using rather than being crippled by negative comments

(The above information is based on Blanchard 1995; Pierce and Newstrom 1995; Hahn and Litwin 1995; Beck and Yeager 1994; Denmark 1993; Unger and Saundra 1993; Wood and Rhodes 1992; Eagly and Johnson 1990; Powell 1988; Hersey and Blanchard 1982)

■ ■ ■ ■

## CHAPTER THIRTEEN

## PARENTS AND THE HOME CURRICULUM

*…every father and mother does an astonishing amount of teaching.*
*Their lessons cover the entire universe, from "Where is God?"*
*to the use of soap, and have a lifetime effect.*

*—Gilbert Highet, 1956*

Every home has a "curriculum" of deliberate teaching, which may include such "subjects" as cleanliness, self-control, honesty, and many others particular to each family. There is also a climate of learning in every home, of which the family is often unaware.

**This includes such things as:**

- ➤ the ways adults react to mistakes and disagreement
- ➤ which activities are valued and given priority
- ➤ how much, and how, curiosity is encouraged
- ➤ opportunities, and encouragement, for taking part in different and varied kinds of activities
- ➤ the effort made to have children experience many different kinds of situations
- ➤ how much and about what adults and children talk to each other, and the part each takes in conversation
- ➤ the unwritten rules about who is allowed, and supposed, to do what

Parents can take action to help their children's learning in and out of school. To do so, they need to be alert to the ways children's learning is, or is not, supported by what goes on in the home. They also need to become more knowledgeable about what favors, and what hampers, children's ability to learn.

**From babyhood on, parents can make sure that both sons and daughters are:**

- ➤ talked to and played with in physical ways
- ➤ given opportunities for and are encouraged in large and small-muscle development and coordination
- ➤ offered experiences with textures, shapes, colors, sounds, and tastes
- ➤ exposed to the widest possible range of things to see, hear, touch, taste, do, and explore, from floating leaves in puddles to rummaging in child-proofed kitchen cupboards and hearing different kinds of music
- ➤ allowed to continue activities they enjoy and are interested in, weighing priorities if interruption appears to be necessary
- ➤ taught to become competently self-sufficient as soon as they can do so, in such things as feeding themselves, getting dressed, fetching, carrying, and tidying
- ➤ encouraged as soon as they are able to talk about their experiences; explain what they are doing; ask questions about their sensations and experiences; and try to put into words how they feel about it
- ➤ given corrective feedback in language use and object handling, with opportunities for repetition and lots of rewards for improvement

*W*ith toddlers and older children, parents must make their own decisions about the degree to which they will encourage non-gender-stereotypic attitudes and behavior. The choice will influence the kind of surroundings they create for their children, the toys, activities, and experiences they provide, and the way they relate to daughters and sons.

But whatever choice is made, children's understanding about appropriate ways of being male and female will be most heavily influenced by what adults around them do, what they say, and how they behave towards others of both genders. A girl may be encouraged to play with trucks; but if her mother says: "There's something wrong with the car, I'll have to ask your father to take it in to be serviced," the message she will hear is that knowing about and dealing with cars is not a woman's responsibility. Similarly, a boy allowed to play with dolls who overhears his father say: "John's wife wants him to get up in the middle of the night to feed the baby. I'd sure never go for that," is unlikely to grow up with a participatory attitude towards fathering.

It helps children to be clearly told when they are old enough how their family feels about gender roles, and about the appropriate attitudes and behavior for males and females. Parents might take such talks with their children as chances to clarify their own ideas, and to consider whether their actions and attitudes bear out what they say. Conflicting messages, when parents say one thing but model another, are very confusing and harmful for children.

Whether the family is on the more or the less traditional side of gender issues, children also need to understand that there are differences of opinion and beliefs among people in their own society and in the wider world about these matters. They should, moreover, be given some guidance on how to handle being confronted by those whose ideas on the issue differ from their family's.

In handling conflict, families who teach both sons and daughters not to seek confrontation but to be strong in defending themselves, who rely heavily on reasoning to solve discipline problems, and teach alternatives to physical aggression for settling arguments, are most likely to raise girls and boys who are confident and assertive but not violent and aggressive, and who can take care of themselves in a confrontation without provoking or escalating it.

For both girls and boys, their family's support can make a big difference in learning how to learn, preparing for the demands of formal education, and getting into the habit of learning with competence, confidence, and enjoyment.

**The following are some basic ways to contribute to children's learning:**

- ➤ Help children treat the mistakes they make not as faults, but as clues to what they still have to learn, or to what they need to do differently.
- ➤ Pinpoint what you think is likely to have caused, or contributed to, failures or mistakes — your children's and your own. Suggest possible ways to prevent or avoid them in the future. With older children, ask for their suggestions on how to prevent or avoid mistakes. Alert them to, and praise them for, improvement.
- ➤ Give specific, useful, reinforcing feedback when you praise: "Great! You remembered to light the oven early enough so it reached the right temperature in time for you to put the risen dough in!" rather than "Great job with the baking!"
- ➤ Watch for a child's over-reliance on adult praise for her self-image. To counteract, emphasize self-assessment skills (see below).
- ➤ When talking with children about their successes and failures, emphasize to both boys and girls the part played by those things they have some control over: careful following of directions, time spent, concentration, willingness both to risk failure and to put in the work needed to overcome it.

➤ Counteract the tendency (more typical in girls) to believe that a poor showing is part of a general pattern, and is an example of stable personality characteristics that predispose for, and predict, failure.

➤ Counteract a child's generalization of failure to overall lack of worth: if she says: "I'm dumb!" correct her firmly and consistently: "You are not dumb — but you sure did a dumb thing ... "

➤ Take an interest in all aspects of schoolwork, asking to see, and have children explain to you, their art work, writings, calculations, and laboratory reports.

➤ Give priority to homework, studying, and reading over chores, socializing, TV watching, and stereo listening.

➤ Read to young children regularly, and continue when they are older with taking turns reading aloud to each other books that the whole family can enjoy.

➤ Teach the importance of setting realistic but challenging goals and working towards them in a disciplined way. (A good rule of thumb is about 75 percent confidence of being able to reach the goal.)

➤ Consider giving children the opportunity to contract for attainable goals. Younger children may enjoy drawing up legalistic written contracts with impressive seals.

➤ Teach self-assessment. Ask children to predict how they will do on a given task, and ask what they base their prediction on. Talk to them about reasons why their prediction was proven accurate or inaccurate by their actual performance. Get them to focus on specifics: How hard is the task compared to others? How does its format, content, and timing affect its level of difficulty? How well-prepared is the child in knowledge, experience, and preparation? What does the child think he or she should do differently next time?

➤ Make it clear consistently and on a continuing basis that you value education and expect that your children will be able to do well.

**To help sons and daughters toward greater reading and writing competence, parents can do much, including some of the following:**

➤ Be readers themselves, alert children to admired others among family and friends who are readers, and provide models for both men and women reading both fiction and nonfiction with interest, enjoyment, and benefit.

➤ Expose children to reading matter written by, and about, people from a wide variety of backgrounds, both women and men.

➤ In talking with children, broaden their horizons and give them more background knowledge they can draw on to help them read with understanding. Discuss information, and give examples and illustrative incidents or anecdotes drawn from various perspectives. Challenge them to look at events and ideas from different points of view, and to consider how their experience and their attitude to it would be different if they stood, figuratively, in someone else's moccasins.

➤ In family conversations, be alert to the dynamics of turn-taking, interruptions, a balance between response to others' ideas and development of one's own, encouragement for the speaker, asking for others' input, conciseness, criticism, and so on (see **CROSSCURRENTS IN COMMUNICATION**, page 16). Alert speakers to their patterns, and how they can capitalize on their own strong points, minimize their weak points, and become more versatile in their speech patterns.

➤ Have both boys and girls help with anything that comes with directions, from recipes to assembling furniture or toys. Let them take over, following the directions themselves, or ask them to read the directions and tell you what to do next.

- Encourage children to talk about what they read, and get them to elaborate and explain with comments such as "Tell me more about...", "Why do you think..." and "Could you explain how...?"
- Suggest to children that they make up alternative courses of action for characters in the stories they read, and to predict what the results of the alternative choices are likely to be ("What if Snow White had not accepted the poisoned apple?").
- Ask children to summarize for you what they are reading about in school, and challenge them to "teach" you well enough so you could answer a quiz. Get them to make up, and give you, a quiz. Ask both girls and boys about various subject areas, not literature or language arts only. How does gravity work? How did women and men, rich and poor, live in the Americas before Europeans' arrival? How do you write a computer program? Make sure that you do not ask only about areas of strength and interest, whether yours or the child's.
- Ask children to find a book for you that they think you would enjoy reading, and write a review of it for you. Ask them to explain why they thought you would be interested. Ask questions based on their review; read the book, and discuss it with them. Suggest other, non-gender-stereotypic, topics you would also be interested in, and ask them to find a book for you in those areas as well.
- Jot down your own reactions to books you read, and share them with children. Encourage them to keep a reading journal or log.
- Talk to children about your own interests: your job, volunteer work, hobbies, pastimes. Encourage them to ask questions, and help them to ask the kinds of initial and follow-up questions that will gain the most, and the most useful, information.
- Leave written messages for each other, and suggest to children that they write letters to absent family members and friends about their experiences in and out of school and about their reactions to books they have read.
- Encourage and help children to collect, record in writing, and keep, information about topics that interest them: the habits and needs of animals and plants; directions to places they visit occasionally; sports scores and performance, their heroes' and their own.
- Suggest that children write directions for baby-sitters, and for the care of pets, plants, gardens and anything else you can think of.

**Even parents with no expertise in the sciences can give their children grounding that will be of benefit in these subject areas, by trying some of the following:**

- Routinely look for opportunities to ask children to predict in many areas, and to look for validation. ("Do you think it will rain soon? What suggests it will?" "It didn't, after all. Why, do you think? "How many laps can you run?" "How long do you think it will take you to read this chapter?")
- Ask questions that guide towards, rather than giving, answers.
- Model problem-solving behavior. ("Let's see, if I do this...")
- Provide opportunities for problem solving. ("How could we figure out a way to..?")
- Encourage divergent thinking. ("What other ways..?")
- Encourage the use of building blocks, woodworking, tinkering, and toys such as Lego and Meccano for girls, and experiences with figure-ground images and puzzles that flip the importance in interpretation between context and detail for boys.
- Encourage both boys and girls not only to look after plants and animals, but to study them by doing things like making detailed drawings of stems, leaves, and flowers and learning to identify different plants outside the home.

➤ Create opportunities for both girls and boys to experience and use physical principles by messing around with levers, gears, magnets, prisms, batteries, and circuits. Give them familiarity with the uses of the widest possible range of tools; teach them to do simple, and then more complex, repair jobs.

**Parents can help their children with mathematics by:**

➤ Becoming convinced that mathematics as both a school subject and a life skill is important, and as much so for girls as for boys.
➤ Playing math games with children in the elementary grades, for example on car trips add the digits on number license plates they sight, and write the sum down, or award points for things seen such as birds, dogs, cows, makes of car, trees, crops, flowers etc.
➤ Playing math games at home, for example asking a child to estimate how many tablespoons to fill a glass half full? a quarter full? how many licks of ice-cream to finish the cone?
➤ Helping children get into the habit of thinking in terms of problem-solving strategies by looking for patterns, drawing pictures, working backward, generating and eliminating possibilities, and estimating and finding ways to check estimates.

(Some of the above activities draw on information from Ohanian 1992.)

P arents can also become aware of the hidden curriculum that exists in the home as well as in school. They can develop an "inner ear" for possible ways that good intentions can misfire, and messages intended to convey one thing that result in unintended effects.

For example:

1.  **Overt statement:** "You're a big boy now, you can figure it out for yourself."
    **Implied and intended message:** "I'm proud of the way you are maturing, and trust you to do it on your own."
    **Possible interpretation by hearer of overt statement alone:** "He/she is rejecting my plea; I can't trust anyone else for help when I need it."

2.  **Overt statement:** "Here, sweetie, let me do it for you."
    **Implied and intended message:** "I love you, and want to save you from difficulty and mistakes."
    **Possible interpretation by hearer of overt statement alone:** "I am not trusted enough to do it right; therefore, I do not have what it takes to be competent."

It is not any one instance of a statement that can be misinterpreted that is a problem, but rather consistent repetition of similar messages and their cumulative effects. Just asking oneself how the messages one sends might come across to the recipients, and what alternative interpretations to one's intentions are possible, will help to avoid potential crossed wires.

Parents may find further ideas that could help in their interactions with their children in the other chapters of this book.

Check the **Resources** sections in all chapters. In some sections, selections marked *(P)* at the end of the entry are specifically recommended for parents. In the rest, parents' interests will dictate their choices.

Belenky, Mary Field, Blythe McVicker Clinchy, Nancy Rule Goldberger and Jill Mattuck Tarule. *Women's Ways of Knowing: The Development of Self, Voice, and Mind.* New York: Basic Books, 1986.
Describes five different perspectives from which women and girls view reality and draw conclusions about truth, knowledge, and authority; shows how women's self-concepts and ways of knowing are intertwined; and how the family and the school both promote and hinder women's development.

Chodorow, Nancy. *The Reproduction of Mothering: Psychoanalysis and the Sociology of Gender.* Berkeley: University of California Press, 1978.
Argues that fathers taking over half the parenting will lead to psychologically healthier children, because their sense of self will be derived from both parents.

Filene, Peter. *Him/Her/Self: Sex Roles in Modern America.* 2nd ed. Baltimore: Johns Hopkins University Press, 1986.
Examines male and female roles from a historical perspective, tracing changes from the Victorian era to the present, and forecasting future trends.

Gilligan, Carol. *In a Different Voice: Psychological Theory and Women's Development.* Cambridge: Harvard University Press, 1982.
Discusses the "ethic of care" and the "ethic of justice," two styles of moral judgment that are gender-associated — though neither is confined to males and females — that have implications for how children are raised, for their self-esteem, and for society.

Gould, Lois. "X: A Fabulous Child's Story." *Ms.*, May 1980.
Often anthologized, (cf. Salamon and Robinson, eds. 1987), this gently humorous story describes an Xperiment, showing what happens when Baby X's parents avoid giving away to anyone by anything they do whether Baby X is male or female. Great discussion starter.

Hunter College Women's Studies Collective. *Women's Realities, Women's Choices.* 2nd Ed. New York: Oxford University Press, 1995.
Readable and balanced account, based on scholarship, of women's changing roles, their definition of themselves, their image in society — in present, past, and globally. Deals with biology, psychology, relationships with other women and men, motherhood, family, education and work.

Kanter, R. and B. Stein. *The Tale of "O": Being Different in an Organization.* New York: Harper and Row, 1980
Outlines what happens when new, and few, people of one kind join any group of people of another kind. Anyone who has ever felt "different" from people around them because of their gender, race, age, size, religion, or job specialty; or has noted the "differentness" or others, will appreciate this discussion of the pressures, discomforts and traps felt by both kinds of people when those who are "different" mix.

Kerr, Barbara R. *Smart Girls, Gifted Women.* 1987. Ohio Psychology Publishing, 131 N. High, Suite 300, Columbus, OH 43215.
Tells of reasons for underachievement by gifted girls; the barriers to achievement that bright women encounter; and how they can be helped to surmount these barriers.

Miedzian, Myriam. *Boys Will Be Boys: Breaking the Link Between Masculinity and Violence*. New York: Anchor Books/Doubleday, 1991.

Well researched, passionate, and readable, presents information on male stereotyping and its violence component, its heavy promotion by media and other aspects of society, and what parents as well as others can do to counteract it.

Thorne, Barrie. *Gender Play: Boys and Girls in School*. New Brunswick, NJ: Rutgers University Press, 1993.

Very readable account of the author's observations of fourth and fifth graders on the playground and in class; the dynamics of gender in single-sex playgroups, interactions within them, and between boys and girls as individuals and as members of mixed gender groups. Her research-supported reflections offer both new insights and guides to action, for parents as well as adults in schools.

■ ■ ■ ■

*About Women on Campus 1* (1), winter 1991. Washington, D.C.: National Association for Women in Education.

*About Women on Campus 1* (2), spring 1992, Washington, D.C.: National Association for Women in Education.

*About Women on Campus,* summer 1993, Washington, D.C.: National Association for Women in Education.

Abrams, M.H., ed. *The Norton Anthology of English Literature,* 1st ed. New York: W.W.Norton & Company, 1962.

Aburdene, Patricia and John Naisbitt. *Megatrends for Women.* New York: Willard Books, 1992.

Adams, James T. "Let the Four Horsemen Ride," in Crosier, 1992.

Adelman, Clifford. *Women at Thirtysomething: Paradoxes of Attainment.* Washington, D.C.: U.S. Dept. of Education, 1991.

Adler, Martha A. "The Checklist: How Equitable is Your Science Education Program?" *Equity Coalition,* 1993/94, University of Michigan.

Adler, Patricia A., Steven J. Kless and Peter Adler. "Socialization to Gender Roles: Popularity among Elementary School Boys and Girls." *Sociology of Education* 65, 169-187, July 1992.

Admissions Testing Program. *National Report on College-Bound Seniors.* Princeton, N.J.: College Entrance Examination Board, 1985.

Agee, James. *Let Us Now Praise Famous Men.* Boston: Houghton-Mifflin, 1989.

Anderson, Terry D. *Transforming Leadership: New Skills for an Extraordinary Future.* Abbotsford, BC, Canada: University College of the Fraser Valley, 1992.

Antony, Mary. "Gender and Science: A Review of Research Literature." *Equity Coalition,* 1993/94, University of Michigan.

Applebee, Arthur N. *A Study of Book-Length Works Taught in High School English Courses.* Albany, N.Y.: Center for the Teaching and Learning of Literature, 1989.

Archer, John and Barbara Lloyd. *Sex and Gender.* Cambridge: Cambridge University Press, 1982.

Asante, M.K. and W.B.Gudykunst, eds. *Handbook of International and Intercultural Communication.* Newbury Park, Calif.: Sage Publications, 1989.

Association of American Colleges and Universities. *On Campus with Women* 23 (4), spring 1994.

Atwood, Margaret. *Good Bones and Simple Murders.* Rockland, Mass.: Wheeler Publishing, 1994.

Atwood, Margaret. *Power Politics.* Toronto: Anansi, 1972.

Axtell, James, ed. *The Indian Peoples of Eastern America: A Documentary History of the Sexes.* New York: Oxford University Press, 1981.

Ayim, Maryann. "Language: The Syntax of Power." Part of a panel discussion on "Theories and Techniques for Feminist Education" at the Sixth Annual Convention of the National Women's Studies Association, Rutgers University, June 24-28, 1984.

Bank Street College of Education. *News from the Center for Children and Technology* 1 (2), October 1991.

Banks, James A. *Multiethnic Education: Theory and Practice,* 3rd ed. Boston: Allyn and Bacon, 1994.

Banks, James A. and Cherry A. McGee Banks, eds. *Multicultural Education: Issues and Perspectives,* 2nd ed. Boston: Allyn and Bacon, 1993.

Baron, Ava. "On Looking at Men: Gender and the Making of a Gendered Working-Class History," in Shapiro, ed. 1994.

Barry, David S. "Growing up Violent: Decades of Research Link Screen Mayhem with Increase in Aggressive Behavior." *Media and Values* 62, summer 1994.

Beck, John D.W. and Neil M.Yeager. *The Leader's Window: Mastering the Four Styles of Leadership to Build High-Performance Teams.* New York: John Wiley & Sons, 1994.

Belenky, Mary, Blythe Clinchy, Nancy Goldberger and Jill Tarule. *Women's Ways of Knowing: The Development of Self, Voice and Mind.* New York: Basic Books, 1986.

Berkowitz, Leonard. "The Effects of Observing Violence." *Scientific American* 210, 1964.

Bernard-Powers, Jane. "Out of the Cameos and into the Conversation: Gender, Social Studies, and Curriculum Transformation," in Gaskell and Willinsky, 1995.

Bernikow, Louise, ed. *The World Split Open: Four Centuries of Women Poets in England and America.* New York: Vintage, 1974.

Betz, Nancy E., Laurie Mintz and Gena Speakmon. "Gender Differences in the Accuracy of Self-Reported Weight." *Sex Roles* 30 (7/8), 1994.

Bigler, Rebecca S. and Lynn S. Liben. "The Role of Attitudes and Interventions in Gender-Schematic Processing." *Child Development* 61, 1990.

Bingham, Marjorie Wall and Susan Hill Gross. *Women in the USSR: From Ancient Russia through the Revolution*. 1980. (See Women in World History Series.)

Bitter, Gary G. "Technology and Minorities." *Computers in the Schools* 9 (1), 1992.

Bjorkvist, Kaj and Pirkko Niemel, eds. *Of Mice and Women: Aspects of Female Aggression*. New York: Academic Press, 1992.

Blaikie, Fiona. "Thoughts Concerning a Feminst Emphasis in Art Education." *Art Education* 45 (2), 1992.

Blanchard, Kenneth H. "Situational Leadership II," in Ritvo, Litwin, and Butler, eds. 1995.

Bloom, Benjamin S. ed. *Taxonomy of Educational Objectives: The Classification of Educational Goals, Handbook I: Cognitive Domain*. New York: David McKay, 1956.

Bloom, Harold. *The Western Canon: The Books and School of the Ages*. New York: Harcourt Brace, 1994.

Bohannan, Laura. "Shakespeare in the Bush," *Natural History* August/September 1966. Reprinted a number of times, for instance in Spradley and McGurdy, eds., 1980.

Bohlin, Roy M. "Computers and Gender Differences: Achieving Equity." *Computers in the Schools* 9 (2/3), 1993

Bornholt, Laurel J., Jacqueline Goodnow, and George H.Cooney. "Influence of Gender Stereotypes on Adolescents' Perceptions of Their Own Achievement." *American Educational Research Journal* 31 (3), 1994.

Bradbard, Marilyn R., Carol Lynn Martin, Richard C. Endsley and Charles F .Halverson. "Influence of Sex Stereotypes on Children's Exploration and Memory: A Competence versus Performance Distinction." *Developmental Psychology* 22 (4), 1986.

Breen, William J. "Black Women and the Great War: Mobilization and Reform in the South," 1982, in Friedman and Shade, eds., 1987.

Bridenthal, Renate, Claudia Koonz, and Susan Stuard, eds. *Becoming Visible: Women in European History*. 2nd ed. Boston: Houghton-Mifflin, 1987.

Brod, Harry. *The Making of Masculinities: The New Men's Studies*. Boston: Allen & Unwin, 1987.

Brown, Alan S., Mary B. Larsen, Susan A. Rankin, and R. Allen Ballard. "Sex Differences in Information Processing," *Sex Roles* 6 (5), 1980.

Brown, Lyn Mikel. "A Problem of Vision: Relational Knowledge in Girls Ages Seven to Sixteen." *Women's Sudies Quarterly* 1 & 2, 1991.

Brown, Robin ed. W*omen's Issues. The Reference Shelf*, Vol. 65, no. 5. New York: H.W. Wilson, 1993.

Bruner, Jerome and Helen Haste, eds. *Making Sense: The Child's Construction of the World*. New York: Methuen, 1987.

Brunner, Cornelia and Margaret Honey. "Gender and Technology," in National Coalition, 1992.

Budgeon, Shelley and Dawn H. Currie. "From Feminism to Postfeminism: Women's Liberation in Fashion Magazines." *Women's Studies International Forum* 18 (2), 1995.

Buel, Joy Day and Richard Buel. *The Way of Duty: A Woman and her Family in Revolutionary America*. New York: Norton, 1985.

Buerk, Dorothy. "Women's Metaphors for Math: Connecting with Mathematics," in National Coalition 1992.

Bull, Peter. *Body Movement and Interpersonal Communication*. New York: John Wiley, 1983.

Bureau of Justice, *Population Today* 21 (3), March 1993.

Caine, Renate, Nummela and Geoffrey Caine. *Making Connections: Teaching and the Human Brain*. Alexandria, Va.: Association for Supervision and Curriculum Development, 1991.

Carlsson-Paige, Nancy and Diane E. Levin. *Who's Calling the Shots? How to Respond Effectively to Children's Fascination with War Play and War Toys*. Philadelphia, PA: New Society Publishers, 1990.

Carnegie Council on Adolescent Development. *Turning Points: Preparing American Youth for the 21st Century*. 1989.

Carpenter, C.J., A.C.Huston and W.Holt. "Modification of Pre-School Sex-Typed Behaviors by Participation in Adult-Structured Activities." *Sex Roles* 14, 1986.

Catsambis, Sophia. "The Path to Math: Gender and Racial-Ethnic Differences in Mathematics Participation from Middle School to High School." *Sociology of Education* 67, July 1994.

Chapman, Anne. *Making Sense: Teaching Critical Reading across the Curriculum*. New York: The College Board, 1993.

Chapman, Anne. "Working with Quantified History: Women in the Labor Force," in Downey, ed., 1982.

Chapman, Anne. "The Textbook as Primary Source." *Social Education* 44 (2), February 1980.

Chapman, Anne, ed. *Approaches to Women's History*. Washington: American Historical Association, 1979.

Chen, Milton. "Gender and Computers: The Beneficial Effects of Experiences on Attitudes." *Journal of Educational Computing Research* 2 (3), 1986.

Clark, Clifford Edward. *The American Family Home , 1800-1960*. Chapel Hill: University of North Carolina Press, 1986.

Clayborne, Mawi Yah. "The Relationship Between the Attitudes of Urban Students and Mothers towards Computers." *The Journal of Negro History* 60 (1), 1991.

Clem, Stephen C. and Z.Vance Wilson. *Paths to New Curriculum*. Washington, D.C.: National Association of Independent Schools, 1991.

Clifton, James A., ed. *Being and Becoming Indian: Biographical Studies of North American Frontiers*. Chicago: Dorse Press, 1989.

Cohen, Beth, ed. *The Distaff Side: Representing the Female in Homer's Odyssey*. New York: Oxford University Press, 1995.

Cohen, Deborah L. "More Fathers Take on Role of Child Care, Study Finds." *Education Week*, September 29, 1993.

Cohen, Richard, *Peer Mediation in Schools: Students Resolving Conflict*. Glenview, Ill.: Scott-Foresman, 1995.

The College Board. *AP National Summary Reports*. New York: The College Board, 1994.

The College Board. *College-Bound Seniors: 1994 Profile of SAT and Achievement Test Takers*. New York: The College Board, 1994.

*College Board Review* #165. Early winter 1992/93.

*The College Board News*. January 1990.

Collins, Georgia C. "Art Education as a Negative Example of Gender-Enriching The Curriculum," in Gaskell and Willinsky, 1995.

Coltrane, Scott and Kenneth Allan. " 'New' Fathers and Old Stereotypes: Representations of Masculinity in 1980s Television and Advertising." *Masculinities* 2 (4), winter 1994.

Conger, Jay A. *Learning to Lead: The Art of Transforming Managers into Leaders*. San Francisco: Jossey-Bass, 1992.

Cookson, Peter. "Race and Class in America's Elite Preparatory Boarding Schools." *The Journal of Negro History* 60 (1), 1991.

Cosman, Carol, Joan Keefe and Kathleen Weaver, eds. 1978. *The Penguin Book of Women Poets*. New York: Penguin Books, 1978.

Countryman, Joan. "Is Gender an Issue in Math Class?" in National Coalition 1993.

Craig, Steve, ed. *Men, Masculinity and the Media*. Newbury Park, Calif.: Sage Publications, 1992.

Crawford, Mary and Margo MacLeod. "Gender in the College Classroom: An Assessment of the 'Chilly Climate' for Women." *Sex Roles* 23 (3/4), 1990.

Crawford, Mary. "Agreeing to Differ: Feminist Epistemologies and Women's Ways of Knowing," in Crawford and Gentry, eds., 1989.

Crawford, Mary and Margaret Gentry, eds. *Gender and Thought: Psychological Perspectives*. New York: Springer-Verlag, 1989.

Crawford, Mary and Roger Chaffin. "Cognitive Research on Gender and Comprehension," in Flynn and Schweickart, eds., 1986.

Creedon, Pamela J., ed. *Women in Mass Communication*. 2nd ed. Newbury Park, Calif.: Sage Publications, 1993.

Crosier, Louis M. "To New Dorm Faculty," in Crosier, ed., 1992.

Crosier, Louis M., ed. *Healthy choices, Healthy schools: The Residential Curriculum*. Washington, D.C.: Avocus Publishing, 1992.

Current Population Reports. *Special Studies, Series P-3 #184: Demographic State of the Nation*. Washington, D.C.: Department of Commerce, Bureau of the Census, February 1993.

Current Population Reports. *Special Studies. Child Support and Alimony 1983*. Washington, D.C.: Department of Commerce, Bureau of the Census, July 1985.

Cushner, Kenneth, Averil McClelland and Philip Safford. *Human Diversity in Education: An Integrative Approach*. New York: McGraw Hill, 1992.

Dalton, Kathleen. *A Portrait of a School: Coeducation at Andover*. Andover, Mass.: Phillips Academy, 1986.

Davis, Donald M. "Portrayals of Women in Prime-Time Network Television: Some Demographic Characteristics." *Sex Roles* 23 (5/6), 1990.

Davis, Laurel R. "Male Cheerleaders and the Naturalization of Gender," in Messner and Sabo, 1990.

Deats, Sara Munson and Lagretta Tallent Lenker. *Gender and Academe: Feminist Pedagogy and Politics*. Lanham, Md.: Rowman & Littlefield, 1994.

Deaux, Kay and Mary Kite. "Gender Stereotypes," in Denmark and Paludi, eds., 1993.

Demos, John. *A Little Commonweath: Family Life in the Plymouth Colony*. New York: Oxford Press, 1970.

Denmark, Florence L. "Women, Leadership. and Empowerment." *Psychology of Women Quarterly* 17, 1993.

Denmark, Florence L. and Michele A. Paludi. *Psychology of Women: A Handbook of Issues and Theories*. Westport, Conn.: Greenwood Press, 1993.

Downey, Matthew T., ed. *Teaching American History: New Directions*, Bulletin No. 67. Washington, D.C.: National Council for the Social Studies, 1992.

Dunn, Judy. "Understanding Feelings: The Early Stages," in Bruner and Haste, eds. ,1987.

Eagly, A.H. and Johnson, B.T. "Gender and Leadership Style: A Meta-Analysis." *Psychological Bulletin* 108, 1990.

Eakins, Barbara Westbrook and R. Gene Eakins. *Sex Differences in Human Communication*. Boston: Houghton Mifflin, 1978.

Eccles, Jacquelynne, Allan Wigfield, Rena D. Harold and Phyllis Blumenfeld. "Age and Gender Differences in Children's Self and Task Perceptions During Elementary School. *Child Development* 64, 1993.

Eccles, Jacquelynne. "Bringing Young Women to Math and Science" in Crawford and Gentry, 1989.

*Education Week*, October 26, 1994.

*Education Week* July 14, 1993.

*Education Week*, November 13, 1991.

*Education Week*, October 16, 1991.

*Education Week,* September 5, 1990.

Elliott, D.L. and Arthur Woodward, eds. *Textbooks and Schooling in the United States: 89th Yearbook of the National Society for the Study of Education, Part I.* Chicago: University of Chicago Press, 1990.

Ellyson, Steve L., John F. Dovidio, and B.J.Fehr. "Visual Dominance in Women and Men," in Mayo and Henley, eds.,1981.

Ellyson, Steve L., John F. Dovidio, and Clifford E. Brown. "The Look of Power: Gender Differences and Similarities in Visual Dominance Behavior," in Ridgeway, ed., 1992.

Entwhistle, Doris R. and David P. Baker. "Gender and Young Children's Expectations for Performance in Arithmetic." *Developmental Psychology* 19, 2. 1983

*Equity Coalition for Race, Gender, and National Origin.* Fall 1993-spring 1994. Programs for Educational Opportunity, Dept. of Education, University of Michigan, Ann Arbor.

Erickson, R. and J. Shultz. "Students' Experience of the Curriculum," in Jackson, ed., 1992

Eron, Leonard. "Prescription for the Reduction of Aggression." *American Psychologist,* March 1980.

Fagot, Beverly I. and Richard Hagan. "Observations of Parent Reactions to Sex-Stereotyped Behaviors: Age and Sex Effects." *Child Development* 62, 1991.

Fallon, Patricia, Melanie A. Latzman, and Susan C. Wooley, eds. *Feminist Perspectives on Eating Disorders.* New York: The Guilford Press, 1994.

Farnham, Christie, ed. *The Impact of Feminist Research in the Academy.* Bloomington: Indiana University Press, 1987.

Feiring, Candice and Michael Lewis. "The Child's Social Network from Three to Six years: The Effects of Age, Sex, and Socioeconomic Status," in Salzinger, Antrobus, and Hammer, eds., 1988.

Fejes, Fred J. "Masculinity as Fact: A Review of Empirical Mass Communications Research on Masculinity," in Craig, ed., 1992.

Fennema, Elizabeth. "Mathematics, Gender and Research," in Woodrow Wilson, 1993.

Fennema, Elizabeth and Gilah C.Leder. *Mathematics and Gender.* New York: Teachers College Press, 1990

Fierman, Jaclyn. "Why Women Still Don't Hit the Top," in Syrett and Hogg, eds., 1992.

Fiol-Matta, Liza and Mariam K. Chamberlain. *Women of Color and the Multicultural Curriculum: Transforming the College Classroom.* New York: The Feminist Press, 1994.

Fiske, Edward B. *Smart Schools, Smart Kids: Why Do Some Schools Work?* New York: Simon and Schuster, 1991.

Flynn, Elizabeth A. and Patrocinio P. Schweikart, eds. *Gender and Reading: Essays on Readers, Texts, and Contexts.* Baltimore: Johns Hopkins University Press, 1986.

Fox, Thomas. "Race and Gender in Collaborative Learning," in Reagan et al., eds., 1994.

Fox-Genovese, Elizabeth. *Within the Plantation Household: Black and White Women of the Old South.* Chapel Hill: University of North Carolina Press, 1988.

Frader, Laura Levine. "Women in the Industrial Capitalist Economy," in Bridenthal, Koonz, and Stuard, eds., 1987.

Franck, Irene M. and David M. Brownstone. *Women's World: A Timeline of Women in History.* New York: HarperCollins, 1995.

Friedman, Jean E. and William Shade, eds. *Our American Sisters: Women in American Life and Thought.* 3rd ed. Lexington, Mass.: D.C. Heath, 1982.

Galambos, Nancy L., David M. Almeida and Anne C. Petersen. "Masculinity, Femininity, and Sex Role Attitudes in Early Adolescence: Exploring Gender Intensification." *Child Development* 61, 1990.

Garibaldi, Antoine M. "Educating and Motivating African American Males to Succeed." *The Journal of Negro Education* 61 (1), 1992.

Garner, James Finn. *Politically Correct Bedtime Stories.* New York: Macmillan,1994.

Gaskell, Jane and John Willinsky, eds. *Gender In/Forms the Curriculum.* New York: Teachers College Press, 1995.

Geadelmann, Patricia L. et al. "Sex Equity in Physical Education and Athletics," in Klein, 1985.

Gerbner, George. *Women and Minorities in Television: A Study in Casting And Fate.* (A report to the Screen Actors Guild and the American Federation of Radio and Television Artists, June 1993). Philadelphia: Annenberg School for Communication, University of Pennsylvania, 1994.

Gerzon, Mark. *A Choice of Heroes: The Changing Faces of American Manhood.* Boston: Houghton Mifflin, 1982.

Gibbs, Nancy. "Office crimes." *Time,* October 21, 1991.

Gilbert, Sandra M. and Susan Gubar. *The Norton Anthology of Literature by Women: The Tradition in English.* New York: W.W. Norton, 1985.

Gilligan, Carol. *In a Different Voice.* Cambridge, Mass.: Harvard University Press, 1982.

Ginorio, Angela B. *Warming the Climate for Women in Academic Science.* Washington, D.C.: Association of American Colleges and Universities Program on the Status and Education of Women, 1995.

Goldstein, Jeffrey H. "Sex Differences in Aggressive Play and Toy Preference," in Bjorkqvist and Niemela, eds., 1992.

Gottlieb, Beatrice. *The Family in the Western World from the Black Death to the Industrial Age.* New York: Oxford University Press, 1993.

Graber, Julia A. et al. "Prediction of eating problems: An Eight-Year Study of Adolescent Girls." *Developmental Psychology* 30 (8), 1994.

Graddol, David and Joan Schwann. *Gender Voices*. Cambridge, Mass.: Basil Blackwell, 1989.

Green, Harvey and Mary E. Perry. *The Light of the Home: An Intimate View of the Lives of Women In Victorian America*. New York: Pantheon, 1983.

Greenfield, P.M. *Mind and Media: The Effects of Television, Video Games and Computers*. Cambridge, Mass.: Harvard University Press, 1984.

Gumperz, John J., ed. *Language and Social Identity*. Cambridge: Cambridge University Press, 1982.

Gutman, Herbert. *The Black Family in Slavery and Freedom, 1750-1925*. New York: Random House, 1977.

Haaken, J. "Field Dependence Research: A Historical Analysis of a Psychological Construct." *Signs* 13 (2), 1988.

Hahn, Sophie and Anne Liwin. "Women and Men: Understanding and Respecting Gender Differences in the Workplace," in Ritvo, Liwin, and Butler, eds., 1995.

Hall, Christine C. Iijima and Matthew J. Crum. "Women and 'Body-isms' in Television Beer Commercials." *Sex Roles* 31 (5/6), 1994.

Hall, Roberta M. and Bernice Sandler. *The Classroom Climate: A Chilly One for Women?* Washington D.C.: Project on the Status and Education of Women, Association of American Colleges, 1982

Halpern, Diane F. *Sex Differences in Cognitive Abilities*. Hillsdale, N.J.: Lawrence Erlbaum Associates, 1986.

Harding, Sandra. *The Science Question in Feminism*. Ithaca, N.Y.: Cornell University Press, 1986.

Hargreaves, Jennifer. *Sporting Females: Critical Issues in the History and Sociology of Women's Sports*. New York: Routledge, 1994.

Harris, Anne Sutherland and Linda Nochlin. *Women Artists: 1550-1950*. New York: Alfred A. Knopf, 1977.

Hartman, Susan M. *American Women in the 1940s: The Home Front and Beyond*. Boston: Twayne Publishers, 1982.

Haskell, F. "Artemisia's Revenge?" *New York Review of Books*, July 20, 1989.

Haub, Karl. "Average Lifetime Births, 1990: Births per U.S. Woman?" *Population Today* 21 (9), September 1993.

Haub, Karl. "Storms over Norms." *Population Today* 20 (11), November 1992.

Hayden, Dolores. *The Grand Domestic Revolution: A History of Feminist Designs for American Homes, Neighborhoods, and Cities*. Cambridge, Mass.: The MIT Press, 1981.

Hayghe, H.V. "Are Women Leaving the Laborforce? Recent Interruptions in Women's Laborforce Gains do not Appear to Signal a Reversal in Their Trend of Increasing Participation." *Monthly Labor Review*, July 1994.

Hayghe, H.V. and S.M. Bianchi. "Married Mothers' Work Patterns: The Job-Family Compromise." *Monthly Labor Review*, June 1994.

Hayghe, H.V. "Working Wives' Contribution to Family Income." *Monthly Labor Review,* August 1993.

Hecht, Michael, Peter Andersen, and Sidney Ribeau. "The Cultural Dimensions of Nonverbal Communication," in Asante and Gudykunst, eds., 1989.

Hedges, Elaine and Wendt, Ingrid. *In Her Own Image: Women Working in the Arts*. New York: The Feminist Press, 1980.

Hein, Hilda and Carolyn Korsmeyer. *Aesthetics in Feminist Perspective*. Bloomington: Indiana University Press, 1993.

Henley, Nancy M. *Body Politics: Power, Sex, and Nonverbal Communication*. New York: Simon & Schuster, 1977.

Hersey, Paul and Kenneth H. Blanchard. *Management of Organizational Behavior: Utilizing Human Resources*. 4th ed. Englewood Cliffs, NJ: Prentice-Hall, 1982.

Hesse, P. and Cross, S. "Star Wars or Rainbows as Defense against Evil? Messages about Conflict Resolution on Boys' and Girls' Television." Presented at the International Society of Political Psychology, Thirteenth Annual Scientific Meeting, Washington D.C., July 11-14, 1990.

Hewitt, Nancy A., ed. *Women, Families, and Communities: Readings in American History*. Glenview, Ill.: Harper-Collins, 1989.

Higginbotham, Elizabeth. "Designing an Inclusive Curriculum: Bringing Women into the Core." *Women's Studies Quarterly* 18 (1 & 2), spring/summer 1990.

Hijiya, Jim. "Changing United States History Survey Textbooks." *The History Teacher* 28 (2), February 1995.

Hindig, Andrea, ed. *Women's History Sources: A Guide to Archives and Manuscript Collections in the United States*. Ann Arbor, Mich.: R.R. Bowker, 1979.

Hood, Jane C., ed. *Men, Work, and Family.* Newbury Park, Calif.: Sage Publications, 1993.

Horgan, Dianne D. *Achieving Gender Equity: Strategies for the Classroom*. Boston: Allyn and Bacon, 1995.

Hughes, Jean O. and Bernice R. Sandler. *In Case of Sexual Harassment: A Guide for Women Students*. Washington, D.C: Project on the Status and Education of Women, Association of American Colleges, 1986.

Hughes, Jean O. and Bernice R. Sandler. *Peer Harassment: Hassles for Women on Campus*. Washington, D.C: Project on the Status and Education of Women, Association of American Colleges, 1988.

Hunter College Women's Studies Collective. *Women's Realities, Women's Choices*. 2nd ed. New York: Oxford University Press, 1995.

Huston, Aletha C. and C. Jan Carpenter. "Gender Differences in Preschool Classrooms: The Effects of Sex-Typed Activity Choices," in Wilkinson and Marrett, eds., 1985.

Hyde, Janet Shibley and Laurie A. Frost. "Meta-Analysis in the Psychology of Women," in Denmark and Paludi, eds., 1993.

Hyde, Janet Shibley. "Meta-Analysis and the Psychology of Gender-Differences." *Signs* 16, 1990.

*Information Please Almanac*. New York: Houghton Mifflin, 1995.

Ingram, Glee. *Together We Can: An Awareness Training Program in Sex-Role Stereotyping for Elementary and Secondary Teachers and Counselors*. Washington, D.C.: U.S. Department of Health, Education, and Welfare, Women's Educational Equity Act Program, n.d.

Jackson, P.W. ed. *Handbook of Research on Curriculum*. New York: Macmillan, 1992.

James, Edward T., Janet Wilson James, and Paul Boyer eds. *Notable American Women: A Biographical Dictionary* 1607-1950., Vol.4 , 1950-75, ed. Barbara Sicherman. Cambridge, Mass.: Belknap Press, 1971.

Johnson, Carol Shulte. "Sexism in Language: The Case for Including Everybody," in Weiner, 1980.

Johnson, Catherine B. et al. "Persistence of Men's Misconceptions of Friendly Cues across a Variety of Interpersonal Encounters." *Psychology of Women Quarterly* 15, 1991.

Johnson, James E. and Jaipaul L. Roopnarine. "The Preschool Classroom and Sex Differences In Children's Play," in Liss, ed., 1983.

Jordan, Sarah Unsworth. "Gender in the Dorm," in Crosier, ed., 1992.

Kahle, Jane Butler. "Women in Science: Where Do We Go from Here?" in National Coalition, 1992

Kahn, Coppelia. "Coming of Age in Verona," in Lenz, Greeene, and Neely, eds., 1980.

Kalish, Susan. "American Families: Greater Diversity but Slower Change Ahead." *Population Today* 20 (9), September 1992.

Kanegis, Arthur. "New Heroes for a New Age: Stories of Nonviolence Inspire the Best in Us." *Media & Values* 63, Fall 1993.

Katz, Phyllis A. and Keith K. Ksansnak. "Developmental Aspects of Gender Role Flexibility and Traditionality in Middle Childhood and Adolescence." *Developmental Psychology* 30 (2), 1994.

Katz, Phyllis A. and P. Vincent Walsh. "Modification of Children's Gender-Stereotyped Behavior." *Child Development* 62, 1991.

Kazemek, Francis E. "Reading and the Female Moral Imagination," in Gaskell and Willinsky, 1995.

Keller, Evelyn Fox. *Reflections on Gender and Science*. New Haven: Yale University Press, 1985.

Keller, Evelyn Fox. *A Feeling for the Organism: The Life and Work of Barbara McClintock*. New York: Freeman, 1983.

Kelly, Ursula A. "The Feminist Trespass: Gender, Literature, and Curriculum," in Gaskell and Willinsky, 1995.

Kelly-Gadol, Joan. "Did Women Have a Renaissance?" in Bridenthal, Koonz, and Stuard, eds., 1987.

Kerber, Linda. *Women of the Republic: Intellect and Ideology in Revolutionary America*. Chapel Hill: University of North Carolina Press, 1980.

Kilbourne, Jean. "Still Killing Us Softly: Advertising and the Obsession with Thinnness," in Fallon, Katzman, and Wooley, eds., 1994.

Kimmel, Michael S. and Michael S. Messner eds. *Men's Lives*. New York: Macmillan, 1989.

Kimmel, Michael S., ed. *Changing Men: New Directions in Research on Men and Masculinity*. Newbury Park, Calif.: Sage Publications, 1987.

Klein, Susan S.,ed. *Handbook for Achieving Sex Equity through Education*. Baltimore: Johns Hopkins University Press, 1985.

Kneedler, Peter E. "Differences between Boys and Girls on California's New Statewide Assessments in History/Social Science." *Social Studies Review* 27 (3), spring 1988.

Kochman, Thomas. *Black and White Styles in Conflict*. Chicago: University of Chicago Press, 1981.

Kolb, Frances. *Portraits of Our Mothers*, Windsor, Conn.: National Women's History Project, n.d.

Kortenhaus, Carole M. and Jack Demarest. "Gender Role Stereotyping in Children's Literature: An Update." *Sex Roles* 28 (3/4), 1993.

Kramer, Pamela E. and Sheila Lehmann. "Mismeasuring Women: A Critique of Research on Computer Ability and Avoidance." *Signs* 16 (1), autumn 1990.

Kratwohl, David R., Benjamin S. Bloom and Bertram B. Masia. *Taxonomy of Educational Objectives: The Classification of Educational Goals. Handbook II: Affective Domain*. New York: David McKay, 1964.

Kriesberg, Louis, Terell A. Northrup, and Stuart J. Thorson, eds. *Intractable Conflicts and their Transformation*. Syracuse, NY: Syracuse University Press, 1989.

Kuhn, Thomas S. *The Structure of Scientific Revolutions*. 2nd ed. Chicago: University of Chicago Press, 1970.

Lakoff, George and Mark Johnson. *Metaphors We Live By*. Chicago: University of Chicago Press, 1980.

Lamison, Leatha. "Income, Poverty, and Wealth." *Current Population Reports*, July 1992.

Landes, Joan B. *Women and the Public Sphere in the Age of the French Revolution*. Ithaca: Cornell University Press, 1988.

Landrine, Hope, Stephen Bardwell and Tina Dean. "Gender and Alcohol Use: A Study of the Significance of the Masculine Role." *Sex Roles* 19, 1988.

Laudan, Larry. *The Book of Risks*. New York: John Wiley, 1994.

Lauter, Estella. "Re-enfranchising Art: Feminist Interventions in the Theory of Art," in Hein and Korsmeyer, eds., 1993.

Lauter, Paul. "Feminism, Multiculturalism, and the Canonical Tradition." *Transformations* 5 (2), fall 1994.5

Lauter, Paul. *Canons and Contexts*. New York: Oxford University Press, 1991.

Lauter, Paul. "Reconstructing American Literature: A Strategy for Change," in Spanier, Bloom, and Boroviak, eds., 1984.

Lawton, Millicent. "Four of Five Students in Grades 8 to 11 Sexually Harassed at School, Poll Finds." *Education Week*, June 9, 1993.

Lazarus, Wendy and Laurie Lipper. *America's Children and the Information Superhighway: A Briefing Book and National Action Agenda.* Santa Monica, Calif.: The Children's Partnership, 1994.

Lazier, Linda and A.G.Kendrick. "Women in Advertisements." in Creedon, ed., 1993.

Leder, Gilah C. "Gender Differences in Mathematics: An Overview," in Fennema and Leder, 1990.

LeGuin, Ursula K. *Dancing at the Edge of the World: Thoughts on Words, Women, Places.* New York: Harper and Row, 1989.

LeGuin, Ursula K. *The Language of the Night: Essays on Fantasy and Science Fiction.* Rev. ed. New York: HarperCollins, 1989.

Lenz, Carolyn Ruth Swift, Gayle Greene and Carol Thomas Neely, eds. *The Woman's Part: Feminist Criticism of Shakespeare.* Urbana: University of Illinois Press, 1980.

Lerner, Gerda. "The Lady and the Mill-Girl: Changes in the Status of Women in the Age of Jackson," in Friedman and Shade, eds., 1982.

Lerner, Gerda. *Teaching Women's History.* Washington, D.C.: American Historical Association, 1981.

Lerner, Gerda, ed. *Black Women in White America: A Documentary History.* New York: Random House, 1973.

Levin, Tamar and Claire Gordon. "Effect of Gender and Computer Experience on Attitudes towards Computers." *Journal of Educational Computing Research* 5 (1), 1989.

Levy, Darline Gay; Harriet Branson Applewhite, and Mary Durham Johnson, eds. *Women in Revolutionary Paris: Selected Documents Translated with Notes and Commentary.* Urbana: University of Illinois Press, 1979.

Levy, Darline Gay and Harriet Branson Applewhite. "Women and Political Revolution in Paris," in Bridenthal, Koonz, and Stuard, eds., 1987.

Lewin, Tamar. "Women Are Becoming Equal Providers: Half of Working Women Bring Home Half the Household Income." *The New York Times* May 11, 1995.

Lewis, Magda Gere. *Without a Word: Teaching beyond Women's Silence.* New York: Routledge, 1993

Lewis, Robert. "Equity Eludes Women." *AARP Bulletin* 32 (10), November 1991.

Liben, Lynn S. and Margaret L. Signorella. "Gender-Schematic Processing in Children: The Role of Initial Interpretations of Stimuli." *Developmental Psychology* 29 (1), 1993.

Linn, Eleanor. "Science and Equity: Why this Issue is Important," in *Equity Coalition* 1993/94.

Linn, Marcia C. and Anne C. Petersen. *"Facts and Assumptions about the Nature of Sex Differences,"* in Klein, 1985.

Linn, Marcia C. and Anne C. Petersen. "Emergence and Characterization of Sex Differences in Spatial Ability: A Metaanalysis." *Child Development* 56, 1985.

Liss, Marsha B., ed. *Social and Cognitive Skills: Sex Roles and Children's Play.* New York: Academic Press, 1983.

Liss, Marsha B. "Learning Gender-Related Skills through Play," in Liss, ed., 1983.

Lloyd, Barbara. "Social Representations of Gender," in Bruner and Haste, eds., 1987.

Loftus, Elizabeth F., Mahzarin R. Banaji, Jonathan W. Schooler, and Rachel A. Foster. "Who Remembers What? Gender Differences in Memory." *Michigan Quarterly Review* XXVI (1), winter 1987.

Lorber, Judith. *Paradoxes of Gender.* New Haven: Yale University Press, 1994.

Lugaila, Terry. "Households, Families and Children: A 30-year Perspective." *Current Population Characteristics*, November 1992.

Lyman, Peter. "The Fraternal Bond as a Joking Relationship: A Case Study of the Role of Sexist Jokes in Male Group Bonding," in Kimmel, ed., 1987.

Machung, Ann. "Talking Career, Thinking Job: Gender Difference in Career and Family Expectations of Berkeley Seniors." *Feminist Studies* 15, 1989.

Madhere, Serge. "Self-esteem of African-American Pre-adolescents." *The Journal of Negro History* 60 (1), 1991.

Maher, Frances A. and Mary Kay Thompson Tetreault. *The Feminist Classroom.* New York : Basic Books, 1994.

Maher, Frances. "Pedagogies for the Gender-Balanced Classroom." *Journal of Thought* 20 (3), fall 1985.

Maltz, Daniel N. and Ruth A. Borker. "A Cultural Approach to Male-Female Miscommunication," in Gumperz, ed., 1982.

Mark, Sandra Fay. "To Succeed or not to Succeed: A Critical Review of Issues in Learned Helplessness." *Contemporary Educational Psychology* 8, 1983.

Marshall, Sandra P. and Julie D. Smith. "Sex Differences in Learning Mathematics: A Longitudinal Study with Item and Error Analyses." *Journal of Educational Psychology* 79 (4), 1987.

Martin, Jane Roland. "The Radical Future of Gender Enrichment," in Gaskell and Willinsky, eds., 1995.

Martin, Lynn Carol and Jane K. Little. "The Development of Gender Stereotype Components." *Child Development* 61, 1990.

Martin, Lynn Carol and Charles F. Halverson. "The Effects of Sex- Stereotyping Schemas on Young Children's Memory." *Child Development* 54, 1983.

Mayo, Clara and Nancy M. Henley, eds. *Gender and Non-Verbal Behavior.* New York: Springer-Verlag, 1981.

McClelland, John R. "Visual Images and Re-imaging: A Review of Research in Mass Communication," in Creedon, ed., 1993.

McCormick, Theresa Mickey. *Creating the Non-Sexist Classroom: A Multicultural Approach.* New York: Teachers College, Columbia University, 1994.

McDonald, Scott. "Sex Bias in the Representation of Male and Female Characters in Children's Books." *Journal of Genetic Psychology* 150 (4), December 1989.

McIntosh, Peggy. "Interactive Phases of Curriculum Development: A Feminist Perspective." Working Paper # 124, Wellesley College Center for Research on Women, Wellesley, Mass., 1983.

McLaren, Arlene and Jim Gaskell. "Now You See It, Now You Don't: Gender as an Issue in School Science," in Gaskell and Willinsky, eds., 1995.

McQuade, Donald and Robert Atwan, eds. *The Winchester Reader.* Boston: St. Martin's Press, 1991.

Mee, Cynthia S. "Middle School Voices on Gender Identity." *Women's Educational Equity Act Publishing Center Digest*, March 1995.

Messner, Michael A. and Donald F.Sabo, eds. *Sport, Men, and the Gender Order.* Champaign, Ill.: Human Kinetics Books, 1990.

Miedzian, Myriam. *Boys Will be Boys: Breaking the Link between Masculinity and Violence.* N.Y.: Doubleday, 1991.

Miller, Judi Beinstein. "Women's and Men's Scripts for Interpersonal Conflict." *Psychology of Women Quarterly* 15, 1991.

Miller, Laura. "Women Found to be Making Gains on College-Entrance Exam Scores." *Education Week*, September 7, 1994.

Mills, Carol J. "Sex Typing, Self-Schemata, Memory, and Response Latency." *Journal of Personal and Social Psychology*, 1983.

Mimms, Elizabeth M. "Race Equity and Science Education: An Interview with Charles Payne," in *Equity Coalition* 1993/94.

Minnich, Elizabeth Kamarck. *Transforming Knowledge.* Philadelphia: Temple University Press, 1990.

Miura, Irene T. and Robert D. Hess. "Enrollment Differences in Computer Camps and Summer Classes." *The Computing Teacher* 11 (8), April 1984.

Moi, Toril. *Sexual/Textual Politics: Feminist Literary Theory.* New York: Methuen, 1985.

Mortimer, Jeffrey. "How TV Violence Hits Kids." *The Education Digest*, October 1994.

Muller, Gilbert H. and John A. William. *Bridges: Literature Across Cultures.* New York: McGraw-Hill, 1994.

Mundorf, Norbert, Stuart Westin, Nikhilesh Dholakia and Winifred Brownell. "Re-evaluating Gender Differences in New Communication Technologies." *Communication Research Reports* 9 (2), 1992.

Munsch, Robert N. *The Paper Bag Princess.* Toronto, Canada: Annick Press, 1980.

Myers, Mitzi. "Gender, Genres, Generations: Artist-Mothers and the Scripting of Girls' Lives: A Review Essay." *NWSA Journal* 2 (2), spring 1990.

*NAIS/CWIS Newsnotes.* Washington, D.C.: National Association of Independent Schools, Council for Women in Independent Schools, fall 1993.

*NAIS/CWIS Newsletter.* Washington, D.C.: National Association of Independent Schools, Council for Women in Independent Schools, winter 1992.

National Coalition of Girls' Schools. *Math and Science for Girls: The Task Force Reports. Teaching Strategies for Girls in Math and Science.* Concord, Mass.: National Coalition of Girls' Schools, 1991.

National Coalition of Girls' Schools. *Math and Science for Girls: The Complete Proceedings.* Concord, Mass.: National Coalition of Girls' Schools, 1992.

Neuls-Bates, Carol, ed. *Women in Music: An Anthology of Source Readings from the Middle Ages to the Present.* New York: Harper and Row,1982.

Neuschel, Kristen B. "Creating a New Past: Women and European History," in O'Barr, 1989.

Newcombe, Nora and Judith Semon Dubas. "A Longitudinal Study of Predictors of Spatial Ability in Adolescent Females." *Child Development* 63, 1992.

*New York Times Educational Supplement.* August 1989.

Niceley, H.T. "A Door Ajar: The Professional Position of Women Artists." *Art Education* 45 (2), 1992.

Noddings, Nel. "Gender and the Curriculum," in Jackson, ed., 1992.

Northrup, Terrell A. "The Dynamic of Identity in Personal and Social Conflict," in Kriesberg, Northrup, and Thorson, eds., 1989.

Norton, A.J. and L.F. Miller. "Marriage, Divorce, and Remarriage in the 1990s." *Current Population Reports,* 1992.

Norton, Mary Beth. *Liberty's Daughters: The Revolutionary Experience of American Women, 1750-1800.* Boston: Little, Brown, 1980.

Oak Knoll School. *Listening for All Voices: Gender Balancing the Curriculum.* Proceedings of a conference held at Oak Knoll School, Summit, N.J. , June 20-23, 1988.

O'Barr, Jean, ed. *Women and a New Academy: Gender and Cultural Contexts.* Madison: University of Wisconsin Press, 1989.

Ohanian, Susan. *Garbage Pizza, Patchwork Quilts, and Math Magic: Stories about Teachers Who Love to Teach and Children Who Love to Learn.* New York: Freeman, 1992.

Ong, Walter J. *Fighting for Life: Contest, Sexuality, and Consciousness.* Ithaca, N.Y.: Cornell University Press, 1981.

Perry, William G. *Forms of Intellectual and Ethical Development in the College Years.* New York: Holt, Rinehart, and Winston,1970.

Peterson, Penelope L. and Elizabeth Fennema. "Effective Teaching, Student Engagement in Classroom Activities, and Sex-Related Differences in Learning Mathematics." *American Educational Research Journal* 22 (3), 1985.

Pierce, Jon L. and John W. Newstrom. *Leaders and the Leadership Process: Readings, Self-Assessments, and Applications.* Boston: Austen Press/Irwin, 1995.

Pitsch, Mark. "A Force to Be Reckoned With." *Education Week*, June 21, 1995.

Pope, Deborah. "Notes towards a Supreme Fiction: The Work of Feminist Criticism," in O'Barr, 1989.

Postman, N., C. Nystrom, L. Strate, and C. Weingartner. *Myths, Men and Beer: An Analysis of Beer Commercials on Broadcast Television*. Washington, D.C.: AAA Foundation of Traffic Safety, 1987.

Powell, Gary N. 1988. *Women and Men in Management*. Newbury Park, Calif.: Sage Publications, 1988.

Power, Thomas G. "Mother-and-Father Infant Play: A Developmental Analysis." *Child Development* 56, 1985.

Presser, Harriet B. "The Housework Gender Gap." *Population Today*, 21 (7/8), July/August 1993.

*Project on the Status and Education of Women* 20 (2). "On Campus with Women." Association of American Colleges, fall 1990.

*Project on the Status and Education of Women* 17 (3). "On Campus with Women." Association of American Colleges, winter 1988.

Rabinowitz, Peter J. "Our Evaluation of Literature Has Been Distorted by Academe's Bias Towards Close Reading of Texts." *The Chronicle of Higher Education*, April 1988.

Ramirez, M. and A. Castaneda. *Cultural Democracy, Bicognitive Development and Education*. New York: Academic Press, 1974.

Ravitch, Diane. "History and the Perils of Pride." *Perspectives*, March 1991.

Ravitch, Diane and Chester E. Finn. *What Do Our 17-Year-Olds Know? A Report on the First National Assessment of History and Literature*. New York: Harper & Row, 1987.

Reagan, Sally Barr, Thomas Fox and David Bleich, eds. *Writing with: New Directions in Collaborative Teaching, Learning, and Research*. Albany: State University of New York Press, 1994.

Reid, Pamela T. and Michele A. Paludi. "Developmental Psychology of Women: Conception to Adolescence," in Denmark and Paludi, eds., 1993.

Resnick, L.B. *Education and Learning How to Think*. Washington, D.C.: National Academy Press, 1987.

Richins, M.L. "Social Comparison and the Idealized Images of Advertising." *Journal of Consumer Research* 18, 1991.

Ridgeway, Cecilia L., ed. *Gender, Interaction, and Inequality*. New York: Springer-Verlag, 1992.

Ridgeway, Cecilia L. and David Diekema. "Are Gender Differences Status Differences?" in Ridgeway, ed., 1992.

Ries, Paula and Anne J. Stone. *The American Woman 1992-93: A Status Report*. New York: W.W. Norton, 1992.

Ritvo, Roger A., Anne H. Litwin and Lee Butler, eds. *Managing in the Age of Change*. New York: NTL Institute and Irwin Professional Publishing, 1995.

Robinson, B.W. and E.D. Salamon. "Gender Role Socialization: A Review of the Literature," in Salamon and Robinson, 1987.

Root-Bernstein, Robert Scott. *Discovering*. Cambridge, Mass.: Harvard University Press, 1989.

Rosenfelt, Deborah S. " 'Definitive' " Issues: Women's Studies, Multicultural Education, and Curriculum Transformation in Policy and Practice in the United States." *Women's Studies Quarterly* 3 & 4, 1994.

Rosser, Sue V. *Female Friendly Science*. New York: Pergamon Press, 1990.

Rowe, Mary P. *Dealing with Harassment Concerns*. (pamphlet). New Haven, Conn.: Office for Women in Medicine, Yale School of Medicine, 1985.

Ryscavage, Paul. "Gender-Related Shifts in the Distribution of Wages." *Monthly Labor Review*, July 1994.

ker, Myra and David Sadker. *Failing at Fairness: How America's Schools Cheat Girls*. New York: Charles Scribner's Sons, 1994.

Sadker, Myra and David Sadker. "Sexism in the Schoolroom of the '80s," in Salamon and Robinson, eds., 1987.

Salamon, E.D. and B.W. Robinson. *Gender Roles: Doing What Comes Naturally?* New York: Methuen,1987.

Saluter, Arlene F. "Marital Status and Living Arrangements: Current Population Reports," *Population Characteristics.*, series P20-468, March 1992.

Salzinger, Susanne, John Antrobus and Muriel Hammer, eds. *Social Networks of Children, Adolescents, and College Students*. Hillsdale, N.J.: Lawrence Erlbaum, 1988.

Sandler, Bernice Resnick and Ellen Hoffman. *Teaching Faculty Members to Be Better Teachers: A Guide to Equitable and Effective Classroom Techniques*. Washington, D.C.: Association of American Colleges, 1992.

Sargent, Pamela, ed. *The New Women of Wonder: Recent Science Fiction Stories by Women about Women*. New York: Random House, 1977.

Saywell, Shelley. *Women in War: First-Hand Accounts from World War II to El Salvador*. New York: Viking Penguin, 1985.

Scarborough, Janet, Elisabeth A. Middleton and Sarah J.Walker. *A Selected High School Reading List in Women's Studies: A Resource for Educators with Guide Included*. Austin, Tex.: Women's Studies, The University of Texas at Austin, 1994.

Schmittroth, Linda, comp. and ed., *Statistical Record of Women Worldwide*. Detroit: Gale Research, Inc., 1991.

Schultz, Debra L. *Risk, Resiliency, and Resistance: Current Research on Adolescent Girls*. New York: Ms. Foundation for Women and the National Girls Initiative, 1991.

Schuster, Marilyn R. and Susan R. Van Dyne, eds. *Women's Place in the Academy: Transforming the Liberal Arts Curriculum*. Totowa, N.J.: Rowman & Allanheld, 1985.

Scott, Donald M. and Bernard Wishy. *America's Families: A Documentary History*. New York: Harper & Row, 1982.

Scott, Joan Wallach. "Women's History and the Rewriting of History," in Farnham, 1987.

Scott, Kathryn P. and Candace Garrett Schau. "Sex Equity and Sex Bias in Instructional Materials," in Klein, 1985.

Segel, Elizabeth. "Gender and Childhood Reading," in Flynn and Schweikart, eds., 1986.

Shade, Barbara J. "Afro-American Cognitive Style: A Variable in School Success?" *Review of Educational Research* 52 (2), 1982.

Shanker, Albert. "Strength in Numbers." *Academic Connections*, fall 1988.

Shapiro, Ann-Lous. *Feminists Revision History*. New Brunswick, N.J.: Rutgers University Press, 1994.

Sharps, Matthew J., Jana L. Price and John K. Williams. "Spatial Cognition and Gender: Instructional and Stimulus Influences on Mental Image Rotation Performance." *Psychology of Women Quarterly* 18, 1994.

Sidel, Ruth. *Battling Bias: The Struggle for Identity and Community on College Campuses*. New York: Viking, 1994.

Siegel, Mark A. and Nancy R. Jacobs, eds. *The Women's Changing Role*. Plano, Tex.: Instructional Aids, Inc., 1982.

Sitton, Thad, George L. Mehaffy, and O.L. Davis. *Oral History: A Guide for Teachers (and Others)*. Austin: University of Texas Press, 1983.

Sizer, Theodore R. *Horace's School: Redesigning the American High School*. Boston: Houghton Mifflin, 1992.

Skolnick, Joan, Carol Langbort, and Lucille Day. *How to Encourage Girls in Math and Science: Activities, Projects, Ideas, and Techniques*. Englewood Cliffs, N.J.: Prentice-Hall, 1992.

Slavin, Robert E. "Cooperative Learning and the Cooperative School." *Educational Leadership*, November 1987.

Slavin, Robert E. "When Does Cooperative Learning Increase Student Achievement?" *Psychological Bulletin* 2, 1983.

Smith-Lovin, Lynn and Dawn T. Robinson. "Gender and Conversational Dynamics," in Ridgeway, ed., 1992.

Sobel, Mechal. *The World They Made Together: Black and White Values in Eighteenth-Century Virginia*. Princeton, N.J.: Princeton University Press, 1987.

Spanier, Bonnie, Alexander Loom, and Darlene Boroviak, eds. *Toward a Balanced Curriculum: A Sourcebook for Initiating Gender Integration Projects*. Cambridge, Mass.: Schenkman Publishing, 1984.

Sperry, Roger W. "The Impact and Promise of the Cognitive Revolution." *American Psychologist* 48 (8), August 1993.

Spradley, James P. and David W. McGurdy, eds. *Conformity and Conflict: Readings in Cultural Anthropology*. Boston: Little, Brown, 1980.

Sprafkin, Carol, Lisa A. Serbin, Carol Denier and Jane M.Connor. "Sex-Differentiated Play: Cognitive Consequences and Early Interventions," in Liss, ed., 1983.

Spruill, Julia Cherry. *Women's Life and Work in the Southern Colonies*. New York: W.W. Norton, 1972 reprint of 1938 edition.

Stage, Elizabeth K. et al. "Increasing the participation and achievement of girls and women in mathematics, science and engineering." In Klein, 1985.

Stansfield, ed. "Tightening Up the Residential Program: Form Faculty Accountability," in Crosier, ed., 1992.

Starrels, Marjorie E. "Husbands' Involvement in Female Gender-Typed Household Chores." *Sex Roles* 31 (7/8), 1994.

*Statistical Abstract of the United States*. 1994.

Stern, Fritz ed. 1956. *The Varieties of History*. New York: The World Publishing Co., 1956.

Stevenson, Louise L., ed. *Women's History: Selected Course Outlines and Reading Lists from American Colleges and Universities*. vol. I. New York: Markus Wiener, 1993.

Stites, Richard. "Women and the Revolutionary Process in Russia," in Bridenthal, Koonz, and Stuard, eds., 1987.

Stites, Richard. *The Women's Liberation Movement in Russia: Feminism, Nihilism, and Bolshevism, 1860-1930*. Princeton, N.J.: Princeton University Press, 1978.

Stomfay-Stitz, Aline M. *Peace Education in America, 1828-1990: Sourcebook for Education and Research*. Metuchen, N.J.: Scarecrow Press, 1993.

Strate, Lance. 1992. "Beer commercials: A Manual on Masculinity". in Craig, ed. 1992.

Striegel-Moore, Ruth H., Lisa R. Silberstein, Neil E. Grunberg, and Judith Rodin. "Competing on All Fronts: Achievement Orientation and Disordered Eating." *Sex Roles* 23 (11/12), 1990.

Strobel, Peg and Marion Miller, eds. *Women's History-Vol. II (European and Third World History): Selected Course Outlines and Reading Lists from American Colleges and Universities*.Rev. ed. New York: Marcus Wiener,1988.

Style, Emily. "Curriculum as Window and Mirror," in Oak Knoll, 1988.

Sutton, R.E. "Equity and Computers in School: A Decade of Research." *Educational Research* 61 (4), winter 1991.

Swerdlow, Amy, Renate Bridenthal, Joan Kelly, and Phyllis Vine. *Families in Flux*. rev. ed. New York: The Feminist Press, 1987.

Syrett, Michael and Clare Hogg, eds. *Frontiers of Leadership: An Essential Reader*. Cambridge, Mass.: Blackwell, 1992.

Tannen, Deborah. *You Just Don't Understand: Women and Men in Conversation*. New York: William Morrow, 1990.

Tapasak, Renee C. "Differences in Expectancy-Attribution Patterns of Cognitive Components in Male and Female Mathematics Performance." *Contemporary Educational Psychology* 15, 1990.

Tatar, Maria. *Off with Their Heads ! Fairy Tales and the Culture of Childhood*. Princeton, N.J.: Princeton University Press, 1992.

Taylor, Harriet G. and Luegina C. Mounfield. "Exploration of the Relationship between Prior Computing Experience and Gender on Success in College Computer Science." *Journal of Educational Computer Research* 11 (4), 1994.

*Teacher Magazine*. Sept./Oct. 1989.

Templin, Charlotte. "The Male-Dominated Curriculum in English: How Did We Get Here and Where Are We Going?" in Deats and Lenker, eds., 1994.

Tetreault, Mary Kay Thompson. "Classrooms for Diversity: Rethinking Curriculum and Pedagogy," in Banks and Banks, eds., 1993.

Tetreault, Mary Kay. "Integrating Women's History." *History Teacher* 19 (2), 1986.

Thorne, Barrie, Cheris Kramarae and Nancy Henley. *Language, Gender and Society*. Rowley, Mass.: Newbury House Publishers, 1983.

Thorne, Barrie. "Girls and Boys Together. . . But Mostly Apart," in Kimmel and Messner, eds., 1989.

Thorne, Barrie. *Gender Play: Girls and Boys in School*. New Brunswick, N.J.: Rutgers University Press, 1993.

Thorngren, Connie M. and Barbara S. Eisenbarth. "Games Yet to Be Played: Equity in Sports Leadership." *Women's Educational Equity Act Publishing Center Digest*. June 1994.

Tilly, Louise A. *Industrialization and Gender Inequality*. Washington, D.C.: American Historical Association, 1993.

Timmerman, Mark G. "Sleeeping and Eating: Skills We Need to Teach," in Crosier, ed., 1992.

Timmerman, Mark G. "You Are What You Don't Eat: Our Culture's Contribution to the Development of Eating Disorders," in *NAIS CWIS Newsletter* 1992.

Tiptree, James. "The Women Men Don't See," in Sargent, ed., 1977.

Tobias, Sheila. *They Are Not Dumb, They Are Different: Stalking the Second Tier*. (An occasional paper on neglected problems in science education.) Tucson, Arizona: Research Corporation, 1990.

Tobias, Sheila. "Insiders and Outsiders." *Academic Connections*, winter 1988.

Treichler, Paula A. and Cheris Kramarae. "Women's Talk in the Ivory Tower." *Communication Quarterly* 31 (2), 1983.

Ulrich, Laurel Thatcher. *Good Wives: Image and Reality in the Lives of Women in Northern New England, 1650-1750*. New York: Random House, 1982.

Unger, Rhoda and Saundra "Sexism: An Integrated Perspective," in Denmark and Paludi, eds., 1993.

United Nations. *The World's Women 1970-1990: Trends and Statistics*. New York: United Nations, 1991.

United States Department of Commerce, Bureau of the Census. "Child Support and Alimony," *Current Population Reports*, 1985

United States Department of Commerce. *Historical Statistics of the United States, Colonial Times to 1970*. Washington, D.C.: Bureau of the Census, 1975.

United States Department of Commerce. *Annual Statistical Abstract of the United States*. Washington, D.C.: Bureau of the Census.

United States Department of Education. *The Condition of Education*. Washington, D.C.: National Center of Educational Statistics, 1992.

United States Department of Labor. "Twenty Facts on Women Workers." (Fact Sheet No. 88-2.) Washington, D.C.: Women's Bureau, 1988.

United States Department of Labor. *Perspectives on Working Women*. Washington, D.C.: Bureau of Labor Statistics, 1980.

United States Government Merit System Protection Board. "Sexual Harassment in the Federal Workplace: Is it a Problem?" excerpted in Siegel and Jacobs, 1982.

University of Michigan School of Education Center for Sex Equity in Schools. "Sexual Harassment Is No Laughing Matter." *Title IX Line* 4 (1), fall 1983.

Van Dyne, Susan. "Notes on a Decade of Change." *NWSA Journal* 2 (2), spring 1990.

Vaughter, Reesa M, Devyani Sadh and Elizabeth Vozzola. "Sex Similarities and Differences in Types of Play in Games and Sports." *Psychology of Women Quarterly* 18, 1994.

Vozar, David. Yo, *Hungry Wolf: A Nursery Rap*. New York: Doubleday Books for Young Readers, 1993.

*Wall Street Journal*, November 22, 1994.

Washington, Valora and Joanne Newman. "Setting Our Own Agenda: Exploring the Meaning of Gender Disparities Among Blacks in Higher Education." *The Journal of Negro Education*. 60 (1), 1991.

Webb, Noreen M. and Cathy M. Kenderski. "Small-Group Interaction and Achievement," in Wilkinson and Marrett, eds., 1985.

Weiner, Elizabeth Hirzler, ed. *Sex Role Stereotyping in the Schools*. 2nd rev. ed. Washington, D.C.: National Education Association, 1980.

Whang, P.A. and G.R. Hancock. "Motivation and Mathematics Achievement." *Contemporary Educational Psychology* 19, 1994.

Whitson, David. "Sport in the Social Construction of Masculinity," in Messner and Sabo, 1990.

Wilkinson, Louise Cherry and Cora B. Marrett, eds. *Gender Influences in Classroom Interaction*. New York: Academic Press, 1985.

Willinger, Beth. "College Men's Attitudes towards Family and Work," in Hood, ed, 1993.

Willis, Sue. "Mathematics: From Constructing Privilege to Deconstructing Myths," in Gaskell and Willinsky, 1995.

Wilkinson, Louise Cherry and Cora B. Marrett, eds. *Gender Influences in Classroom Interaction.* Orlando, Fla.: Academic Press, 1985.

Wilson, Joan Hoff. "The Illusion of Change: Women and the American Revolution," in Friedman and Shade, eds., 1982.

Witkin, H., C. Moore, D. Goodenough, and P. Cox. "Field-Dependent and Field-Independent Cognitive Styles and Their Educational Implications." *Review of Educational Research* 47, 1977.

Witkin, H. and S. Asch. "Studies in Space Orientation, Part III: Perception of the Upright in the Absence of a Visual Field." *Journal of Experimental Psychology,* 38, 1948.

Wolf, Naomi. *The Beauty Myth.* New York: William Morrow, 1991.

Wolfe, Arnold S. and Colleen McNally. A Gender and Visual Literacy: Towards a Multidisciplinary Perspective," in Deats and Lenker, 1994.

Women's Action Coalition. *WAC Stats: The Facts about Women.* New York: The New Press, 1993.

Women's Bureau. "Earnings Differences Between Women and Men." *Facts on Working Women* #93-5.

Wood, Wendy and Nancy Rhodes. "Sex Differences in Interaction Style in Task Groups," in Ridgeway, ed., 1992.

Woodrow Wilson National Fellowship Foundation. *Wooodrow Wilson Gender Equity in Mathematics and Science Congress.* Princeton University, 1991.

Woodward, Arthur and David L. Elliott. "Textbooks: Consensus and Controversy," in Elliott and Woodward, 1990.

*World Almanac and Book of Facts.* Mahwah, N.J.: Funk & Wagnalls, 1995.

Yung, Judy. *Chinese Women of America: A Pictorial History.* Seattle: University of Washington Press, 1986.

Zinsser, Judith. *History and Feminism: A Glass Half Full.* New York: Twayne, 1993.


PUBLISHERS OF ANNOTATED CATALOGS OF MATERIALS ON WOMEN AND GENDER:

Association of American Colleges and Universities, Washington, DC

Council on Interracial Books for Children, Inc., New York, NY

The Feminist Press, New York, NY

Garland Publishing, Hamden, CT

Greeenwood Publishing Group Inc., Westport, CT

The Haworth Press, Binghampton, NY

Indiana University Press, Bloomington, IN

National Women's History Project, Windsor, CA

Organization for Equal Education of the Sexes, Inc., Blue Hill, ME

Oxford University Press, New York, NY

Princeton University Press, Princeton, NJ

Programs for Educational Opportunity, University of Michigan, Ann Arbor, MI

Routledge, New York, NY

Rutgers University Press, New Brunswick, NJ

Sage Publications Inc., Thousand Oaks, CA

Scarecrow Press, Metuchen, NJ

Temple University Press, Philadelphia, PA

University of Michigan Press, Ann Arbor, MI

University of Nebraska Press, Lincoln, NE

The University Press of Kentucky, Lexington, KY

Wellesley College Center for Research on Women, Wellesley, MA

Women, Ink.: Women and Development, New York, NY

Women's Educational Equity Act Publishing Center, Newton, MA


AUDIOVISUAL DISTRIBUTORS:

American Audioprose Library, Inc. Authors on Cassettes, Columbia, MO

Ladyslipper, Inc. Recordings by Women, Durham, NC

New Day Films (& Video), Hohokus, NJ

The Cinema Guild, Inc. Film & Video, New York, NY